22708

DEATH OR DECORATION

RONNIE WAITE

NEWTON

DEATH OR DECORATION

First Published in Great Britain by
Newton Publishers (1991)
Hartfield Road, Cowden, Kent TN8 7JW

ISBN: 1 872 308 08 2
PRICE: £14.95

Every effort has been made by the author and publishers to trace owners of copyright material.

Printed by: **Unwin Brothers Limited,**
              The Gresham Press
              Old Woking
              Surrey GU22 9LH

ACKNOWLEDGEMENTS

This book would not have 'got off the ground' but for the enthusiasm and help of many friends and of my family. My grateful thanks to all of them. In particular I am indebted to Hans Onderwater of the Netherlands for his exemplary research into the air battle over Holland, and to Bill Chorley, author of the book, "To See the Dawn Breaking."

In the early stages of my book, I received valuable help from Jill and Peter Hawker. Peter has a special interest in my narrative, being the nephew of the First World War fighter ace, Major Lanoe Hawker VC, DSO, who had shot down 47 enemy aircraft before becoming a victim of Von Richthofen, the 'Red Baron'.

I acknowledge with thanks, the use of photographs supplied by Peter Dobson, Ken Mould, the Air Ministry and the Imperial War Museum, also the original painting by the war artist Roland Davies of the 'Sphere' magazine. My thanks to Derrick Smith for the humorous drawings, except the first two which were drawn by Mickie.

In some instances names of people mentioned in the book have been changed to avoid distress or embarrassment.

CRANWELL COLLEGE. Service Flying Training School.
Top row from left: (2nd) D. Wallington (3rd) I. Tasker (5th) T. Skinner (6th) W. Fletcher.
2nd row from left: (6th) H. Drake (7th) McCombe (8th) Allinson.
Bottom row from left: J. Wright (3rd) W.R. Waite (5th) Sgt McLeod (?).

iv

DEATH OR DECORATION

CONTENTS

Crew of Halifax awaiting the signal for take-off. Navigator and B/A at their stations in the forward position. The waiting time was often long and anxious.

LIST OF PHOTOGRAPHS

LIST OF ILLUSTRATIONS

ABOUT THE AUTHOR

Ron Waite was born at Reading in 1912. After leaving school, he qualified as an ophthalmic optician and took an appointment assisting in the School Eye Clinics in Bristol. It was there that he met Mickie, a ladies' hairdresser. They were married in 1930 and have a daughter, two sons and five grandchildren. Ron started his own optician business in Bristol, which he left in 1940 when he volunteered for pilot duties in the Royal Air Force. After the war in 1948, an unsuccessful partnership caused him to step into an entirely different life when he was offered the tenancy of a famous XVI Century Inn in Weymouth. This was followed by several years as mine host of a charming country hotel.

After the fledglings had flown the nest, his desire for a quieter mode of life led him to buy a business with a Sub-Post Office in Bath. The business was not very successful but the Post Office thrived. Situated on the busy main London Road, the Office attracted several minor crimes before a major one in 1969. One November day, two gansters stole a car from the city centre and five minutes later, Ron found himself looking down the sawn-off barrels of a shotgun, with the hammer ready cocked. He decided it was prudent to carry out the masked gunman's demand to 'fill the bag'!

In 1972, Ron and Mickie bought a small terraced house near the sea in Weymouth. He took the opportunity to return to ophthalmic work after taking refresher courses. At sixty five he was the oldest student at Aston University.

Now retired, Mickie and Ron live happily and modestly in Weymouth, sharing water-colour painting as their main hobby.

FOREWORD

Writing about people in war is a great responsibility and extremely difficult to do adequately. In this book Ronnie Waite has fulfilled the requirements admirably and I am confident that those who were part of the world that is the substance of this story will not be disappointed; others will find a fascinating story containing knowledge of a very special world that those who were privileged to enter will never forget and may look back to as the best time of their lives.

At the time that Ronnie came to No 76 Squadron there was an acute shortage of experienced Halifax pilots due to exceptionally heavy losses. On one daylight operation only two aircraft returned, one flown by the Squadron Commander, as I remember, and the other by Harry Drummond, a very fine pilot who was able to maintain close formation with the C.O.'s aircraft so that the combined gunpower held the German fighters at bay.

The fighters were expected to be on the ground refuelling, having been lured aloft earlier by a diversionary raid, but something had gone wrong with the timing, and they were still airborne. I was on leave when the operation took place, otherwise I should probably not be here today. The shortage of pilots and crews probably caused Ronnie's precipitated despatch on operations.

I vividly remember my 'conversion'. I was taken on a tour of a Halifax by one of the squadron pilots who then proceeded to do a take-off, circuit of the airfield and a rather bumpy landing with me in the second pilot's seat. There were no dual controls. He then suggested I did a few take-offs and landings, and to my surprise left the aircraft. What the crew members thought I did not ask.

Fortunately after a rather heavy first landing we got on fine. I had already completed a tour of operations and two months on Atlantic Patrol on Whitley V aircraft with 102 Squadron before joining 76 Squadron, which was the sort of background originally intended for pilots joining the Halifax force. Ronnie was definitely thrown in at the deep end.

I was posted to No 1658 Heavy Conversion Unit to command 'B' Flight. Jock Calder was the 'A' Flight Commander. I remember that we shared an office at first. Eventually, 'C' and 'D' Flights were established commanded by Harry Drummond and 'Hammie' Hamilton. Ronnie was an instructor on my flight.

In connection with his flying experiences Ronnie mentions that many of the HCU aircraft were 'clapped out'. This is not a reflection on the servicing crews. They did their best but highly stressed machines such as aircraft do develop faults. Obviously the older the aircraft the greater the risk, and the most up-to-date aircraft are inevitably required in the operational squadrons. Even there things can go wrong as Ronnie's experience shows.

My experience of RAF ground personnel has been that they are exceptionally dedicated, always carrying out their work well even in the most appalling conditions without any shelter.

The HCU's soon proved their worth. Complete trainee crews from the Operational Training Units were introduced to the Halifax by experienced instructors and given a comprehensive course of ground and air experience designed to prepare them fully for operational squadron duties. The air experience included day and night bombing practice and cross-country flights of a duration similar to a normal operational sortie. The aim was to ensure that crews attained a satisfactory standard before being posted to their squadrons.

In June 1944 I was posted to Lissett as Commanding Officer of No 158 Squadron, a command which I handed over to W/Cdr G.B.Read in March 1945.

I remember Ronnie Waite as a first class Halifax instructor and a good friend. In this book, "Death or Decoration", he has produced a very readable and interesting account of his memories. I commend it to you.

Wing Commander Peter Dobson

DSO, DFC, AFC, RAF (Ret'd)

CHAPTER 1

AT WAR

On the 3rd September, 1939, I had spent the day at Mullers Orphanage in Bristol. It had been some years since the last of several hundred children had lived their communal life there. I recall them as happy, rosy-cheeked children, who cheerfully accepted the uniformed discipline. The atmosphere of pristine cleanliness still prevailed, with the white, scrubbed floors and warm pinewood furnishings. There was no hint of repression in the large stone-grey buildings and lofty rooms, only one of order.

The Orphanage had been taken over by the City Council and was used for cultural and educational purposes. Now that war threatened, some rooms were being used for Civil Defence. Like many other citizens, I had joined to do what I could. In one room a dozen ladies, with ages as varied as their skills, were making triangular bandages, or applying tourniquets to mock victims.

On this bright Sunday morning, I had been delegated to give instruction on the driving of delivery vans which had been converted to ambulances. I found myself attempting to show a charming, plump middle-aged lady - who had previously only driven her beloved Austin Seven - how to drive a retired and decrepit Brookes laundry-van. The gearbox had ideas of its own when reverse gear was selected, and screeched its objection. Outside, barrage balloons were going up and down indecisively - such was the confusion of Britain on the brink of war.

Precisely at 11 o'clock, all ears were glued to the wireless sets throughout the country. We dropped what we were doing and stood in a quiet group as Big Ben laboriously boomed the hour. As we listened, we could feel the mute silence of the entire country. Neville Chamberlain's voice was slow and deliberate as he announced:

"Great Britain is now in a state of war with Germany." The tremor in his voice indicated the emotion he felt as he addressed the Nation. There was a sense of relief that after months of tension; the crunch had at last come.

As the weeks went by, there seemed an air of disappointment that nothing dramatic was happening. Some Bristolians were even having bets that German bombers could never reach a town so far west. However, momentous events were to follow. This narrative is a personal recollection of the people and those dramatic wartime years.

I was an ophthalmic optician: my wife Mickie had been a ladies hairdresser with Leoni-Jeanne. The 'Leoni Girls' were well known for their

1

modern, smart appearance, and were never short of an escort. Mickie was no exception, she was blonde, lively and popular. We had not fallen in love at first sight, but, after a few meetings, we fell in love and were certain it would last. In 1938 we married, and in January 1940, in sub-zero temperatures, baby Diana arrived in the early hours of the morning.

One night, in the Spring of 1940, the time was around midnight and we were asleep in bed. Gently, through my subconsciousness, I heard an unfamiliar sound. It was the muffled throb of distant engines with an irregular, unsynchronised beat. I was instantly alert. Giving Mickie a gentle nudge, I whispered - as if afraid of being overheard:

"Wake up dear...can you hear that sound?"

Propping herself up on one elbow as she listened, she replied:

"It sounds like an aeroplane, but hasn't got the usual sound." There had not been an air raid warning, and we were more puzzled than afraid. The sound grew nearer and then - scrunch-scrunch-scrunch, as bombs were falling. These were the first bombs we had ever heard; we looked at each other in stunned disbelief.

Scrambling out of bed, we grabbed Diana from her cot and installed her inside the gas-proof cylinder, a weird contraption which had been issued for use with very young babies. The canister completely enclosed the baby, a hand-pump connected from the outside provided fresh air and a perspex viewing panel was fitted in front of the baby's face. Mickie had read somewhere, that it was a good idea to wear a saucepan on one's head for protection, so there she sat, with a two-quart stew-pot on top of her blonde curls, and the handle over her right eye at a rakish angle! We were all huddled together beside the wardrobe. Had it not been for the seriousness of the situation, our appearance would have been hilarious.

We had been closeted in this way for about five minutes when, in the road outside, we heard a bell clanging and a voice shouting, "TAKE COVER...TAKE COVER!" Within seconds, the wailing sound of the air raid sirens filled the air, then all was silent for the next twenty minutes.

We sat wondering what would happen next, when the low, tentative note of the siren quickly ascended into the "ALL CLEAR." We removed Diana from her personal gas-mask cylinder and I left them to take a look outside. There was a crispness in the air and the night seemed oddly quiet, when suddenly - scrunch-scrunch-scrunch more bombs rained down. As I rushed indoors, I saw the flashes of the bombs as they fell in the vicinity of the city centre. There had been no warning but we decided we had better take up our shelter positions again.

A short while later, the Air Raid Warden's voice could be heard calling "ALL CLEAR...ALL CLEAR" - the only correct signal we had received that night. The German bombers had returned to their fatherland.

Ophthalmic Opticians were in a reserved occupation class, consequently, for at least a year, I would not have been required for military service.

CHAPTER 1   AT WAR

TAKING COVER – BRISTOL FASHION

Until the bombing, I had not felt any particular hatred of the Germans, but now that Bristol - our city - my city, had been attacked I had an overwhelming desire to get my own back.

The following morning, I went to a temporary recruiting office in a disused warehouse near Temple Meads. Offering my services as a prospective pilot, the Warrant Officer in charge, asked me a few difficult questions..."How good are you at maths, particularly trigonometry?" and so forth. It was twelve years since I had left school, and I saw that my chances of becoming a pilot were very slim. In trying to cover up my lack of confidence, I was perhaps over-assertive in my replies to his questions. It was with some surprise that a few days later I received a letter asking me to return to the office.

The same Warrant Officer told me that I was to go to Oxford where I would attend interviews and have medical and aptitude tests. Six other aspiring pilots were going with me; being the eldest, I was given the rail warrant for the group.

The only other occupant in the train compartment, besides the seven of us, was a clergyman. We were all strangers and the conversation was mainly speculation about the kind of questions we would be asked when we were in Oxford. One of our party was in doubt about the motto of the RAF, most of us had some idea but were uncertain of the exact translation.

DEATH OR DECORATION

The clergyman, who had been sitting opposite me, leant forward and surreptitiously pushed a piece of paper into my hand: on it was written 'PER ARDUA AD ASTRA' - through hardship to the stars. He had written this unobtrusively behind the cover of his newspaper. I shall always remember his simple, kindly act, I wonder if he does too.

The first two days at Oxford we spent going through a series of stringent medical checks. There were the usual heart, blood and vision tests and some more unusual ones; being spun in a revolving chair and then having to walk a straight line. Another was to stand on one leg, blindfolded, with arms outstretched for two minutes. The educational tests were simple mathematics and general knowledge written papers. The climax was the all-important interview with a board of senior RAF officers; this was the 'Star Chamber' we all feared. I knew that 'sporting types' were well favoured. There seems a reasonable basis for this, rugby and rowing blues probably have some of the special qualities required to make a good pilot.

As far as I was concerned, this was the moment of truth. At school, sport, I would have said, was my worst subject. I was very good at table-tennis and made a bit of a splash as a highboard diver, neither were team games. Aggressive, physical sports were not my forte. I entered the interview room with much trepidation. My worst fears were somewhat abated when they heard that I had started my own business at the youthful age of twenty-two, especially at a time of financial depression. The inevitable question came:

"Ah, Waite...what sports do you play?"

"Well, Sir," I replied, "my business takes up so much of my time, I really haven't a lot left for sport."

Frowns appeared on the faces of my inquisitors - I could hardly boast about the occasional game of 'ping-pong' or billiards with my friend Spilsbury! I had to find an idea and quickly, to stand a chance - what about horses? I had ridden them. I do not like them all that much, I am a bit afraid of them and I dislike their smell.

We had good friends who were farmers; at their weekend parties almost everyone rode horses. Mickie had always admired a good horseman, so, in order to maintain my status in her eyes, I had been forced to have a go. I rode twice. On the first occasion I fell at a small fence. The second attempt was no more successful: whilst trying to keep with the mainstream during a gallop, I came off. This time it was not really my fault as the left stirrup leather had broken.

To return to the interview. With a stroke of brilliance, I said:

"I do a bit of riding, Sir."

The effect was astonishing. My interviewers raised their eyebrows in surprise and admiration. Following this success, and before they could enquire further, I told them about my farmer friends. The Wing Commander then remarked:

4

CHAPTER 1 AT WAR

"They mount you I suppose?"

I was afraid they would pursue the subject with more embarrassing questions, such as 'which hunt do you ride with?' Inspiration came to my aid as I quickly replied:

"Yes, Sir...mostly hacking of course."

They seemed satisfied with my responses and I was dismissed. As I left the room, I sensed that perhaps all was not lost. Later the same day, I was informed that I had been accepted for pilot training. I took the Oath of Allegiance and Attestation, which completed my two days at Oxford, days which certainly had the most dramatic effect on my entire future.

I was surprised to discover later that, of the original seven applicants, only one other had been accepted for pilot training - I was the eldest of the group and he, the youngest.

The RAF told me that I would be notified of the time and where I would have to report, which might be several weeks later. In the meantime I joined the newly-formed Home Guard. This was a very enthusiastic body of men, mostly veterans of the First World War. Weapons were almost non-existent and there was great excitement when a crate of American Ross P4 rifles arrived. Unlike the British Lee-Enfield, it had aperture sights, and was a longer rifle. Like most young men, my only experience had been with an air-rifle, and I was delighted to be issued with a real weapon. One of the older members made a very derogatory remark that my marksmanship would most likely be a danger to the platoon.

During our first visit to the firing range however, I managed to get all of my rounds on the target, whilst the man who made the sneer missed the target with three of his rounds!

My farmer friend - Glyn Teek - was a member of the Wells Company. Glyn was dark complexioned, with jet black hair, over six foot tall, and a powerfully built young man. His company had organised a big shoot for two hundred men. Although I was a member from the Bristol area, Glyn had organised permission for me to join his crowd.

There was a lively atmosphere as we assembled on the wild and windy hills of the Mendips, where the firing range was situated. Glyn's platoon was almost the last to shoot. I was in a group of five, who having been issued with five rounds of ammunition, were instructed to fire from the prone position at the two hundred yard range. Down at the butts a disc was raised in front of the target to indicate what the marksman had scored.

The target indicator confirmed that my first three rounds had scored bulls. I tried to remain calm, hoping that my success would continue - especially as I was a guest. My fourth shot produced a bull. I felt nervous as I prepared for my final round and had difficulty in keeping the target in the aperture sight. I rested the rifle for a moment, raised it again, and got everything in line. Carefully squeezing the trigger, I scored another bull.

Ten minutes later, men were returning from duty on the butts.

DEATH OR DECORATION

"Some fellow has just scored five bulls," I overheard one say.
"Yes...he got a seven inch group," added another.
I could hardly believe they were talking about me, until the Company
Commander - Major Weeks - called for me, to offer congratulations. Since
so many of the men were countrymen, I expected that many would have
equalled, if not exceeded my score. We went to the Farrington Inn
afterwards for a few drinks and several men came up to me seeking advice.
Glyn was highly amused, being aware of my inexperience.

*　　*　　*

We were still living in the flat above the business premises which we had
occupied since we were married. During the previous week, I had prepared
a dug-out shelter in the back garden. One beautiful summer day I was
returning from Home Guard duty when, high in the clear blue sky, I saw
several squadrons of aircraft.

They were approaching Bristol from the south, and what appeared to be
fighter aeroplanes were providing a protective circle around them. I was
just wondering what they could be when the sirens wailed.

I arrived home in time to get Mickie and the baby into the shelter.
Before joining them, I took a look at the planes through a powerful
telescope which I had. The formation was now flying over Filton, home of
the large Bristol Aeroplane Company. As I focused on the leading plane, I
saw black objects falling from it - I don't know why I should have wasted a
second wondering what they were - it should have been obvious that I was
seeing bombs actually leaving the plane. As I jumped into the shelter, we
heard the thud of the bombs exploding.

When the bombing ceased, I ventured to take a look outside. There were
no planes in sight, but I saw several parachutes with men dangling from
their white canopies. Neighbours quickly assembled talking animatedly
about the raid.

Shortly afterwards, ambulances raced in quick succession towards the
city centre and the Royal Infirmary. We were surprised to see private cars
with stretchers strapped to the roofs, carrying dead or injured. We learnt
later that casualties had been heavy, and the ambulance service had not
been able to cope on its own. Private cars had been commandeered to serve
as ambulances.

Whatever happened later in the war, it could not be denied that this
time, the Germans had only attacked a military target - the aircraft factory
at Filton. The city was temptingly laid out beneath them, in perfect
visibility, but no bombs had been dropped on it.

Mickie's parents owned the Carlton Restaurant jointly with her sister
Winnie and her husband Alf. It was situated close to the city centre, in
Park Row. Realising the risk from air attack, Alf had reinforced the cellar,

6

making it an excellent shelter. The family decided that when I left for the RAF, it would be best for Mickie and the baby to live with them, in a flat above the Restaurant. For a short time before leaving, I stayed with them at the Carlton.

Mamma was a dark, vivacious little lady, who never accepted caution as a virtue. During a raid one night, we were all in the shelter playing cards, when she said:

"Ron...let's go up on to the balcony to see what is going on". The rest of the family knew it was useless to try and dissuade her once her mind was made up. With all-round disapproval, I went with her. The balcony was high up on the third floor and looked over the whole of the eastern and southern side of the city.

Searchlights were fingering the black sky, seeking the enemy. We watched an aeroplane caught in a beam; immediately several others moved on to it. The plane looked like a silver fish, thrashing about on a fisherman's line, as the German pilot tried to extricate himself from the beams. We hoped that the anti-aircraft shells which burst around would shoot it down. Deep in my heart, I felt pity for the plight of the poor devils trapped in their machine.

We did not think of the risk of bombs as we stood on the open balcony, watching the drama. Bombs were not the only danger - we heard a terrific swishing noise right in front of us - it came from a balloon barrage cable which must have broken loose. Mamma returned to the cellar; I was almost hypnotised into staying on a little longer. It was quiet for a while until I saw a flash from the ground. In a second it grew into a mushroom of red and yellow flames, mixed with dust and what appeared to be large chunks of debris flying into the air. A large bomb must have landed about a mile away.

Returning to the cellar, I told the family about it, also saying that I thought it had landed in the St. Werberghs area, near where Alf's parents lived. Early next day, we drove there. The district was cordoned off and the Civil Defence were not allowing people through; Alf explained about his parents, and we were allowed entry. Fortunately we found them safe but suffering from shock. The bomb had fallen across the road demolishing several houses completely. The 'Evening Post' newspaper reported the story later.

The family where the bomb fell were killed but, as the fire services were sifting through the rubble, they heard the plaintive cry of a baby. As they worked, they discovered a chest of drawers amongst the ruins - more or less intact - inside one of the drawers they found a baby, quite unharmed, just as it had been placed there by its parents for safety.

We spent a happy day with my parents who lived at Keynsham, near Bristol, probably the last chance I would have of visiting them before leaving for the RAF. As dusk fell we decided it was time we returned to the Carlton. Before we left, my mother checked to make sure the 'blackout' curtains were properly closed, she was very careful about this as she said:

"Can't have those German bombers seeing light from OUR windows." I was certain she believed the faintest chink of light would reap a load of bombs directly on 'The Laurels'.

"Better get moving, son," advised my father, "to get back before 'Jerry' starts anything."

Diana was already fast asleep as I lifted her carrycot on to the back seat of my Ford 'Eight'.

It was a fine night and the car was purring along nicely, even on wartime, low-grade petrol. When we were halfway up the long hill approaching Bristol, the sky was suddenly lit by a brilliant, phosphorescent light. It appeared as a great ball of silver light exploding into thousands of luminous droplets. As they drifted very slowly downwards, the ground was illuminated like daytime, it would have been easy to read a newspaper. The roofs of buildings stood out starkly against the sky. As more of these great candelabra fell, the church spires seemed to spear the sky, as if to hold off an approaching danger. Certainly we had never seen anything so menacing before.

"It looks as if we are for it...we'll hurry back to the Carlton, where we have got a good shelter." I said.

Mickie's voice - usually restrained - sounded commanding:

"I want you to stop right away - we will take shelter near here."

"I think you are right...I will turn off the main road." I replied.

I soon found a turning, which I took. The hooded car headlamps gave little light from their war-regulation slits, making it difficult to avoid the ditches. We soon came across a farm. While I took the carry cot from the car, Mickie went to the door which was opened right away by a comely, motherly woman. Before we could ask for shelter, she said:

"Come in quickly." Seeing the baby sleeping peacefully drew the remark, "Ah, precious little mite."

We entered the large stone- flagged kitchen where a low-powered light hung from the middle of the room. Outside, all hell was breaking loose as the dull thud of exploding bombs mixed with the loud cracks from the anti-aircraft gunfire, made a formidable overture.

"Put the cot under the table," said the farm lady, "there is room for you to squeeze under as well."

The oblong oak table was massively built, and looked as if it could withstand a direct hit, we felt quite safe beneath it. The whining sound of one bomb was so near we thought it must fall on the house. A crack appeared as the ceiling shook, causing plaster to fall. We did not know at the time that this was the nearest miss, and remained very frightened until the raid ended. After an hour, the bombing became more spasmodic and eventually stopped. When the siren sounded the 'ALL CLEAR', we emerged from under the table to find that altogether nineteen people had been sheltering in the farmhouse kitchen. As we left the farm, we were horrified to see that the sky over the whole city area was lit by red and orange flames, capped by a pall of black smoke.

We dismissed the idea of pressing on to Bristol and decided to return to my parents. It was almost midnight and we were surprised to find the 'Old Ship Inn' open. It was doing a roaring business. The customers thronging the bar, were now relaxed after the ordeal, creating quite a party atmosphere, due to the dangers all had shared.

Early next morning as we set off for Bristol, an umbrella of smoke hung over the city. Many buildings in the centre were still burning unattended, the fire services had been overwhelmed by the severity of the attack. We became increasingly apprehensive for the safety of Mamma and Pop. The area around Bristol Bridge had been devastated. The spire of St. Nicholas Church was all that remained of that landmark. The leaning tower of Temple Church was accentuated by the flattened buildings which now surrounded it, and the 15th century church of St. Peters was also gutted.

We could hardly believe the destruction, as buildings and streets which were so familiar only yesterday, were now unrecognisable. Sometimes it was difficult to find a track for the car wheels over the rubble; firemen's hoses, empty of water, were snaking everywhere.

As we rounded the hairpin bend at the bottom of Park Row, we saw that the Carlton was still intact and breathed an immense sigh of relief. The family were unharmed and in good spirits, despite the rough night they had endured.

I had been staying at the Carlton for about ten days when I received instructions to report to the Aircrew Reception Centre at Babbacombe.

Saying 'good-bye' during the war, was always an emotional time. On this, our first parting, my thoughts were partly occupied with the journey ahead and what the immediate future held for me. It was almost certainly worse for Mickie, who never allowed her outward appearance to show how deeply upset she was inside. Years later, she told me that as soon as I left, she would turn - almost frenziedly - to do some domestic work -anything to avoid missing me. Mickie said she would come to the station to see me off, but I declined, preferring to say our farewells at home.

CHAPTER 2

INITIAL TRAINING WING

In peacetime, Temple Mead Station - a fine structure designed by Brunel - was bright and bustling with activity but, on this November night, it was dimly lit and the refreshment room had double, light-trapping doors. The acrid aroma of steam, mixed with other indescribable odours, old canvas mail bags and discarded food bins, had not changed.

The train I caught was a slow one, stopping at every station and halt on its journey to Torquay. When it squealed to a stop, it was impossible in the darkness, to see at which station we had arrived. While the heavy doors were being slammed, a porter called out the station name. As we travelled further west, I found this ritual interesting - almost entertaining. The voice at one station would be a high-pitched tenor, at another a fruity baritone. I was surprised how much the accents changed during our progress westward.

"Ya- un...this is Ya-un." (spelt Yatton).

Later, at Taunton, the name was hardly recognisable.

"Tah-un...Tah-un...change yer fer Exeter."

By the time we had reached Newton Abbot, the voices had become slower and distinctly Devonian. Even in the year 1940, England was still a very parochial country.

Torquay railway station was some distance from the town centre and about three miles from Babbacombe. It was past midnight; in the darkness I could just discern two airmen in uniform. I spoke to them and we agreed to wait - hopefully - for a taxi which we could share. Both men wore a crescent shaped white 'flash' in their caps. I felt very much the new boy as I asked:

"What does that piece of white material in your caps indicate?"

Together and with obvious pride, they replied:

"We are cadet pilots under training."

Twenty minutes later, a taxi arrived. After dropping the other two airmen I continued on to Babbacombe. It was 2 a.m. and Babbacombe was deathly silent. I found an hotel which had been taken over by the RAF. I entered the front door, unchallenged; the atmosphere inside was warm, stuffy and heavy with slumber, a contrast to the fresh night air outside. In a small room off the foyer, I found the Duty Corporal, who did not seem pleased at being disturbed. Opening sleepy eyes, he took a cursory look at my papers, then took me to a small room, barely furnished, with an iron bedstead upon which rested three mattress-type cushions. I later discovered these were called 'biscuits' - after the outsize dog biscuits they resembled. When lying on them, they seemed just as hard. Covering myself with a grey service blanket, I soon fell asleep.

At about 6 o'clock in the morning, some movement in the corridor outside disturbed me. When I first awoke, I could not imagine where I was. In a very few minutes the place was buzzing. Mooching around, someone told me that if I could borrow some 'irons' (cutlery), I would be able to get food in the dining hall. I saw a few men, some in uniform, others in 'civvies', emerging from the dining room. On a table near the entrance stood a large bin of steaming water where each man rinsed his irons as he left. Seeing one with a friendly looking face, I asked:

"Would you please lend me your irons? I have just arrived."

Using the term 'irons', made me feel initiated into this strange new life. The porridge was not bad, with plenty of sugar and milk, the two sausages which followed, were not the smooth-coated, luscious variety to which I had been accustomed. In the middle of the large white pottery plate, lay two finger-length brown specimens with fossilized skins. My appetite was such that I 'wolfed' them without flinching.

Loftily, I had expected my arrival at Reception Wing to have been anticipated - rather like a guest at a party; I was soon to discover that I was 'less than dust.' I queued with other new arrivals, to give information about my next of kin, my religion, who I wanted to be informed if!! Next, I had to stand naked, with long, short and tall men for an FFI (free for infection); an inspection to ensure that we were not suffering from VD (Venereal disease). Life was not dull, and one never knew what the next assignment might entail.

We had not received any drill instruction so, when about thirty of us were formed up in the road, in columns of three, still wearing a variety of clothes - double-breasted business suits, Harris tweed jackets with baggy grey flannels, and so on, we must have looked a very motley bunch.

We marched off, or rather - shambled off - to a small warehouse where we were given a palliasse each. The next building held a mountain of straw from which we stuffed our palliasses. It would have helped had we been given instruction about this because too much straw made a bed of rock, too little and one slept on one's bones! Exactly the right amount made a very comfortable mattress.

During the next fortnight, I was accommodated in what had been a small boarding house called 'Coastview', on the top of the cliffs at Babbacombe. It was here - as prospective pilots - we discovered how to lay out our personal equipment. Blankets had to be folded in a very precise way and laid at the head of the bed. Placed upon these, in a predetermined position, would be the face flannel and shaving gear. At the foot of the bed, shoes - highly polished - shoe polish and brushes had similarly to be laid out in precise and accurate fashion. I was amazed that corporals,

CHAPTER 2   INITIAL TRAINING WING

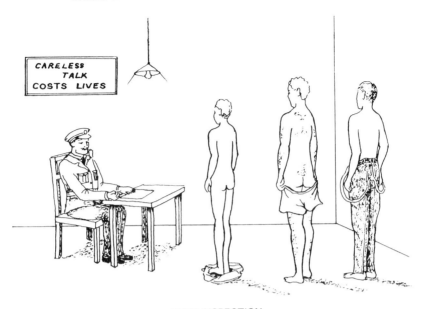

"FFI" INSPECTION

sergeants and even officers treated this daily bed lay out with such dedicated seriousness.

There were about twenty of us billeted at 'Coastview', and what a varied lot we were. There was a blond, giant of a man named Georgeson, who was a charming Norwegian, Stanislaus, had, I believe, left a good job with the BBC to join the RAF, he was a tall, studious looking fellow. Another of our throng, was Julian Amery - the son of a Cabinet Minister - who also aspired to become a pilot. It was impossible not to notice the large stonegem ring he wore. In post-war years, I saw him often on Television, when he became a member of Parliament, I might have doubted whether it was the same Julian - but the ring confirmed it. He had not altered much, a shade more portly perhaps.

One foreigner in our group stood out as an interesting character. He was American or Mexican, and was conspicuous because of his unusual clothes. He wore a Stetson hat and his boots - leather of course - were fitted at the ankles to take spurs. He was an athletic, sun-tanned man, who told us that he was already a pilot and had fought in several South American conflicts. He was I suppose a mercenary and I was bound to wonder how he came to be accepted for the RAF.

Every morning, our ablutions had to be carried out in two very small wash rooms. Sometimes up to half-a-dozen of us would all be trying to shave at the same time, sharing a mirror, sixty percent of which was brown-mottled with damp. It was necessary to keep moving, to try and find a clear piece of mirror - those nearest had the best chance. It was difficult to avoid shaving some other fellow's face! I soon found out that, if I got up only ten minutes earlier I had the washroom to myself and avoided the crush at breakfast.

One day, all new recruits were ordered to attend a lecture in a former summer theatre, instead of a summer show with comedians and dancing girls, the subject of venereal disease. There was a capacity audience of several hundred men. The hall was stuffy and had a distinct aroma of new serge uniforms.

The Medical Officer delivering the lecture, obviously intended putting the fear of God into us - and to a certain extent succeeded. The main theme of his message was - don't go with girls. If one did and caught a 'packet', there would be no sympathy, and the treatment would be harsh and very painful. In other words, the remedy would be as bad as punishment. The intimate medical details the doctor revealed, caused many faces to turn grey and several men fainted.

Three weeks later, the thirty-six erstwhile civilians, had become an orderly Flight of airmen as we marched smartly, in columns of three, to Torquay and the ITW (Initial Training Wing). Leading us on the march was our Flight Officer - Flying Officer Lewington. He was a friendly man, well built and with an upward turn to the corners of his mouth which gave him a perpetual smile.

We became 'D' Flight No. 5 ITW. During our training, we were quartered in Templestowe, a former hotel now stripped of luxury fittings and carpets, replaced by service furnishings. The first taste of life at ITW was frugal and disciplined. From 6.30 in the morning to 5.30 in the evening, every moment was accounted for. Most of us felt that the amount of drill and physical training we had to endure was excessive, but by the end of the eight weeks course, we took pride in our drill and marching ability and became accomplished in some very difficult drill movements.

The sergeants were tough with us; in their eyes, we were just a 'shower' of 'gormless Charlies'. They treated us as such and we could do little to retaliate.

The Sergeant in charge of our flight, was a savage little sod named Pollard. He was less than average height and solidly built. His head was square shaped, with pale blue eyes which flitted, looking for trouble. His limited vocabulary was more than compensated for by his knowledge and use of expletives.

In the early days, small things could cause smouldering resentment. There was the occasion when Metcalf, a quiet gentlemanly fellow, had some difficulty with the collar of his winter greatcoat. The collar band had to be fastened by two hooks and eyes, which were difficult to manipulate. He had not managed to fasten them before the morning parade was called. The sergeant, with his pacing stick tucked aggressively under his arm, marched up to Metcalf and stuffed two fingers inside his collar, at the same time shouting how it should be fastened. The Sergeant was enraged over such a small misdemeanour. He shook poor Metcalf who was almost purple as the fingers pressed against his throat. The rest of the Flight were seething with resentment and muttering, "We will kill the bastard." The surprising thing was, that by the end of the course, we were almost attached to the 'bastard'.

In each Flight, a cadet was monitored to take charge of marching in the absence of both the Flight Officer and the Sergeant, and was given the overrated title of Flight Commander. Flying Officer Lewington told me that I was to take this role, and I assumed it was because I was eldest in the Flight. I protested, as there were two other men who, although younger, were regulars who had volunteered for air crew duty. Their names were Milton and Paige. I suggested to Fg Off Lewington that one of them should have the job but he would not change his mind.

The duties were not too onerous, except on one occasion. We had attended a lecture on navigation in a building in the centre of Torquay. There was no one to take over the Flight, so it was my duty to march the men up the very busy Union Street. With as much authority as I could muster, I got them lined up in columns of three, and took up my position five paces in front. Over my shoulder, I shouted - as loudly as my nervousness would allow:

"FLIGHT...IN COLUMNS OF THREE...QUI.I.CK MARCH."
We moved off magnificently. I could hear the rhythmical - blonk-blink of the marching feet behind me.

I have to admit to a feeling of pride as we marched up the busy street and could 'feel' a few admiring glances from the shoppers on the pavement. Halfway up Union Street were traffic lights, and if these were red, I would have to halt the Flight. After awhile, I could scarcely hear the marching feet behind me, I put this down to the traffic noise, which was quite heavy. I desperately wanted to look back, as I felt all was not well, but the rule book forbade this: at all times I had to look to the front. As we approached the traffic lights, the worst happened - they changed to red. I 'about turned', ready to halt the Flight, and was shattered to see they were at least 80 yards down the street! Milton and Paige, who were in the front rank, had purposely reduced the marching pace by half. By the time the Flight caught up, the damned traffic lights had changed again.

The practical joke they played on me worked perfectly to everyone's amusement, except mine. I also had the risk - as the lights changed - of having some men on one side of the crossing and the rest on the other.

After the first week we got used to our tough hard-swearing Sergeant and discovered he did have a sense of humour. Our regular morning march, took us down a side road flanked with large Victorian houses. One morning, we were marching down the road, deserted at this early hour, when, for no apparent reason Sergeant Pollard shouted out, "FLI.I.GHT...EYES

RIGHT'. Thirty heads snapped to the right as if by clockwork, expecting to see an officer on the pavement, whom we would have to salute, instead, we were astonished to see a well endowed lady, almost naked, looking from her ground floor window! The sergeant waited until the whole Flight had passed, before giving the command, "EYES FRONT".

After this episode, we held Sergeant Pollard in much greater esteem. The odd thing was, for several mornings afterwards, we had this one-sided rendezvous with the lady in the window. We never found out whether she knew she could be seen, was an exhibitionist, or just wanted to cheer up the lads.

I quite enjoyed marching and drill, but physical training was not my 'scene'. P.T. seemed to have the reverse effect on me - the more I did, the worse I felt. The cross-county run I could have coped with better, had it been two miles instead of five.

However, I found a system whereby I could 'skive off'. The usual run was to Paignton, Cockington and return. I discovered that half-a-mile out, there was a sharp bend in the road where there was a tiny cafe. I used to put a sixpence in the sole of my running shoes. As I was invariably a back runner, I was able to make a quick dash at the bend in the road and nip into the cafe unobserved. I doubt if the proprietor was very well pleased to have an airman hanging around for an hour, with one Chelsea bun and a cup of tea. I awaited the return of the rest of the runners, and rejoined them as adroitly as I had left them earlier.

It was a very full life at Initial Training Wing, with lectures on navigation, Air Force law, armaments and other subjects. The sessions on the morse code could have been boring, but our instructor had a bright idea, instead of tapping out endless five letter words, he tapped out sexy stories, that way we had to stay awake and alert, to learn the tantalising endings!

*　*　*

The Prudential Assurance Company had evacuated its Head Office from the city of London, and several hundred of its female staff were moved to Torquay. In December 1940, the Company organised a dance party and invited the RAF to provide two hundred airmen as guests. Wisely, the senior officers did not ask for volunteers - the response from girl - starved airmen would have been overwhelming. I was one of those detailed to attend, and admit to a glow of pleasure at having the chance of enjoying the company of a lot of girls wearing party frocks. I cannot remember any details of the dance, but it brought back memories of many happy dances in Bristol before the war.

ITW held few surprises for us, but we were annoyed one morning to be aroused at 5.30 and told to be on Parade at 6.30. It was one of those cold, damp miserable mornings, and we were mystified when a Royal Navy coach arrived which we had to board. Flt Off Lewington was with us, and ignoring all our questions, just bore an amused grin at our bewilderment.

After an hour's travelling, the coach stopped at the small village of Starcross on the bank of the River Exe. The Flight was divided into two sections. One half was ferried to a submarine, the remainder, including myself, were taken aboard an old First World War destroyer. Its slender hull, high superstructure and four funnels dated it as - antiquated. The vessel was one of a number loaned to Britain by President Roosevelt.

We had been at sea for a short time on this chilly February morning, and were still unaware of the reason for this exercise. The submarine submerged and about fifteen minutes later, an orange buoy bobbed to the surface, which we circled in the destroyer. The buoy disappeared and we steamed off in a different direction. This action was repeated several times, and we could only guess that it was a submarine hunting exercise. It seemed to have no practical value to us, but made a very interesting break in our routine.

As the end of the course drew closer, those of us who were either keener - or less bright - sometimes swotted in the evenings for the exams which loomed ahead. Time did not allow deep friendships to develop. Two men I came to know better than the others, were Johnny Wright and David Wood. Johnny was well above six feet tall, and was more religiously active than most of us. One thing we both had in common, was our enjoyment of discussion and sometimes argument, on serious topics - an interest not usually shared by the younger fellows.

David was one of the six who shared the room at the top of Templestowe with me. His home was in Grantown-on-Spey, amongst some of the best whisky distilling country in Scotland; it was not surprising he was popular in our room, after bringing with him a bottle of the finest Scotch malt ever distilled! David - a very cheerful fellow, wore a permanent grin. His auburn hair, which seemed glued to his head in a mass of ripples, was never out of place or appearing in need of attention. David loved his native Scotland, we never minded him talking about it - it sounded such a happy community. His colourful description of the Highland parties, with the dancers dressed in tartan kilts and sashes, made us Sassenachs quite envious. I never saw David again after we left Torquay. A couple of years later, I was very sad to hear that he had been killed in North Africa.

The three month course at ITW came to an end: those who had passed for pilot training would be sent to an RAF station to commence flying, those who had failed, could re-muster for training as navigators, wireless operators or air gunners. As the entire squadron waited in rows on the final Pay Parade, I knew I would be one of the last to be called - the initial of my surname attended to that. It would be fairer, if occasionally they

started with the 'Zs' and worked back! After about three-quarters of an
hour, the corporal's strident voice shouted:

"WAITE."

I stepped smartly forward to the table behind which sat an officer and
sergeant. I saluted, and in the approved manner, replied loudly:

"WAITE...1312297...SIR."

Holding out my right hand, the sum of three pounds two shillings and
seven pence was placed in it by the sergeant. The Parade now over, we
were allowed to 'stand easy.' Excitement was intense as we awaited news of
our fate. In this atmosphere, rumours were rife. There was the proverbial
'know-all' who spread spurious stories which nevertheless, caused niggling
doubts in our minds. Had I reached the rumoured 80% in the navigation
exam? At last, Fg Off Lewington started calling out names.

"Jones, F.L...Sywell."

"Waddington...Watchfield."

"Bateman- Jones...Watchfield."

"Waite...Sywell."

"Sywell...where and what is Sywell?" I asked my neighbours. No one
seemed to know. I was soon to discover that Sywell was not an RAF
Station, but a civilian flying field which had been taken over by the RAF.
Passes and failures were not announced, possibly to save the feelings of the
unfortunate chaps who had failed. So - I had passed.

CHAPTER 3

ELEMENTARY FLYING SCHOOL

Sywell airfield was on the outskirts of Northampton and the journey was long and tedious. Railway station platforms were packed with a variety of servicemen, burdened with holdalls and kitbags, added to this, the soldiers of course, had their rifles. The worst aspect of the journey was trying to find a corner to sit. On this journey, the only spot I could find was in the corridor, where I sat uncomfortably on my kitbag - wondering what the weight was doing to the creases in my best blue trousers!

I was billeted with a very nice family. Every morning, the aircrew bus - actually a large canvas covered van without seats - gathered us up from our different billets. We were thrown about as we bumped along the country road to the airfield. This did not bother us as we looked forward to our new life. We passed the time singing the wartime songs -

"She'll be coming round the mountain when she comes;

She'll be wearing silk pyjamas when she comes;

etc...etcetera.........."

Life was so different from that at ITW, it hardly seemed like the Air Force. The airfield was the headquarters of the Northampton Flying Club. Although it had been taken over by the RAF, it still retained its civilian atmosphere. More than half the staff were civilians, only the flying instructors were RAF personel.

The van, with its twenty or so keen flying pupils, bumped through the airfield gate and stopped in front of a single-storey building. Until now, we had no idea what kind of aircraft we would be flying. Between the buildings, we caught a glimpse of a couple planes parked on the grass. They were small biplanes with two open cockpits. The wings were separated by thin struts and wires - closely resembling the fighter planes of the First World War. Some of my fellow pupils showed disappointment that the aircraft were not Miles Magisters - the more modern trainer monoplanes. I felt quite differently - I was happy to have got this far and was ready to learn on anything. At the time, I did not realise the biplanes were the legendary Tiger Moths, loved by everyone who flew them.

Our first day was rather like a friendly introduction to a new club. We were shown around the lecture rooms and met the instructors who gave lectures on navigation and aeronautics.

Lunchtime provided us with a pleasant surprise. The dining room was bright, with half-a-dozen tables laid with quality cutlery on clean, white table cloths. White-coated stewards were in attendance, giving it the atmosphere of an executives' dining room. This was in such contrast to ITW, where we ate at bare wooden tables, using our 'irons', which we had die-stamped with our service number.

It was a lovely Spring morning when I was due for my first flying lesson. I had not felt such enthusiasm since buying my first belt-driven BSA motorcycle, at the age of seventeen.

With the other pupils, I waited at the Flight Office, where we were to meet our flying instructors. There was an air of excitement as the other pupils shared my enthusiasm. The instructors were older than I had expected; they were tough-looking men who bore an expression of having seen it all before. I viewed them with awe, and hoped before long, to qualify for the 'Wings' they wore on the left breast. During my earlier months in the RAF, I had hardly ever seen an officer or NCO wearing the coveted brevet. I was still sitting, speculating, when I heard:

"WAITE."

I nearly jumped out of my skin.

"Yes, Sir," I replied, as I tried to assess the nature of my instructor.

"I am Flying Officer Maxwell...we are flying in about half-an-hour...Wear flying suit, helmet, goggles and draw a parachute from the store."

"Right, Sir."

"See you here at ten o'clock," said Maxwell, as he walked over to join a Flight Lieutenant.

At the parachute section, a grey-haired man put a seat-type 'chute' on the counter, then, giving me a second look asked:

"Ever worn one before?"

"No...it is a bit of a contraption, isn't it?" I replied.

"OK...I will help you..." as he showed me how to link the various straps and operate the release knob.

"Most important you get those straps tight," my helper told me.

"If you have 'em loose and do a loop, you'll fall out of the bloody plane."

Succinctly put - and never to be forgotten. I had to really put a move on, to get into all the gear and be back at the office on time.

As Fg Off Maxwell arrived, I saluted smartly - a formality instilled in me during earlier training. Maxwell returned my salute casually, showing some irritation.

"Waite...you are allowed to salute once, when you first see me in the morning...any further saluting will be frowned on - understand - this is not the High School Cadets!"

Maxwell was rather a taciturn man, he was economical with words, which made his instructions clear and to the point. I suppose he would be called a good-looking man in his early forties. His granite-like features and athletic build made him look a really tough guy - which he was.

CHAPTER 3   ELEMENTARY FLYING SCHOOL

"You get in the back cockpit," he told me, as he helped me with the harness and smiled for the first time. He plugged in the speaking tube saying:

"This is the throttle...the control column we call the 'stick'...if the rudder bar isn't a comfortable distance, it can be adjusted with that nut," he explained, before climbing into the front cockpit.

"The aircraft's nose interferes with vision when you are taxying...so you have to yaw the nose from side-to-side, to see ahead." Now that I was about to have my first flying lesson, my feelings were mixed. I felt exhilarated, at the same time I was so anxious to do well, I felt scared.

The ritual for starting-up a Tiger Moth was fascinating. Orders were shouted from the pilot to the ground mechanic:

"Petrol ON...switches OFF...CONTACT."

The mechanic then gripped the top of the propeller with both hands and gave it an almighty downward swing. He stepped smartly back, as the prop 'kicked' and flicked back up. This action was repeated once or twice, then came a new instruction:

"Petrol ON...Switches ON...CONTACT."

The propeller was 'swung' again. At the second attempt, the Gipsy engine, with a crackling roar, burst into life. The speaking tube between the cockpits was an elementary affair - just a tube with a mouthpiece - which made the instructor's voice sound thin as he asked:

"Can you hear me all right, Waite?"

"Yes, Sir." I replied - a bit tense with excitement.

Chocks were removed and Maxwell taxied the aircraft away. The Tiger Moth had a steel skid, instead of a tailwheel, which made a bumpy ride over the rough grass. There were no runways at Sywell, a windsock at the top of a mast, indicated the wind direction. After a brief scan of the sky, to ensure that no other planes were approaching, Fg Off Maxwell turned the plane into the wind and pushed the throttle open. It was an odd feeling, sitting alone in the small cockpit -not doing a thing - as the Tiger Moth bounced over the uneven ground, gathering speed. The rush of cool air in the open cockpit was very invigorating.

At first, all I could see was the helmeted head of my instructor in front of me, when suddenly, the tail rose off the ground and I was able to see ahead. As Maxwell was operating the controls in his cockpit, so the dual set in my cockpit were moving. The rudder bar was turning right and left. The control column between my knees was weaving about gently, both seemingly of their own volition. When the airspeed needle indicated about 50mph, the aircraft became airborne; moments later the boundary hedge flashed past below. We climbed steadily to approximately 1,500 feet and my instructor demonstrated the use of the controls, to carry out straight and level flight - not as easy to achieve as may appear.

21

DEATH OR DECORATION

The short demonstration completed, we returned to the airfield. Through the speaking tube, Fg Off Maxwell gave me brief and important details of the speeds and the use of the controls, as we approached to land.

After crossing the boundary, the speed dropped off rapidly and we seemed to float for some 30 yards, just a few feet off the ground, before the tail dropped. The wheels and tail skid touched the ground at the same time, to make a perfect 'three-point' landing. After the plane had come to a stop, Maxwell instructed:

"You can taxy back to the hanger, Waite."

Having this apparently simple manoeuvre thrust upon me, made me sweat a little. I opened up the throttle boldly - too boldly as it happened and pushed the rudder bar too vigorously. This resulted in the Tiger making a zig-zag movement of almost 180 degrees instead of the 30 degrees required. Fg Off Maxwell made no comment, I guessed he thought I could see the error for myself. With less abandon and a lot more care, I eventually arrived safely in front of the hanger.

The following day, Maxwell was off duty, so I was detailed to fly with Flight Lieutenant Bembridge, who was the Chief Flying Instructor. I discovered later that 'Bem' was one of two quite famous brothers who had flown in World War I. He was a 'character'. It was rumoured that, during a dog- fight, he received a bullet in the cheek which had damaged the roof of his mouth. I could quite believe this, as he seemed quite unable to pronounce certain consonants. His voice projected in a strange manner. Flt Lt Bembridge was an immense man, and the way he could shoe-horn himself into the tiny Tiger Moth cockpit, was worth watching. No matter how may Tigers were in the sky at the same time, it was easy to pick out 'Bem' - so much of him was sticking out of the cockpit, it appeared as though he was flying standing up.

I had to muster all my morale, to face this flying lesson with the celebrated Bembridge. We had been flying for about five minutes after take-off, when Bem called through the speaking tube:

"Waite...will you take the control stick."

Taking hold of the stick with my right hand, I answered:

"Yes, Sir."

"Waite...put your feet on the rudder bar."

"Sir, I have done that."

"Alright, Waite...now I just want you to fly the aeroplane straight and level."

"Very good, Sir."

I divided my attention between looking ahead at the horizon and looking at the 'artificial horizon' - an instrument which indicated to the pilot, whether the aircraft was diving or climbing. The rudder bar was not difficult to operate, but the control column was not easy to use correctly. It could be moved in any direction, which caused the nose to go up, or down or sometimes made a wing drop alarmingly. I found myself using it like a stirring rod. Flying straight and level sounded simple enough but I found it difficult to accomplish either. For several minutes - whilst I made the Tiger Moth behave like a drunken Mayfly - Bem sat quietly in his cockpit. I knew I was not doing very well, so why was he not bawling me out I wondered. After a while, through the speaking tube, I heard Flt Lt Bembridge's voice which sounded very moderate - almost gentle:

"Waite...will you take your hands off the stick?"

Placing my hands in my lap, I replied:

"Yes, Sir."

Then, to my astonishment, Bem put his arms high above his head.

"Waite...now take your feet off the rudder bar." For my life, I could not think what Bem was up to, but removing my feet from the bar, I tucked them under me. Bembridge, still with both hands above his head announced:

"I have taken my feet off the rudder bar too."

Look...No Hands

I could not think of anything else to say other than:

"Yes, Sir."

Back came Bem's voice:

"Waite...you see the bloody aeroplane flies better by itself!"

He then explained that the controls should be moved smoothly and gently - a practical lesson I never forgot, and my flying improved from then on.

Preliminary training consisted of learning basic flying, airfield approach and landings. Sitting in the open cockpit of these lively, responsive little biplanes was a joy, and those early days were very exhilarating.

Later, we had to learn aerobatics and the art of spinning - or more correctly - the ability of recovering from a spin. If a modern aircraft went into a spin, the result was usually fatal; it was essential to be able to master this manoeuvre. My first experience of this exercise nearly made me sick. The instructor closed the throttle, and as the Tiger lost flying speed to the stalling point, he applied hard rudder causing the nose to fall immediately. The little plane dropped out of the sky, spinning violently. Below, the fields spun round like a crazy kaleidoscope, only the rush of fresh air on my face overcame my nausea. It seemed nothing could stop the descent until Maxwell centralised the rudder, opened the engine, and the Moth levelled out.

It was the 15th May - Mickie's birthday -a year earlier, I would hardly have expected to be celebrating it with aerobatics. It was a sunny morning, with clear blue skies, the fresh green foliage of the trees at this time of the year, made the day seem full of promise - soon to be fulfilled. When we climbed to 2000 feet, my instructor called through the headset:

"We are going to do some aerobatics...first a slow roll."

I always felt that 'rolls' were the glamour manoeuvres of flying and my heart beat faster at the prospect. Maxwell performed a perfect slow roll, without losing a foot of height. It all happened so quickly I was unable to follow all the control movements.

"OK, Waite...now you do one."

Jeepers! I could hardly remember a single move. However, I started quite well, left aileron - gentle right rudder - bit more power - stick forward, and we are suddenly inverted. Gosh! I was certain my harness was not tight enough, as I dropped a couple of inches out of my seat. The advice I had been given at the parachute section flashed through my mind as my feet came away from the rudder bar. Now that we were upside down, seeing the fields above my head made me distinctly uncomfortable, what do I do next, everything happened so fast - right aileron, ease the stick back - as the earth rotated I realised we were losing height. I knew it was not one of my best moments as I heard Maxwell's anguished voice exclaim:

"GOOD GOD ALMIGHTY!"

The tone of his voice left no doubt that the expletive was not intended as a compliment. At the end of this flying lesson, I sensed a certain lack of cordiality on the part of Flt Lt Maxwell.

During the next two or three weeks, my training progressed normally; other techniques had to be mastered - crosswind and precautionary landings, steep turns, climbing turns, forced landings, even action in the event of fire in the air. The course was really comprehensive. After about ten hours of dual instruction, the average pupil was ready to take his first solo flight. This was without doubt the most exciting part of the course. In between flying, the cadets lounged in the Flight Office, with the same topic in mind - 'going solo'.

"Hello Georgeson, are you nearly ready for solo yet?"

24

"Shouldn't be long now, perhaps another couple of dual sessions. How are you doing, Waite?"

"Holding off a bit too high...if I can sort that out, I shall be ready I think."

The following day, two of my friends went solo. One of them - Alan Stewart -had been a Hollywood film actor. Alan had not only played a role but, as an old Harrovain, had also been the adviser on English Public School life for the film 'Tom Brown's School Days.' When we were in Torquay, almost the entire course went to the Cinema when the film was shown there. Two years later, I met him by chance in London, when I learnt he had become a fighter pilot.

Thomas, the other friend, was not so successful on his first solo; after making a heavy landing, the plane bounced and then turned over on to its back. It was really quite funny to see him hanging upside down, supported by the harness. Before anyone could reach him, he released himself and dropped unharmed two or three feet onto the ground. There was a saying 'You cannot kill yourself in a Tiger Moth.'

The next morning - after a check dual session with Flt Lt Maxwell, he climbed out of his cockpit and said:

"Alright Waite...off you go and do one circuit."

Maxwell patted the fuselage - almost as one would pat a horse - and gave me a quick smile as he left. Were these gestures of hope, or encouragement I wondered. As I sat alone in the aircraft, without the comforting figure of Maxwell in the front cockpit, I had a momentary attack of fear. But was this not the moment I had been waiting for? Voicing my thoughts aloud, I said, 'Come on now...just one good circuit and landing.' Most pilots I suppose, find it difficult to express the feeling of the FIRST SOLO flight, and the realisation that you, and you alone can get yourself back on terra firma.

As I taxied away, the wind-sock at the top of its pole weaved gently - as if to be beckoning. Remembering the drill, after scanning the sky to make sure all was clear, I turned the Tiger into the wind and pushed the throttle open. The little plane bounced over the rough ground which shook the fabric covered wings and struts cruelly. The tail rose from the ground, I centralised the 'stick', and as I eased it gently back, the Tiger Moth left the ground. I was much too busy keeping the wings level and controlling the rate of climb to feel anxious at this stage. Climbing steadily to 800 feet, I levelled out. It was the strangest feeling, and the space between me and the earth below took on a new dimension.

The Gypsy engine purred - I knew it would not let me down. As my confidence grew, I banked to port and starboard to look at the patchwork of fields and tiny buildings below. I flew audaciously close to the pure white cumulous clouds, it gave me a new sense of achievement. If I lost a bit of height in the turns, I did not have my instructor to rebuke me - I was the pilot now - THE pilot. I shouted 'Yippee...Yippee!' with the elation of the moment. This slap- happy abandoned spirit was short-lived, as I had to think of the descent and landing. At this point, I needed to concentrate. The approach speed should be around 65-mph - I was coming in too fast and losing height too rapidly. 'A little less throttle and bring up the nose...that's better', I told myself. I saw that the wind sock was hanging limp from its mast - the wind must have dropped to almost dead calm. I would float a long way on landing.

My approach was good, but things were happening quickly now, and there was little time to think. As the boundary hedge shot beneath, the last vital seconds arrived...close the throttle, stick gently back to 'hold off'...ooh...the nose has gone up - must have been a bit too sudden. Steady...straighten up...the speed seems to have dropped right off. The height is about right - too late now if it is not. Pull the stick right back into my stomach. As the nose comes up, I lose sight of the distant hedge. The Tiger Moth dropped with a bit of a bump, but I was down and had made a fairly good landing.

My first solo flight was proudly entered in my log book and underlined in red. I could hardly wait to return to my billet that night, to write home and tell Mickie about it.

The next afternoon, one of the pupils - fresh-faced, boyish-looking fellow, named Prince - was taking his first solo flight, which drew the attention of almost everyone on the airfield. He weaved about a bit on the approach, which otherwise appeared normal. When he was a few feet from the ground, he 'held-off' rather too high, bounced and landed heavily. Instead of staying on the ground, he opened up the engine and took-off immediately. (We had been instructed that if we made a really bad landing, it was better to 'open up' and go round again.) Prince's landing had not been all that bad, but he must have decided to do another circuit.

His second approach also seemed quite normal, but, when only a few feet from the ground, he roared off again. Although this was slightly puzzling, those who were watching were not unduly worried. However, when he repeated this action for the third time, we realised that something was wrong or that he had got panicky. Intercommunication with the ground was not possible, so we could only watch helplessly, whilst he carried out another nine circuits, close to ground level, without attempting to land!

Whether it was shortage of petrol, or sheer terror, I never knew, but on the twelfth attempt, he made quite a good landing. He was quickly nick-named 'The Prince of Circuits'. Sadly for him, the Chief Flying Instructor removed him from further pilot training.

For the next few weeks of lovely spring weather, I was happily learning to fly and aerobat these splendid little Tiger Moths. During the course, we had to carry out one map-reading, cross-country flight. For my exercise, I was required to fly from Sywell to Cambridge and back, and instructed to land at Cambridge and report to the Flying Control tower, to prove that I had succeeded with my map-reading.

On my way to the aircraft to commence the exercise, I wrenched my ankle. It hurt considerably at the time, but after awhile, the pain wore off. As I flew at 2000 feet, the countryside below looked glorious, with the trees and hedgerows at their best in a variety of greens. Flying over the little town of St. Neots, I wondered how the baby quadruplets were getting on, they were the first to be born in England and survive. However, my main interest in St. Neots just now was to satisfy myself that I was on the correct course for Cambridge.

I was a bit anxious as my ankle began to swell. It became very stiff, so that using the rudder was difficult. Soon the sight of large black hangers in the distance, indicated that Cambridge aerodrome was ahead, and made me oblivious to my painful ankle. I made a reconnaissance circuit of the unfamiliar airfield before coming in to land. After taxying to the Control Tower, I released my harness and climbed gingerly out of the cockpit. By now the ankle was so swollen that I had to remove the shoe lace. I tried to avoid hobbling as I reported to the Airfield Control Officer. Apparently he had noticed, as he asked:

"Something the matter with your foot?"

"Only a slight twist, Sir, I think." I replied casually.

He looked at me dubiously, but gave me permission to take-off and return to Sywell, after endorsing my log.

Back at base, I reported to the CFI. By now I could not put any weight on my foot and was unable to conceal the injury any longer. If I had expected any medal for my press-on spirit, I was quickly disillusioned as he said, sharply:

"You were a bloody fool to fly with a foot like that - dangerous too - go and report to the M.O."

I felt rather deflated but glad to have accomplished my cross- country test.

One evening there was quite a 'flap' on. LAC Moir, a big, blond young Scotsman, who had left Medical School to fly with the RAF, had been detailed for local flying practice. His return was well overdue and the CFI was about to alert the police to carry out a search, when the phone rang.

"Is that Sywell airfield?" enquired the caller.

"Yes...this is RAF Sywell."

"I am speaking for Sir Robert Heslop of Bourne Hall...we have one of your young airmen here."

"Really, is he alright?"

"Yes... it seems he lost his way and landed in a field near the Hall."

The CFI looked out of the window and replied:

"It's getting a bit too dark to fly him out now..."

"That's alright..." cut in the caller, "we will make him comfortable here, and arrangements can be made tomorrow."

"Very good Sir, we will ring you early tomorrow morning."The following day the CFI and a small team of ground staff drove out to the Hall.

"What happened Moir?" questioned the CFI.

Moir, who had already passed his map-reading test, somewhat shamefaced replied:

"Really not sure, Sir...I just lost my bearings."

The CFI, noting the wind direction, and sizing up the field, said:

"There will be no trouble in flying out, except for a few high branches in that hedge down there."

"Oh, we can easily have those cut down," suggested Sir Robert. The gardener with the help of two airmen, soon had the lofty branches lopped off. The CFI took off alone in the Tiger Moth - to cut down the weight for take-off. The others returned to Sywell in the van.

The instructors were puzzled to know how Moir could have lost his way so near to base. To his most intimate friends, Moir confided that he had met Sir Robert's youngest daughter at a dance, and was crazy about her! - 'faint flyer never won fair lady' would have been a very apt axiom for Moir's amorous enterprise.

It was near the end of the course, when a small incident happened whilst I was solo flying. Once again, it was perfect weather with clear blue skies. I was happily flying at around 2000 feet - minding my own business and enjoying the countryside below. Suddenly, I heard a terrific noise of engines all around me - completely drowning the sound of my own engine. In the same split second, four Spitfires roared past, barely within wing-span distance. The pilots - who were obviously in communication with each other - seeing a lone Tiger, decided to give it a 'beat up.' They knew it must be a 'sprog' pilot flying it and thought they would show him who's who in the Royal Air Force! When the initial surprise had worn off, I felt enormously flattered that such superior beings as fighter pilots had singled me out for such an honour.

The whole Elementary Flying Course took little over a month to complete, which included about eight hours spent in that little monster - the Link Trainer - a flying simulator which almost drove everyone mad.

Life at Sywell had been great, and flying Tiger Moths, unforgettable. Nothing was ever mentioned about the war operational flying ahead of us and the frightening casualty statistics. We still had much to learn before attaining the coveted 'wings'. We were promoted to Leading Aircraftsmen, entitling us to sew the Propeller Badge on our sleeves. My Flying Log Book was endorsed - Proficiency as Pilot - Average. Fair enough I thought - might have been higher, then again I might have failed, as happened to quite a few trainees. We all left Sywell with a much stronger sense of the role we had to play in the RAF.

CHAPTER 4

CRANWELL - SERVICE FLYING

Our elementary flying training now completed, some pupils were posted to stations for training on more advanced, single-engined aircraft, the rest being sent for training on twin-engined planes. It was the ambition of almost all trainees to become fighter pilots, an ambition which I shared. My disappointment at being directed for twin-engined flying was compensated, when I found that I was going to Cranwell, with about half-a-dozen of my fellow pupils.

Cranwell College was known to be probably the finest flying academy in the world. Its very imposing and lovely buildings, set in large lawns, reflected the importance of the establishment.

We were taken from the little town of Sleaford in a small crew bus. As it swung through the ornate, wrought-iron gates and round the circular drive, we caught our first glimpse of the College. We were very impressed; it was grander by far than we had expected. At the top of a flight of wide stone steps, tall columns dominated the facade. As I climbed the steps for the first time, I felt that I really was a Royal Air Force Cadet. During wartime, not all trainees who qualified became Officers but the majority were offered Commissions.

The dining hall was no less imposing than the rest of the building. Six rows of long tables faced the 'top table' where the Senior Officers sat. At the end of the hall, some ten or twelve feet from the floor, a Minstrel Gallery gave a hint of an occasional banquet. We had a meal - seated at table number six, allocated to the newest course - after which we were directed to our rooms.

The bedroom I was to share with Tony McLeod had a large window, draped with heavy brocade curtains. After putting our clothes away, we decided to explore the College. There were several large ante- rooms, one of which was exclusively for the use of our course. In keeping with the rest of Cranwell, it was spacious and generously furnished with heavy oak tables and hide-upholstered chairs. It took most of the evening to explore the facilities for recreation, which included a fine swimming pool, tennis courts and a fully equipped gymnasium.

Since we had left Sywell early in the morning, it had been a very full day, and Tony and I decided to retire early. I found the crisp, snow-white linen sheets refreshingly cool; the fringed bedspread too, was white and worked with RAF emblems.

29

DEATH OR DECORATION

I slept very soundly and would not have wakened so early, had it not been for a loud swishing sound and sunlight suddenly pouring into the room. Rubbing my eyes, I strained to see who had drawn the curtains. Whilst trying to recollect where I was and how I had got there, a thin voice called out:

"Good morning, Gentlemen. It's 6.30 and time to get up."Looking at a rather diminutive man of about forty, dressed in a white jacket, I thought: "I can't believe it; there must be some mistake." But there was no mistake; this was Cranwell and even cadet pilots received a certain amount of privileged treatment.

Breakfast was informal but a feeling of orderliness prevailed, accentuated by the presence of white-coated stewards, who seemed to display a kind of aloof deference to cadets. After breakfast, we assembled for a talk about the course. I was allocated to 'E' Flight, No. 2 Squadron. The usual Flight photograph was taken and form filling completed, including details of religion and next-of-kin which I had always felt to be slightly ominous.

Then the door was thrust open and an upright, beefy man made an impressive entrance. His sleeve displayed a Crown badge, the emblem of the commanding rank of Station Warrant Officer. His purpose was to lecture us on the standard of behaviour that would be expected of us during our stay at Cranwell. He carried out this duty with uncommon oratory, finishing with the admonition:

"And, Gentlemen, you will not leave your 'ats lying abaght; you will 'ang yours 'ats in the 'all, on the 'ooks provided for that purpose."Pausing for a moment, to allow the full impact of his words to take effect, he then right-turned and marched out, giving a disdainful look at this latest bunch of raw, war-course recruits as he left.

We discovered that discipline was strict but fair, the College being run with the utmost efficiency. Each morning, after a short Colour-hoisting Parade, we marched away to a martial tune, played by a lone bagpiper in regimental dress. On Sundays and Station Commander's Parades, the full Royal Air Force band was in attendance.

Each working day had a fully organised programme of lectures on a variety of subjects which included navigation, meteorology, Air Force law, etc., or flying training. The aircraft we were taught to fly was the Airspeed Oxford, a cabin-type, low-winged monoplane powered by two Cheetah radial engines.

The summer of 1941 was a scorcher. The earth was parched and the heat made flying in the perspex-covered cockpits swelteringly hot. In the College, during lectures given by staff instructors, it was difficult to avoid 'nodding off.' One particular Warrant Officer, who had obviously been in the Service since his youth, contrived to keep us awake with anecdotes or amusing similes.

During a lecture on the use of the P8 compass, he was stressing the importance of aligning the red point of the compass needle with the red spot on the grid ring. His sonorous voice penetrated the most inattentive ear with:

"Never forget when you are flying - always put red on red, and I don't mean lipstick on a monkey's backside."

Well, I never forgot to put red on red, so the lesson was well learned as far as I was concerned.

Later, he told a story about a pilot whose mission was to photograph the German defences in Holland. He did not put red on red and returned with photographs of Dublin!

My flying instructor, Fg Off Allies, was tall and about 25 years of age. He had a pleasant, cheerful manner which made learning to fly a new aeroplane really enjoyable. After two or three hours of dual instruction, I was ready to take my first solo flight in an Oxford.

It was another fine summer morning when I met my instructor. His voice was cheerful as he said:

"Good morning, Waite. Whew! It's going to be hot in the plane today."

"Yes, Sir, pity we can't wear shorts."

Making my way through the fuselage, I took the seat on the port side; my instructor took the dual position seat by my side. Before putting on our flying helmets, Allies said:

"This morning we're flying from a field called Barkston Heath. I'll map-read. You can fly the aircraft perfectly well - I'll just be your passenger."

"Very good, Sir."

Beckoning a ground staff airman, he called out:

"Start her up, will you."

Climbing onto the wing, the airman pushed a starting handle into the engine nacelle; after one or two turns, the engine fired. The starboard engine started with equal ease.

"Alright, let's be off." Fg Off Allie's voice sounded optimistic; he seemed to be looking forward to the session. I felt confident as I taxied to the take-off point. After turning the Oxford into the wind, I gave my instructor a quick glance which he returned with a nod of his head. This assured me that all was well. I opened the throttles fully, enjoying the power of the Cheetah engines, and the Oxford surged forward. I felt that my flying was good and accurate, as I followed the changes of course being given me by Allies, who was checking the map on his knee with the ground below.

When we arrived over Barkston Heath, the temporary airfield looked only slightly larger than an ordinary farm field. I decided not to be in a hurry and did a circuit of the field, to spy out the land. In one corner, I saw the black Nissen hut which served as a Flight Office. In the opposite corner, I could see what appeared to be a small, ruined red brick building. When I found the wind-sock, I was pleased to see that it was fairly well extended, indicating a reasonable wind for landing.I felt relaxed and made a good landing. After taxying to the Nissen Flight hut, Mr. Allies looked at me with a reassuring smile and spoke those all important words:

"You are ready for solo...do one circuit and I will wait for you at the Flight hut."

The wind had now dropped to almost calm, so I sought some last minute advice from my instructor:

"The wind has dropped to almost nothing, would a diagonal approach still be best?" I asked him.

"Yes," replied Allies, "if you come in over the ruined building, you will have the longest run...but don't come in too high."

Flying Officer Allies released his harness and left the aeroplane. I waited till he had walked clear. He gave me a quick wave as he disappeared into the hut.

I looked momentarily at the seat Allies had occupied, half wishing he was still there, at the same time, I was desperately keen to get on with my first solo in an Oxford. The Cheetah engines emitted a burst of blue smoke, in protest at having to wait idling on the ground. I took-off, climbing steadily into a blue cloudless sky to the circuit height of 1000 feet. From this height, the field looked very small in which to land an Oxford. At the end of the cross-wind 'leg', I found the ruined building my instructor had spoken of. I scanned the sky for other planes, but none were in sight so I prepared to land. After reducing power, I lowered the undercarriage. At this point, all my attention was given to maintaining the correct speed and controlling the rate of descent.

"Don't panic," I told myself, "it's all going fine."

As I was approaching the ground, suddenly, a large dark shadow swept across my aeroplane. A wave of apprehension froze my blood. The height was now only about 100 feet. I could only afford a brief glance backwards, and to my horror, I saw another Oxford heading straight towards me and barely twenty yards behind.

There was not enough height for me to be able to take avoiding action. A second later, a shuddering crash behind me, shook my aircraft violently, making it uncontrollable. The ground rushed to meet me. The crash was now inevitable, so I pulled the control column back to bring the nose up and lessen the impact. There was a terrific jolt and sound of splintering wood as the plane struck the ground and slithered across the grass - minus the undercarriage.

I must have been temporarily concussed - the reeking smell of petrol soon brought me to my senses. The propeller blades of the port engine were embedded in the ground, whilst those of the starboard engine appeared to be missing with the 'revs' screaming. As my head cleared, my first thought was that the plane might blow up, so I reached frantically, to switch the engines off.

CHAPTER 4   CRANWELL - SERVICE FLYING

A few seconds later I had recovered from the shock of hitting the ground. Releasing my harness, I clambered out of my seat and walked down the fuselage. Then I saw that the centre section had been completely smashed, exposing a mass of splintered wood. Instead of leaving by the entrance door, all I had to do was to step over what remained of the middle section of the plane! I saw that the other Oxford, some 80 yards away, had settled on its belly, but otherwise not looking very badly damaged. I ran towards it and found the pilot slumped over the control column. I was about to try and open the cockpit when a fire tender arrived, and the fire crew took charge of the situation.

Air Collision

Shortly afterwards, a large Rolls Royce vehicle which had been converted into a field ambulance, arrived on the scene. Acton Bond,the other pilot had regained consciousness by this time and, miraculously, did not appear to have any serious injuries. A Medical Orderly asked us how we felt:

"I'm alright," I told him. "Just a small cut on my hand from broken perspex."

"Well, that's not surprising, after a 'prang' like that," said the Orderly, as he helped us into the back of the Rolls.

The journey back to Cranwell, several miles from Barkston Heath, via winding and often bumpy country roads, did nothing to enhance our comfort! We sat silently side-by-side, still too stunned to hold any conversation. Poor Acton-Bond winced as we travelled over the worst sections of the road.

On arriving back at Cranwell, we were both taken to Sick Quarters. After a thorough check I was pronounced uninjured and ready to fly again. Acton-Bond was detained overnight. The following day I was told that he had been moved to the RAF Hospital at Rauceby. I took the first opportunity to visit him there and discovered that his spine had been damaged. I never saw him again. Some time later I heard that he had been discharged from the RAF as unfit for flying duties due to the crash, and had become a successful Producer with the BBC.

Later an odd coincidence occurred when Mickie and I were visiting our farmer friends at Farrington Gurney. We were sitting around having tea and chatting about the weekend parties we had enjoyed before the War. Mr Teek, who generally preferred to listen rather than talk, joined the conversation. In his warm Somerset accent he asked:

"And how are things with you, Ron?"

"Pretty well, thanks, Mr Teek," I replied.

"I hope to get my Wings within two or three weeks, but I was very lucky to walk away from an air collision."

Mrs Teek, always very concerned, said:

"The son of friends of ours, who was going to be a pilot, had a bad accident...poor young Acton-Bond, he is still in hospital, I believe."

"Acton-Bond!!" I exclaimed. "What an amazing coincidence. He was the other pilot involved in my accident."

Back at Cranwell I was still too inexperienced in flying to appreciate my narrow escape from death; very few fliers have walked away from a collision in the air.

Within two days I was called to give evidence at a Court of Inquiry. The Squadron Leader, who took my statement, was quiet and kindly. Where necessary he prompted me gently, to elicit all the facts of the accident. As I had been the pilot of the aircraft closest to landing, it was intimated that I had priority and would, therefore, not be responsible for the accident.

The flying programme continued during that hot summer. It aimed at improving our flying skills with such exercises as precautionary and cross-wind landings, besides lots of instrument flying.

One evening after dinner, several fellows in my Flight were chatting over a beer or two in the ante-room. The general conversation halted sharply when Franklyn said:

"Say fellows, what do you think McLeod and I saw when we were flying near Lincoln?"

No one bothered to reply, but all looked at Franklyn. Having got everyone's attention, he came out with his newsflash:

"Two completely naked girls in a field."

This statement was received with a mixture of jeering disbelief, suspicion, and perhaps, a hint of 'lip-smacking' anticipation. Whatever the individual opinions, all shouted in unison:

"Where?"

The majority also wanted to know:

34

"What were they like?"

McLeod, the Scot, who was older than Franklyn, was more reticent. Not so, Franklyn who launched into a flood of ecstatic description:

"Cor - the smaller, dark one was a 'scorcher'. She was gorgeous lying down; but when she stood up and waved, her figure was - UMMPH!"

McLeod interrupted what was likely to be an even more detailed description of her pulchritudinous charms:

"Aye, and ye lost at least 200 feet in that steep tairn, and damned nearly caused a 'prang'."

Looking For Land Marks

Being of a more practical disposition, I cut in:

"Let's get a map and try and pinpoint the position."

The only map available was an Air Ministry chart. This made the task more difficult as an aerial chart was not designed to enable lascivious young pilots to pinpoint basking beauties. McLeod and Franklyn agreed that the location was probably a farm about 11 miles south of Lincoln.

"The girls were lying on a horse blanket, and I saw some dark green clothes near them," said McLeod.

With this information, I was able to confidently announce:

"They are Land Army girls for certain."

Thereafter, I think all those present took the first opportunity, when flying solo, to discover the farm. I had no success and, as far as I know, neither did anyone else. Franklyn took a bicycle on a safari of the Lincolnshire country lanes, but returned exhausted and totally frustrated.

35

DEATH OR DECORATION

The fine summer weather allowed uninterrupted flying. Occasional haze and low stratus cloud made visibility poor. Pupils flew in pairs for many exercises, taking turns at the controls.

One afternoon, most of the course were detailed to fly on a three-leg, cross- country flight, as an exercise in simple navigation and map reading. The route we had to fly was close to the towns of Kettering and Rugby. We had been warned that, if we met cloud or bad visibility, we were to return to Cranwell and pick up an instructor to fly with us.

It was my turn to be the pilot, whilst my co-pilot, Leslie Allison, had the task of navigating. We were both looking forward immensely to the trip. It was the first break from seemingly endless instrument flying, which was both difficult and tedious.

We had been flying for about twenty minutes and were approaching the town of Melton Mowbray when visibility suddenly fell to less than a mile. Turning to Allison, I said:

"I think we had better return to Cranwell; the weather looks a bit duff."
Leslie agreed, so I turned around and flew back to Cranwell for our instructor.

Arriving over the airfield and preparing to land, we could not see a single Oxford on the dispersal point where our aircraft were normally parked. "That's funny," said Leslie, "not a single Oxford in sight."
I made a quick decision.

"Right, we'll carry on with the exercise. I did not want to be the only one to have 'burked' it."
So, for the second time, I set course over Cranwell; the weather was now quite clear.

After flying for about a quarter of an hour, we were approaching Rugby when the weather became thick again. Before the flight, we had been studying the map and saw that there were some very high wireless masts close to our track. We were flying at 1,000 feet, which I felt was not a safe height to clear the masts. Drawing Leslie's attention to the situation, I said: "I think we'll climb over this murk to 5,000 feet. Will you work out a safe time to descend, well clear of the masts?"

As we climbed through the mist, we lost sight of the roads and fields below. The layer of fog was quite shallow, and at 5,000 feet, we were in bright, blue sky again. Below, lay a vast canopy of white cloud, appearing like cotton wool. Some seven or eight minutes later, Allison nudged my arm:

"It's alright to descend now, we should be well clear of any masts."
Throttling back the engines and slightly lowering the nose, we steadily lost height. At around 1,500 feet, the patchy mist started to swirl around us. It had now become gloomy and, peering through the mist, I suddenly shouted:

"Christ, there's a mast dead ahead of us."
Then I heard Allison exclaim:

"God! There are masts all around us - and aerials draped between them - they're higher than we are!"

I could not afford to waste a split second and slammed both throttles fully open. As I pulled the stick back almost into my stomach, the nose of the Oxford reared up. I broke into a cold sweat when I realised that there was nothing more I could do. It was literally a matter of life or death. The seconds seemed like ages, waiting to see if we would clear those masts, which almost appeared to be beckoning us. This story would have remained untold if we had not cleared them with only a few feet to spare.

It must have been a full minute before either of us had recovered enough to speak. I broke the silence:

"What went wrong, do you think?"

Leslie thought for a moment and replied:

"I don't know. I was sure there was enough time to be clear of the masts."

Then, suddenly, he blurted out:

"I know the reason. During the ten minutes we were climbing, the ground speed would have been a lot less, so we haven't travelled over the ground as far as we thought - that's why we came down too early."

Realising that he was right, I said:

"We were still damned unlucky to be dead on track and to come down in the middle of that forest of aerial masts."

As might have been expected, we were the last to arrive back at Cranwell. Immediately we had landed, we were called to the CFI's office. S/Ldr. Sexton looked up from his desk:

"Waite...Allison, what happened?"

Before I could reply, he said:

"You were instructed to return if the weather deteriorated; why didn't you?"

"Well, Sir," I replied, "we did, but found all the other planes had gone."

Looking at us angrily, he said:

"You should have landed and reported to the Flight office, then you would have found out that the other crews had returned and taken an instructor."

I dared not tell him how near we had been to disaster, but thought it would be propitious to add:

"When we came across the low cloud, I flew above it."

"YOU DID WHAT? You knew you shouldn't have flown above cloud without radio." All I could do was to blurt out :

"Sorry, Sir."

"Sorry be damned. You are a pair of bloody fools. Let that be a lesson to you - alright, off you go."

Whew! that was the second narrow escape of the afternoon; we could have been taken off the course.

DEATH OR DECORATION

Between lectures and flying, we had sport and PT. Drill was secondary. It was assumed we had learnt this at ITW. However, we did have one very interesting and, for me, chastening drill session.

The RAF 'powers that be' felt it was necessary - if we were to become pilots, and possibly officers - to be able to take over a drill parade. For this purpose, we were assembled on the very large Station square.

The exercise, known as 'Shouting Drill', required that one cadet should take charge of a small squad of nine men. He had to stand on one spot and not move, whilst shouting drill commands to his own squad. The problem was that about another six squads were all carrying out a similar exercise at the same time.

An observer would have found the whole thing hilarious. Squads of nine men marched in all directions with six cadets having to stand to attention, each bawling his head off as he tried to drill and control his own squad. All sorts of voices could be heard, from basso-profundo to counter-tenor. I found that my light baritone was totally inadequate and I tried falsetto. This was reasonably effective, and my confidence grew.

After a few "Quick March; About turn; Right turn; About turn;" I sought to impress the drill Warrant Officer in charge with a more intricate bit of drill I had learnt at ITW. So I shouted:

"Right incline."

My squad observed this command to the letter, and marched off diagonally away from me like a small human diamond.

It was such an effective manoeuvre that I completely forgot the necessary command required to bring them back to me! They retreated further and further, in the meantime, two other squads had marched between me and my outfit.

As I watched helplessly, my collar getting tighter with the worry, I saw my fellows change direction and return towards me. I had given them no command, so I could only suppose they had done this out of sympathy. Meanwhile the other cadets 'in charge' were all shrieking orders hysterically, each trying to control his own squad.

The Warrant Office in charge waited until everything was in total chaos then, with his 'pacing stick' tucked menacingly under his arm, bellowed:

"HALT!"

This command only 'tickled the surface' the first time, but his second "HALT" roared out across the square, and everyone halted. Whilst he lectured us on how it should be done, he kept raising himself on his toes, presumably to increase his stature. His moustache tilted up disdainfully on one side, as he told us finally to "Get some in," - a sneering reference to our ineptness.

Training for day flying was now almost complete, and the time for night flying had arrived. Once again we had to fly from the field at Barkston Heath. It was dusk when my instructor, Fg Off Fletcher, and I, took off from Cranwell. The airfield did not have the luxury of an illuminated runway, so a flare path had to be laid. After landing I had to assist with placing the flares. These flares were almost exactly like large watering cans filled with paraffin; the long spouts contained a kind of coarse cotton wick. By the time we had spaced out the flares, it was almost dark. The flares produced quite a large bright orange flame mixed with dense black smoke. Altogether it was a smelly affair.

Returning to the aircraft, I took the pilot's seat next to the instructor. Fletcher gave me the minimum of instructions, and his quiet manner made me feel at ease and gave me confidence. From a small van near the take-off end of the flare path, a Sergeant, using an Aldis lamp, controlled the take-offs and landings.

The night was now dark and clear, and the line of flares flickered eerily, but were quite easy to see. Inside the cockpit, the instrument panel lights, although dimmed, seemed distractingly bright. My take-off cockpit drill completed, I awaited the green Aldis light for permission to take off. In a matter of seconds the bright green light flashed and I taxied to the beginning of the flare path.

I opened the throttles and found it a little difficult at first to keep the aircraft straight. I seemed to be working the rudder bar a bit too erratically. As the plane gathered speed, it was easier to control; before the last flare had flashed past, we became airborne.

The cool night air made flying very steady. From the circuit height of 800 feet, I was surprised to see how distant and short the flare-path looked.

In two or three minutes it was time to turn for the approach to land. As I banked the Oxford, the flare path appeared below at about 45 degrees. With the undercarriage lowered, I was now on the final approach. Fg Off Fletcher, who had been silent during the circuit, said quietly:

"You're coming in a bit too high, lose a bit of height."

Whilst doing this, I waggled about a bit, causing the flare path to appear to weave. I corrected this and found the flares coming up very quickly. It was quite difficult to assess the exact height, and I did not 'hold off' quite soon enough. The wheels hit the ground rather hard, but it was a safe landing, if not very polished.

After two more circuits, I taxied round to the take-off point and did my cockpit check. I expected to do another dual circuit because my landings had been a bit rough. Fletcher turned to me and said:

"Alright, Waite, you are quite safe now - go and do three circuits."

I thought 'if he thinks I'm OK, I must be'...

Fg Off Fletcher gave me a final reminder:

"Oh, just watch your height on the approach. Your speed is correct, but you're coming in a bit too high."

With a firm 'thumbs up' sign, he added:

DEATH OR DECORATION

"Taxy to the Nissan hut when you've finished."

I was now alone, and perhaps just a little scared.

Going solo at night for the first time was another unique experience. Unlike day flying, once airborne, and the flares left behind, the landscape becomes lost in the darkness, the feeling of being launched into space is accentuated. It is not possible to fly by 'feel' any longer and it is essential to concentrate on the instruments. One in particular was a 'godsend' - the artificial horizon, showing a silhouette of the aeroplanes wings floating between two parallel bars. The silhouette takes the attitude the aircraft is actually flying.

There is a rather strange feeling of 'detachment' when flying alone at night. The absence of any distractions helped me to complete my three solo circuits without any problems.

A week later, my name was down for night flying again but with a different instructor, a Flying Officer Streeter. Things did not go at all well this time. We were detailed to fly the second period, which meant starting late - almost midnight. From the beginning, Fg Off Streeter was edgy and nervous. I felt I was doing quite well, but he niggled over every detail:

"What do you think you are doing?" he blustered, which seemed the only remark he could make, as he sat uncomfortably beside me. He seemed incapable of giving simple instructions and advice. After I had carried out what I thought were two perfectly reasonable circuits, I expected he would send me solo, instead, he barked:

"We are packing it in for the night...I will fly her back to Cranwell."

The following night I was down to fly with Streeter again. This time he was much quieter. After a couple of check circuits, he sent me solo, thus completing the total of six circuits and landings I was required to do.

It was now the beginning of August and the end of the Service Flying course; it had taken barely a couple of months. Close formation flying was one of the few remaining exercises to be done. The last obstacle to be overcome - before being awarded the cherished wings - was the CFI'S flying test, the Flight Commander's report and the written examinations.

I had 'boned up' pretty thoroughly on the ground subjects, so they worried me less than the flying tests which intimidated all the cadets. These tests were each of about three-quarters of an hour duration. They were not particularly complicated, but it was difficult to fly at one's best, knowing that every manoeuvre was being watched, and one mistake could mean failure. At the end of the CFI's test, the landing, luckily, was one of my best. After taxying to the dispersal area, I was very relieved when Squadron Leader Tomalin said:

"That wasn't at all bad. You lost a bit of height in the steep turn. Start centralising the rudder earlier should solve the problem."

CHAPTER 4   CRANWELL - SERVICE FLYING

The following day we were told who had passed the exams and flying tests, and all assembled for a talk by Fg Off Sexton. He opened with a few general and humorous remarks, then he addressed us:

"Your really serious flying is about to begin."

Looking around at each cadet individually, he said:

"If any of you feel you haven't the stomach for the job, now is the time to say so."

He followed this rather unexpected remark with:

"No action will be taken at this stage, but later, if you suddenly discover that you are suffering from air sickness or any similar problem, it may not be received sympathetically."

I think we all got the message!

The course ended without any Wings Parade, in fact we were not even sure that we would receive a Commission. I think probably about 75 percent of us were commissioned, the remainder being promoted to Sergeant.

A day or so later, those of us who had obtained Commissions assembled in one of the large ante-rooms. Several representatives from the military tailors, Gieves, had arrived from London to measure us for our Officers' uniforms, greatcoats, etc., which were to be made and delivered to Cranwell within a week.

At the end of each course there was an evening of celebration and tonight it was OUR night. The usual dinner had always been good, but on this occasion many extras were contrived by the kitchen staff. The Officers sat with us at the long refectory table. We were seated alternately; I had a Wing Commander on my right and a Flight Lieutenant on my left.

At first I found it difficult to converse freely, being conscious of the difference in our ranks. I was, after all, still only a Leading Aircraftsman. The Officers who sat with me were excellent company; they made conversation easy, without the slightest hint of condescension. I listened in rapt attention as they told stories of their own adventures in the RAF.

The night was made more memorable by the sound of music coming from the Minstrel Gallery. They were obviously enjoying the festive evening, as they played popular music from the films and Gilbert and Sullivan operettas.

After dinner, our course gave a short concert, more of a variety show really. I was very surprised at the hidden and unexpected talents in some of my fellow pupils. The show was led and organised by Greg Stanislaus, who had been 'something' in the BBC before deciding to fly with the RAF. Most of the items were either sketches or parodies of songs, extolling not only the virtues but, more often, the foibles of our various instructors, none of whom escaped a mention. However, no one overstepped the mark, and it was all carried off with great good humour, no doubt partly due to the lashings of ale consumed. One thing we all discovered at dinner - traditional and vital bit of knowledge - was the correct direction to pass the port!

DEATH OR DECORATION

Friday, the 10th August, was our last day at Cranwell. On that morning, even the most blasé amongst us could not disguise their excitement when the cartons of uniforms arrived from Gieves. The scene was reminiscent of peacetime summer sales, with fellows trying on their gear, turning this way and that, to see how well it fitted. I was pleased with my outfit, particularly the stylish, heavy Melton greatcoat. The item which gave all of us a sense of pride and achievement, was the coveted RAF Wings.

After turning in my original airman's uniform, I was now attired in quality 'officer's blue'. The one part of the uniform which was disliked by everyone, was the peaked cap - particularly when it was new. A cane ring in the rim of the cap ensured that it retained its flat, plate-like shape which we detested. We could hardly wait to get out of sight of the College, to remove the offending ring. Later, during mess binges, we filled the hats with beer, in order to give them a semblance of faithful and long service. I recall once, on Peterborough rail station, seeing an officer wearing a peaked cap which had a tear in the top, through which poked a piece of the lining straw! I was certain he must have been a quite famous pilot to have had the nerve.

On my way to the adjutant's office to collect my leave pass, I saw two sergeants coming towards me - this would be the first time that I would have to return a salute - instead of giving one. When the men were a few paces away, they both raised their right arms. I raised mine, to return a salute when, to my chagrin, instead of saluting, they made a mock adjustment to the forage caps they were wearing. I was fuming at the indignity, whilst they - being used to seeing 'sprog' officers at Cranwell - assumed that we would not have the nerve to give them a dressing down.

I was about to start my first full leave since joining the RAF. I travelled from Paddington with another of my course mates, Ken Mould. Anyone who had pre-conceived ideas that all RAF pilots emerged from the same mould, would have changed their minds at seeing Ken and I together. I was almost six foot tall and slim - almost to the point of being skinny - whilst Ken was about six inches shorter and chubby; his round face wore a permanent, optimistic grin.

At Bath station, we had to go our separate ways, Ken to his home at Salisbury, I to Bristol. Before we parted, a cup of tea seemed a good idea. We had to walk almost the length of the platform, to reach the Refreshment Room. Wearing our spanking new uniforms, we must have looked as though we had just stepped out of the chorus line from "Glamorous Night."

We could not avoid noticing the admiring glances, and we clearly overheard two elderly ladies say - 'aren't our flying boys just marvellous.' We were obviously basking in the glorious trail the Battle of Britain pilots were blazing during 1941. My only conspicuous achievement (?) to date, was to get 'pranged' in the 'Oxford'. Later, when my mother proudly told me that her small home town had collected £6000 for 'Wings for Victory Week', I thought another thousand would have paid for the ill-fated plane.

I never saw Ken Mould again, but heard two years later, that he was very badly injured in a crash- landing.

At Temple Mead station, I soon found Mickie in the crowd. As we walked towards each other, the ecstatic welcome I expected was somewhat subdued. During the crowded bus journey to Keynsham, she scarcely glanced at me, and I felt a distinct frostiness in the atmosphere - I discovered the reason later.

In wartime, all cadets who qualified as pilots from Cranwell College did not automatically receive a Commission. Realising this, I was desperately anxious not to disappoint my family - especially Mickie- should I have failed to become an officer, consequently - at every opportunity - I falsely stressed the advantages of NOT having a Commission. It never occurred to me at the time, that Mickie would tell all her friends, how much better it would be if I became a sergeant pilot! I should, I suppose, have phoned her with the news, but thought she would be delighted with the surprise. She now faced the embarrassing job of 'changing her tune' to her friends - hence her understandable coolness. It did not take her long to recover from the surprise, and was proud to accept my officer status.

It was difficult to know what qualities were looked for by the Board, when determining which men were 'officer material'. A good education, diction and bearing helped no doubt. The Commission parchment...'Given at the Court of St. James...by His Majesty's Command', undoubtedly improved one's social status - apart from the less obvious advantages of First Class travel and uniforms made from the finest cloth.

CHAPTER 5

OPERATIONAL TRAINING UNIT - KINLOSS

I had spent a wonderful leave with Mickie and little Diana, one continual round of 'get-togethers' with relatives and friends. I had an empty, sinking feeling as I was about to take the 450 mile journey to Scotland. My posting to No 19 Operational Training Unit at Kinloss, situated on the Moray Firth, north of Inverness, a journey which would take almost 24 hours.

At Temple Meads, I joined the very long train standing at the LMS platform. Servicemen packed the station, with an increasing number of girls in uniform amongst them. I was glad of my first class rail warrant, which would assure me of a great deal more comfort than hitherto.

The train reached Glasgow at six in the morning, after a seemingly endless journey, with many stops and unexplained delays in the middle of nowhere. I just had time to grab a snack before catching the connection to Edinburgh.

We left Waverley station in brilliant sunshine and at Perth an extra locomotive was added to the train. Interesting names such as Bridge of Allen and Blair Atholl began to appear on station signs. As we snaked around hairpin bends, the views became more and more striking, with small lochs - deep and remote - suddenly appearing. The two engines, straining under the load as we climbed the Cairngorm Mountains, billowed pure white steam against the purple, heather-clad slopes. This was my first visit to Scotland and I found the landscape very impressive, dispelling my earlier depression.

At Pitlochry, amongst the handful of people waiting to board the train, a particular trio caught my attention. A woman and a little girl aged about six, were seeing off a soldier in full army kit. As the guard blew his first warning whistle, the little girl crying bitterly, flew into the arms of her father. Early in the war I decided to say my goodbyes at home - railway station farewells were too dreadful. Gracie Fields' jolly little jingle, "Wish me luck as you wave me goodbye, with a smile, not a tear, make it gay," was very remote from reality.

A small van was waiting at Forres station to take me with several other airmen to RAF Kinloss. Sitting in the back of the swaying vehicle made it difficult to take in much of the small town. I managed to spot the Post Office, but could not see any little pubs, which we might visit when we had some free time. The driver swept through the main gates at Kinloss and we were unloaded with our baggage in front of the Station Headquarters. As this was to be my home for the next few months, I tried to get a 'feel' of the place. Most of the buildings were single-storeyed and made of brick. I sensed a rather less disciplined atmosphere than existed at Cranwell. As I glanced around, I could not fail to notice that the flag in front of the HQ buildings, was fluttering at half- mast. Turning to a Sergeant standing nearby, I enquired:

"Why is the flag at half-mast?".

Almost casually he replied:

"A crew flew into the mountains two nights ago.."

Until now our flying had been reasonably carefree, almost fun; accidents had been rare and none fatal. I suddenly woke up to the fact that wartime flying could be very dangerous. Because of several fatal accidents during the next three weeks, the flag stayed at half-mast!

Reporting to the Adjutant's office, I was told that my quarters were to be in Burgie Hall and that transport would take me there in about ten minutes' time. A Canadian navigator accompanied me on the journey.

"Are you a new arrival, too?" I asked him.

"No. I've been here a week; I came from Cranbourne S.F.T.S.."

"I did my S.F.T.S. at Cranwell," I replied, almost apologetically, for fear of seeming snooty.

"Cranwell, Jeez! You'll find Burgie Hall pretty bloody - it's cold, dank, more like a jail in a forest. I'm trying to get a room at the camp.."

The van climbed the rough and winding road which became steeper as it entered a heavily wooded area. The driver swung the van suddenly left, into a wide drive of loose gravel, and slid to a stop in front of an imposing stone mansion, surrounded on three sides by tall pines. The large, weathered, front door was approached by three wide steps. On each side, symmetrically placed, were six tall curtainless windows. The outside looked formidable. Inside, the very large hall had two immense stone fireplaces on either side. The walls, also of stone, were starkly bare. For a moment, I imagined how it might have looked a couple of hundred years ago, with great pine logs burning in the hearths, the wall bearing the arms and swords of previous owners and the flagstoned floor covered with colourful Persian carpets - it probably had quite a history.

"Sir...SIR.."

My dreaming was interrupted and I turned to the airman who was addressing me.

"I'm sorry, lost in thought..."

"I'll show you your room, more like a dormitory really..."

I followed him up a wide, bare wooden staircase with heavy banisters; large rod fittings on each step showed they had once been heavily carpeted. The room contained four beds, each with a locker beside, otherwise it was devoid of furnishings. The two white opal, office-type shades only accentuated the cheerless room.

Although it was only September, the atmosphere at Burgie Hall was chilly, so we quickly renamed it 'Bogie Hall'. Being about three miles from Kinloss was a distinct disadvantage, and like my Canadian friend, I could not wait to get accommodated in the camp.

After a week spent badgering the Adjutant, I was given a room on the camp at Kinloss. My room was one of ten in a typical brick and concrete hut. It was quite comfortable and very pleasant to have a place of my own.

Two days later, after dinner, I decided to return to the mess for a drink. As I went through the swing door, the hullabaloo coming from inside was terrific. Being a 'new boy', I had not heard of anything special going on, and could hardly get inside and find out what the party was in aid of. It was unlike anything I had previously seen in the Air Force - and I had experienced a party or two. A number of fellows, mostly without tunics, had formed a crowded circle, cheering on some activity taking place in the middle. As I went to the bar to get a pint of beer, I found it difficult to take my eyes away from the action for fear of missing something. With a tankard firmly grasped in my hand, I joined the roistering throng. In the centre of the ring, two chaps were staggering around, each with another seated firmly on his shoulders.

The battle in progress was called 'King's Horses.' The aim of each rider was to unseat his opponent by fair means or foul. The 'horses' were having a rough time, charging around under the weight of their riders, who were hanging on tenaciously, with their feet gripped firmly around the backs of their mounts. The support for the pair of combatants was enthusiastic and raucous. Now and then, one pair of the contenders would stumble into the circle of cheering supporters. This made an excellent opportunity for everyone to join the fray. It did not matter who was supporting whom: some would be trying to shove the rider back on, others were just as vigorously trying to dismount him. Hostilities came to an end with no decisive winner, with horses, riders and supporters all finishing up in a perspiring heap on the floor.

I did not know at the time who the contestants were, without their tunics it was not possible to know their rank, but I thought they had an appearance of seniority. We were all in dire need of topping up our beer tankards. Whilst waiting at the bar, I asked the fellow next to me:

"Who were the two contestants?."

He looked at me in surprise and said:

"Gawd, you must be new, don't you know who they are?"

"No, not the foggiest."

"The smaller one, going a bit thin on top, is Group Captain Maw, who has just been posted. The other, the big fellow, is his replacement - Group Captain Jarman, a tough customer, from what I've heard."

DEATH OR DECORATION

There was a lull in the physical activities, spent very advantageously imbibing refreshing tankards of ale. The intelligence officer, who was a good pianist, sat at the battered upright piano. There was no hushed silence for a concerto, instead, the strains of Waltzing Matilda came forth, with plenty of loud pedal work. It seemed everyone else but me knew every word of the paraphrased verses. Instead of Waltzing Matilda, the title line was 'Ops in a Whitley.' I recalled a couple of the verses later, and before the end of the course at Kinloss, I could sing all eight verses:

First Verse: The first silly bastard, opened up his throttles wide,
     Went down the runway - one, two, three,
     And he sang as he swang and pranged it on the
     boundary,
     Who'll come on ops in a Whitley with me?

Chorus: Ops in a Whitley, Ops in a Whitley,
     Who'll come on ops in a Whitley with me?

Second Verse: The third silly bastard, he got over Germany,
     Up came the 'flak' like a Christmas Tree,
     And the rear gunner sang as the navigator s..t himself,
     Who'll come on ops in a Whitley with me?

Chorus: Ops in a Whitley, Ops in a Whitley,
     Who'll come on ops in a Whitley with me?

This party made me aware, subconsciously, that I was entering a new phase in the wartime Air Force, when the dangers, which we all shared, produced a closer bond of comradeship and brotherhood.

Most of the instructors were men who had finished their first tour of bomber operations in Whitleys and were supposedly having their rest period - some 'rest period' - teaching new pilots how to fly these cumbersome-looking aircraft. In fact the Whitley, nicknamed the 'flying coffin' because of its box-like shape, was a very gentle beast. It was tough as old boots and could take even the roughest of landings without embarrassing the pilot.

The morning for our first flying session was perfect - clear skies and just enough breeze with a Scottish nip in the air to keep the senses alert. The crew bus, containing its complement of instructors and pupil pilots, set off for the airfield. The only one I knew was Johnny Wright who had been with me on all the courses since ITW.

My instructor, Flying Officer Daniels, was tall, dark and quite good looking. His manner was quiet and intense, but conveyed a confidence which helped to dispel any apprehensions I might have felt.

The field was level and without runways. At the far end, a row of trees indicated the boundary. I had a co-pupil, Plt Off Parker; the three of us walked across to where one of several Whitleys was waiting, its Rolls-Royce Merlin engines already ticking over. We walked around the aircraft whilst Fg Off Daniels pointed out the salient features. Like our instructor, the Whitley had done her fair share of bombing raids over Germany and she showed it. As the aeroplane sat sedately on the grass, it almost seemed to be wearing the expression of one who had seen it all and would show tolerance to the new 'sprog' pilots.

Fg Off Daniels, having finished his brief description of the aircraft, said: "OK chaps -let's get in."

Near the tail of the long box-like fuselage was the entrance door. Waiting behind Parker, to follow him in, I could just make out the letters DY which had been painted out with the dull grey-black colour of the rest of the fuselage. These were the identification letters of 78 Squadron, from which the old aeroplane had been retired.

As we climbed through the doorway, a very distinctive smell assaulted the nostrils, one with which we were to become very familiar. It was a sweet, sickly mixture of glycol, hydraulic oil and something indefinable - probably old, cold sweat! Clambering through the length of the fuselage was a bit difficult with barely five feet of headroom, and various obstructions such as flare chute, Elsan toilet, and particularly the main wing spars to negotiate.

I was the first to be given dual instruction, I sat in the left (port side) seat and listening attentively whilst I was told the cockpit check procedure. Taxying out to the take-off position was not as difficult as I had expected because the Whitley was less 'bouncy' than the Airspeed Oxfords we had flown at Cranwell.

The initial exercises went well enough. Those aeroplanes were old, ugly but kind; they had no vices. Two days later, my instructor considered me safe enough to take the Whitley on my first solo flight. Unlike previous 'first solos', I had a skeleton crew of a second pilot - who was a co-pupil - a rear gunner and a navigator. This flight and the other training flights over the next few days were uneventful.

One Saturday, we had some free time, with Johnny Wright and a new friend, 'Fletch', I went to Inverness. Walking back from the station at Forres, the sky to the east was lit up by great wavy streaks of light. We stopped in our tracks, wondering what this phenomenon might be, when Fletch, with a hint of disdain in his voice at our ignorance, announced:

"They are the Northern Lights; haven't you heard of them?"

"Of course we have," Johnny and I said in unison.

"I didn't think they were so spectacular." I added.

We stopped to admire those weaving, flame-like lights for a few minutes before making our way to the mess.

Although it was not that late, the mess seemed very quiet, especially for a Saturday. We mused for a while, had a final drink and went to our quarters. The next morning, we were to discover the reason for the 'atmosphere' in the mess the previous night. It appeared that, quite late in the evening, a Flight Lieutenant had decided that things were too quiet. He walked to the sleeping quarters in a long hut of single rooms. Entering a bedroom where one of his colleagues had decided to go to bed early, in a slurred voice he said:

"Come on, get out of it, come over and have a drink.."

His friend, realising he was the worse for drink, said:

"GO AWAY. I'm not going anywhere, and if I were you, I'd get my head down, too."

Thereupon, the Flight 'Looey' pulled out a service revolver and fired five rounds into the pillow, circling his friend's head. I never heard any details of what happened then, but it was generally believed that the Flight Lieutenant suffered a breakdown as a result of his experiences, and was immediately removed to a hospital. Officers never carried firearms under normal circumstances and it was a mystery how he had obtained the weapon. No real harm had been done and the incident was soon forgotten. The Flight Lieutenant was not seen again in Kinloss.

Day flying now completed, the time had arrived for night flying. This always gave rise to an atmosphere of increased excitement. Perhaps the roar of the Merlins, accentuated by the red hot exhausts breathing out blue flames, seemed more sinister at night.

Daylight was fading rapidly as we climbed into the crew bus for the start of the journey to the airfield. I was one of the first on board and sat at the rear next to Plt Off Parker, who was flying with me for our first night of dual instruction. A couple of seats in front, Johnny Wright was sitting alone, with his flying helmet on the seat beside him. In the front, several instructors were chatting quietly. Parker turned to me and remarked:

"Looks as if the Met fellows were right and it's going to be a fine night."

"Yes, and a full moon too." I added.

I noticed that Johnny sat with his head inclined forward his brow cupped in his hand as if resting. I was about to draw Parkers attention to him, thinking that perhaps Johnny felt unwell, when I realised that his attitude was that of prayer; the slight movement of his lips confirmed this, and I knew that he was a devout Christian. Johnny, whom I had known since ITW days, was over six feet tall. His very large round grey eyes gave him a benign countenance and had he been wearing a clerical collar, one would not have been surprised. He had a gentle sense of humour but the noisy frivolity of Service life did not come easily to him.

Arriving at the airfield, there was a malevolent look to the black bomber as it stood silhouetted against the evening sky. We crawled through the fuselage to the cockpit and were ready to begin the exercise. The instructor said:

"OK Waite, you go first."

Under his watchful eye, I carried out the cockpit check. I poked my head out of the side panel to watch the movement of the rudder, elevator and ailerons to ensure they were working correctly, followed by the engine check for boost, magneto drop and so on. Fg Off Daniels then said:

"I will taxy out.."

When we had reached the position where the Airfield Control Caravan was parked, a line of paraffin flares stretched across the field; their flickering yellow flames contrasted eerily with the full moon which had climbed unpretentiously into the sky. I had expected that Daniels would do the first circuit and was surprised when he said:

"Alright, Waite...she's all yours. When you get the 'green', turn onto the flarepath and take- off.."

"OK Sir." I replied.

He then added a last instruction:

"Watch your airspeed, start to lift off at about 90 and climb at not less than 110."

The old Whitley moved forward sluggishly at first then slowly gathered momentum. The sturdy Oleo legs of the under-carriage did a good job of ironing out the roughness of the ground. I glanced at the airspeed, now hovering near about 90 mph., and eased the control 'stick' gently backwards, the aircraft responded by lifting off. Soon after the last flare disappeared, we flew low over the pine trees which fringed the edge of the airfield. It was indeed a beautiful night. The flight path took us over Findhorn Bay, and it was difficult not to be sidetracked by the moonlight sparkling on the water in the lovely little inlet. Both Parker and I carried out several circuits and landings, but neither of us went solo on this occasion.

The following night's programme was much the same. During the third take-off, as we were gathering speed, I allowed the Whitley to swing slightly to starboard. It was not bad enough for the instructor to take over, and he made no comment, but as a result of the swing, it took longer to become airborne.

We were flying rather low, and as we crossed the hedge at the airfield boundary, we felt the Whitley jolt slightly. I wondered for a moment what might have caused it and glanced at Flying Officer Daniels. Neither of us said anything and he just raised his eyebrows in slight surprise and the matter was forgotten.

After several more circuits, our instructor was satisfied that both Parker and I were safe, and we were sent off to carry out three solo circuits and landings each - a hurdle every pupil pilot is glad to have behind him.

The next day, we were not included in the night flying programme, so it was an excellent chance to have an evening off in Forres and quaff a few jugs of beer to celebrate. The RAF shuttle bus dropped us near the Station Hotel where we 'hot-footed' to what was absurdly called the 'Saloon Bar' -

which was indeed Spartan - with just enough comfort to stop one from feeling miserable. There was probably a good business reason for this, as one had to drink more in order to achieve a reasonable state of cheerfulness. A dozen or so local men, were drinking in small groups. Although ladies were probably not barred, none were to be seen.

The attitude of the local towards us - Air Force chaps - was neither friendly nor unfriendly, they treated us rather as people from outer space - not to be meddled with. They paused briefly in their drinking to glance at us, then returned to their glasses. Ian Parker, Johnny Wright, 'Fletch' and I were the only Air Force personnel in the bar.

We were quietly supping our pints of McEwan's Scotch ale, when I heard the word aeroplane crop up in the local's conversation. Putting a finger to my lips for my companions to keep quiet, we listened. The man with the thinning hair and sallow, hollow cheeks, asked:

"Did you heer aboot the bus from Findhorn last neet?"

"No, what was that, Alistair? I've heard noot," was the reply from the gingery one.

Alistair did not reply at once; he was obviously savouring the story he had to tell. From under his coarse, black eyebrows, his eyes glanced from one companion to the other:

"Well, my missus, Moira, was coming back to Forres and she said that all the passengers from Findhorn were very excited.."

"What happened?" cut in one of his listeners.

"Whae a minute and I'll tell ye," grumbled Alistair, making the most of his story.

"The driver of the bus said that along the stretch of road, wheer it bends and runs alongside the airfield, an airplane roared overhead, making a terrible din."

"There's nothing unusual in tha'," interrupted another of his companions.

"Maybe not," replied Alistair, "but the driver said there was a bang on the roof and he almost lost control of the bus. When they got out at Forres, the driver took a look and theer was a greet dent in the roof."

As I listened, I realised the bump we had felt in the Whitley the previous night, must have been due to the undercarriage grazing the roof of the bus as it passed below! Wartime restrictions allowed only the minimum of light on buses, which would have made it impossible to see from the air. I shuddered at the thought that, had I been flying but a few inches lower, there would almost certainly have been a tragedy. I whispered to Ian Parker:

"That was us last night. Do you remember, we felt a bit of a jolt on our third circuit?"

We tried to affect an appearance of nonchalance, as we drank up and left. The locals stopped drinking and followed us with their eyes, appearing a bit mystified at our rather abrupt departure.

AC2. Ron Waite (RAF.VR) at No. 5 ITW (Initial Training Wing) Torquay Jan. 1941, wearing the 'white flash' of pilots under training.

Dorothy 'Mickie' Waite (née Watts) wife of the author, with Diana (aged 5 months) at Bristol June 1940.

Ready for take-off, Ron: in Defiant Mk.I, at Leconfield.

Flt Lt Simpson DFC. Gunnery Leader

WAAF Radio operator on Radio-telephone duty, 1658 HCU Riccall 1943.

'B' Flight group including, Ted, Ronnie, Frankie, 'Tubby' and 2nd from right Flt Lt Bill Kofoed DFC. (New Zealand)

Flying Instructor watching his 'fledgling'. Ronnie at Riccall wearing unofficial flying suit!

Plt Off W. Fletcher at 19 OTU Kinloss. October 1941.

Wg Cdr 'Jock' Calder DSO, DFC., when CO 'A' Flight 1658 HCU. Riccall. 1942/3

Plt Off Johnnie Wright at 19 OTU Kinloss. (Killed on operations)

Halifax (R9430) being flown on single engine (starboard inner) by Sqn Ldr
Dobson DFC at Riccall on 22 June 1943. Photo taken from Halifax flown by
Fg Off Waite.

Survivors of the crew after battle with German night fighters during the raid
on Dusseldorf 31st July 1942. Lt to rt. Ronnie Waite pilot. Harry Greenwood
F/E (killed 1.10.42) W. Geddie WOP (killed 16.9.42) Bob Poole NAV
(wounded) Sam Glasgow A/G. J. Miller B/A (wounded) Missing from photo.
J.McAuley A/G killed during the battle.

Sqn Ldr Joe Ward DFC, AFC. 'C' Flight Commander 1663 HCU. Rufforth. 1944.

Flt Lt Frank Collins (Navigator, later awarded DSO for extreme courage when wounded during a mission) Wg Cdr Pete Warner DFC. (later killed on operations in the Middle East) 76 Sqn. Middleton St. George. 1942.

76 Squadron F. Sgt Johnny Harwood (Later became Sqn Ldr awarded the DFC.) F. Sgt Kenny Clack DFM (immediate award for attack on the Tirpitz 27 April 1942)

Middleton St. George. F. Sgt Kenny Clack DFM (later killed by night fighter during the notorious Nuremberg raid 30 March 1944) Fg Off. Ronnie Waite, Sgt. Tommy Thompson (Canada, later killed on the Nuremberg raid)

Outside 'B' Flight Office, No.76 Squadron, Middleton. St.George. Lt to Rt. Ted Greenway, Ronnie Waite, Frank Collins, Tubby Lawes, Sgt. Rutt.

Halifax II of 76 Squadron being loaded with 3 × 1000 lb HE Bombs and 12 cans of incendiary bombs, for the first thousand bomber raid on Cologne, 30th May 1942.

"Do you think they suspected?" asked Ian.

"They gave us a canny look - think it would be best to avoid that bar for a while," was my advice.

Daytime flying continued; most of the exercises being circuits and landings, with some instrument flying. I did not enjoy the latter, it was very necessary of course, as our future night operations would depend upon accurate instrument flying.

The time had now arrived to do general night flying. I had a different co-pupil to fly with me. Our new instructor, Flight Sergeant Bulpit, was an impressive man, about twenty five years old, well built and always cheerful.

It was now October and I was looking forward to my first experience of a night cross-country flight. Bradbury and I were to fly with our instructor. I did not handle the controls myself during the three hour flight, my only duty was to lock the throttle nuts after take-off.

Four nights later, I was again on the list for a cross-country exercise. At 21.30 hours, I reported to the Flight Office where I joined the other members of the crew. Flight Sergeant Bulpit entered our names in the Flight Authorization Book. The rest of the crew consisted of a navigator, wireless operator and airgunner.

The weather was perfect and a brilliant full moon lit the cloudless sky. Each member of the crew scrambled aboard Whitley Z6730, carrying the particular gear necessary for his work during the flight Flt Sgt Bulpit sat in the left-hand pilot's seat with Bradbury next to him, in the second pilot's position. There was really no suitable place for me, so, being a spare 'bod' I took the bomb aimer's station in the nose of the aircraft. As the Whitley accelerated on take-off and the tail lifted off the ground, the nose lowered. Sitting in the forward position, I felt uncomfortably close to the ground as the 'plane raced over the uneven grass. We had been climbing for about ten minutes, when the navigator came forward and shouted in my ear:

"Will you let me have your helmet; the 'clot' of a wireless op. has left his behind."

I agreed saying:

"I haven't got a plugging-in point for the intercom anyway."

From now on I was not in communication with the rest of the crew.

Having reached a height of about eight thousand feet, we were flying straight and level on a set course. Sitting there, without a helmet, I felt detached from the world; only the steady beat of the Rolls-Royce Merlin engines gave me any sense of reality. They seemed to be purring contentedly in the crisp night air which was well below freezing at this height. The north facing crags were still snow-capped and were dramatically illuminated by the moon.

I was not sure of our position, but I believed it to be somewhere above the Grampian Mountains. My thoughts went back to school days and how small the United Kingdom appeared in an atlas. Now, looking down, this area of mountains and forests seemed vast, and the peaks very close, as they slid past below the Whitley. Here and there, quite high up in the mountains, small lochs and tarns stood out, placid and black against the snow.

My contemplation of the panorama was interrupted when the navigator tapped me on the shoulder. I was so lost in thought that he made me jump.

"The skipper says the port engine is 'playing up'...seems the temperature has risen suddenly. Will let you know if anything develops," he told me.

The navigator had to shout the words in my ear to make me hear above the din of the engines. I just grimaced acknowledgement. The message made me more aware of the engines and I began to imagine I could hear peculiar noises.

About ten minutes later, there was another tap on my shoulder and a more dramatic message:

"The skipper is stopping and feathering the port engine; we're returning to base right away but losing a bit of height."

The navigator disappeared in to the darkness of the fuselage. Within a few minutes he returned yet again:

"We've worked out an ETA back at base but the skipper says we're still losing height."

"Sounds distinctly dodgy." I replied.

"There is a chance we may have to bale out. Have you got your 'chute?" Pointing to my bottom, I said:

"Yes, I'm sitting on it. Hope the wireless op. hasn't left his behind as well as his helmet."

The navigator made the appropriate grimace, gave a thumbs up sign and disappeared again.

The forward escape hatch was just in front of where I was sitting. I gave it a close inspection, in case we had to jump. It would be my job to open and jettison the hatch, should it be necessary. There was nothing I could do but sit and wait. It was difficult to remain impassive, being unable to hear the conversation between the crew.

The landscape below now took on an entirely different aspect. The mountains and lochs had a forbidding appearance. Landing by parachute in this remote wilderness was a frightening thought - might never be found - worse still, supposing one landed on an icy tarn - no hope at all! Before my stimulated imagination could dream up further horrors, the navigator arrived with a more cheerful message:

"Skipper says we should be able to make base and land on one engine," adding, "He wants you to come back into the crash position."

Looking out, the snow-clad slopes of the mountains were now behind us. In the distance I could vaguely make out the edge of a coastline. I realised this must be Moray Firth. Feeling confident that Flt. Sgt. Bulpit would be able to make a safe landing on one engine, my anxiety disappeared.

CHAPTER 5   OPERATIONAL TRAINING UNIT - KINLOSS

In the darkness I made my way through the fuselage to the crash position where I joined the others and we braced ourselves for the emergency landing. We heard the engine note change to high revs and the clonking of the undercarriage as it came down to the landing position. Seconds later there was a jolt and squeaks from the tyres - we knew that we had made it. Whew!

Another of the instructors at Kinloss was a great 'character'. With the surname Gunn, his Christian name just had to be Tommy. In unimportant matters he seemed to have a great propensity for doing the wrong thing. He had an old Riley car, which he used regularly for evening visits to the local hostelries in Findhorn, a charming little coastal village on the tip of Findhorn Bay. On this particular night, there was a very sharp frost - just the sort of night to enjoy a pint or so of good Scotch ale in front of a log fire in the village inn. No one was the least surprised to find Tommy doing just that.

The Cluny Arms was a friendly little inn, smaller than the hotel in Findhorn which boasted six letting bedrooms. The only vehicle around, was Tommy's old Riley which was parked outside the Cluny Arms. Tommy was not a large man but his sturdy figure gave an impression of strength. He looked 'right', sitting in a plain wooden armchair with a tankard of beer firmly in his grasp.

It was around seven o'clock in the evening and all the regulars were already settled in their usual places. No other customers were expected, so when the door opened, everyone turned to inspect the new arrival. The tall figure of Constable McEwan stood in the doorway. Removing his hat with the black and white chequered band, he looked around at the half a dozen or so occupants of the bar and enquired:

"Anyone heer own a black Riley saloon car?"

"It's mine," owned up Tommy. "Anything wrong, Constable?"

"I'm not sure," replied the Constable, "but if ye dinnna mind, Sir, perhaps ye could step outside for a wee minute."

"Sure," replied Tommy, as he followed McEwan from the bar.
Standing beside the car, Tommy shivered - not through fear of any wrongdoing, I hasten to add - I do not think he could be afraid of anything, but, after the cosiness of the pub, the cold outside was bitter.

"I expect ye forgot to put your new licence on the car, Sir." said the Constable with more than a hint of suspicion in his voice. They both peered closely at the licence.

"Ah...um...yes, I think it was an oversight," said Tommy hopefully. "I'll get a new one right away."

"Ye've got a driving licence on you, of course," he enquired.

"Yes, I think so," replied Tommy, diving into an inside breast pocket. He produced it and, with a broad confident smile, handed it to the Constable. McEwan studied it closely for some time before saying:

"Ah, weel now, this was an oversight too, I suppose. It's ten months out of date."

There was silence whilst the Constable mulled over the best action to take.

"I think ye'd better see the Sergeant at the station, Sir. When can ye come?"

"Next Thursday night is the first time," replied Tommy.

"Very well, Sir, next Thursday, ask for Sergeant Innes."

Two days later I was surprised to see Tommy dressed in his best 'blue', instead of the more casual aircrew dress worn in the mess for supper. Then I realised it was Thursday and the day for Tommy's reluctant interview with Sergeant Innes in Forres. He was standing at the bar, imbibing a couple of pints, fortifying himself for the interview. Tommy was being 'ribbed' by his friends at the bar.

"What's your defence going to be - operational fatigue, Tommy?" asked one.

"Can't be that," said another in mock derision, "He hasn't been airborne for a month."

After a final 'chaser', Tommy went off with more encouraging remarks from those remaining at the bar.

The police station was a detached building, surrounded on three sides by a sandbag barrier, six feet high and about five feet in front of the main wall. The night was pitch dark, but a glimmer of light on the ground indicated the entrance. Tommy, now quite buoyant, entered. The policeman at the desk looked up slowly:

"Yes, Sir?"

"I have an appointment with Sergeant Innes."

"Ah, yes, come this way."

Before following him, Tommy enquired:

"Where's the toilet?"

The directions were rather complicated for Tommy to follow. The policeman told him:

"There's a nearer one just outside - turn left, follow the sandbags around - turn left again at the corner, and it's the second door."

Tommy nodded cheerfully, and went into the darkness outside, which seemed even blacker after the bright light of the office. Feeling his way gingerly, it seemed to him that he had done a couple of circuits of the premises without finding a single door. By now, the effects of the couple of pints of beer he had drunk in the bar were beginning to tell and the need for a toilet was becoming urgent.

A few yards further on, a slit on the ground indicated a door. Tommy gave a push; nothing happened. It was blackout time - nobody could possibly see - so he decided it was safe to relieve himself there and then. The feeling of intense satisfaction was abruptly shattered when he heard a handle being turned. By now, in full flood, a sudden stop was quite impossible. The door opened and there stood the Sergeant! Tommy, who was never short of an excuse, if not a reason, could only blurt out:

"Very sorry, Sergeant; lost my way."

This totally inadequate excuse was reflected in the fierceness of the Sergeant's voice:

"Ye'ed better come inside before ye face more serious charges."

In the warmth of the interview room, both Tommy and the Sergeant were more relaxed.

"Well, your in a fair amount of trouble, Flight Sergeant - driving licence - vehicle tax out of date, and now urinating in a public place. What have ye got to say about it?."

Tommy, trying to appear as shame-faced as possible, like a small boy caught filching apples, could only reply:

"I'm very sorry, that's all I can say. We've been flying our 'pants off' for the last few weeks and I completely overlooked it."

"Well, as ye know, we think a lot of you flying fellows and try to be lenient, but you've really broken the rule book this time."

"Yes, I realise that," confessed Tommy.

The police sergeant stood up, clasped his hands behind his back and thought in silence for a moment.

"I'll take no further action this time, Flight Sergeant, but there have been a lot of minor breaches of the law lately, so you can spread it around the camp that we'll not be as lenient in future."

Tommy, trying not to show his surprise at being let off the hook so unexpectedly, murmured his thanks and left.

Back in the mess, he celebrated by buying a round for everyone at the bar.

"That fellow Innes, kept calling me Flight Sergeant...if I had told him I was a Flight Lieutenant, he might have given me more 'stick'."

*   *   *

The month of October had been rather dull, all work and no social activities. Then it was announced that there would be a guest party night and the gloom lifted away. Wives and girl friends would be invited, together with local dignitaries from the area. Sadly, I would be unable to have Mickie there, as she and Diana were almost five hundred miles away, staying with our farmer friends at Farrington Gurney.

The functional austerity of the mess, with its drab painted brick walls, acquired a remarkable face-lift, mainly through the enthusiasm of the WAAF personnel. They somehow managed to transform it into something approaching an Hawaiian Beach club.

The Commanding Officer of a nearby Highland Regiment, obligingly arranged for us to have the services of an excellent dance band. The soldier musicians only numbered seven, but they produced a very good sound. Even the most accomplished dancers - and there were a few of them - would not be able to complain that their style had been cramped. Everyone was dressed in smartest 'blue' and all were on their best behaviour, eagerly awaiting the arrival of the local 'talent'. Even those who were always the first at the bar, were restricting their drinking to a modest half-pint. The atmosphere was unnaturally quiet, rather like that in a theatre just before the curtain rises.

We had rarely seen a lady wearing a dress instead of a uniform in the mess, so, when the first feminine voices were heard coming from the entrance hall, all eyes turned in that direction. The first three ladies to enter, accompanied by their RAF escorts, looked absolutely gorgeous in their party dresses, or so they seemed to our unaccustomed eyes. Within a few minutes, guests were streaming in. The band opened up with a lively number, 'One O'Clock Jump', and the party really got under way.

Everything was 'going like a bomb'. I was at the bar, enjoying a drink with a few friends, and wishing that Mickie was there - I always felt that her gaiety added a certain sparkle to a party. Just then, the Wing Commander came over to our little group. He seemed in a very good mood and said cheerily:

"Hello, Fletcher. Good party isn't it?"

Having noticed that our drinks were modest half-pints of bitter, he felt it safe to ask:

"Ready for another drink, chaps?"

We responded in unison:

"Thank you very much, Sir."

"Three halves of bitter, please," he ordered from the steward.

Raising our glasses, we chanted together:

"Cheers, Sir."

Looking in turn at the three of us, the Winco spoke to me:

"Could I tear you away for a moment, Waite?"

Wondering what could possibly be the reason for his request, I followed him.

"I have a niece from Eastbourne here, she's on her own. Would you mind looking after her for a while; I have to meet the AOC when he arrives."

"Good heavens!" I thought, "why pick on me?" but replied as confidently as possible:

"I'll do my best, Sir."

Following the Wing Commander, I wondered what was in store for me - how old and what sort of person his niece would be. We approached a girl, about eighteen years old, quite tall, slim and wearing a blue dress, which did nothing to glamorise her rather ordinary appearance; she gave me the impression of a girl waiting for her first 'date' at a school dance. The Wing

58

Commander dispelled any awkwardness we might have felt by the matter-of-fact way he introduced us:

"Ah, Theresa, this is Pilot Officer Waite. He will look after you for a few minutes as I have to meet the AOC."

As he walked away, I wondered how to open up the conversation, without appearing either dull, or too smart, when she said:

"My name is Theresa...it sounds a bit holy and everyone calls me Tress."
I was about ten years her senior and was surprised at her ready initiative. Instead of my having to put HER at her ease, she made me feel comfortable right away. She did not have a glass in her hand, which gave me the opportunity to ask her:

"You haven't a drink Tress, what would you like? Oh, by the way, I'm Ronnie." She hesitated for a moment, probably not being sure what drink she should order.

"How about a sherry or gin and tonic, to start the evening," I suggested.

"I'll have a gin and orange please," she replied with a friendly smile.
Perhaps entertaining this young lady was not going to be such a chore after all. I ushered her to a spare table, saying:

"There's quite a crowd at the bar. I'll be as quick as I can."
Her uncle was talking with Group Captain Jarman as I approached, and gave me a reassuring glance.

Tress had been educated at Wentworth, which was probably why she was able to converse freely and with assurance. She told me she had left school at the end of the summer and was now living with her aunt in Eastbourne. She did not fancy joining any of the women's services and had put her name down for the Land Army.

"I'm finding life rather boring, waiting to be 'called up'. This is an exciting change for me," she confided.

The party was going with a swing - a full bar and all tables occupied. A dozen couples on the small crowded dance floor swayed to the slow, romantic beat of 'At Last'. I thought that it would perhaps be unwise to ask Tress to dance to this 'smoochy' cheek-to-cheek number, so we sat with our drinks, watching the dancing. As soon as the dance had ended, the room filled with chatter and laughter. There had scarcely been a break when the bandleader announced:

"Before we have a tea interval - no sarcastic remarks please - everyone on the floor for 'Flying Home'."
One short quickstep - an ideal chance, I felt, to ask:

"Would you like to dance this one before the interval, Tress?"
She took my hand as we made our way to the dance floor. 'Flying Home' had a nice rhythm, easy for dancing. Even so, I was not really looking forward to it. I was very surprised and relieved to find that Tress danced with such ease and obvious enjoyment. I had quite a false notion that a

Wentworth girl would be rather prim and perhaps gawkish. How wrong I had been, and was annoyed with myself for making such a brash assumption.

The interval in the dancing was an excellent chance for me to introduce Tress to 'Fletch', John and other friends who were drinking at the bar. They had no partners of their own and vied with each other for the opportunity to entertain this young lady. I was glad to share the responsibility for seeing that she had a good time.

I had the last dance with Tress and wondered what we should do when it was over. I need not have worried; the Wingco, who was already looking around for her, soon spotted us and asked casually:

"Have you had a good time, Theresa?"

I now almost felt like an old friend as I said:

"Goodnight Tress...I have enjoyed your company, hope we'll meet again sometime."

Her reply was flattering:

"I thought it might be rather boring but I have had a lovely evening...and you are such a good dancer."

"A good partner makes every man a 'Fred Astaire'," I said, attempting to return the compliment.

Without a sign of affectation, she gave me a quick goodnight kiss, before leaving with the Wing Commander.

* * *

Training had slowed down, with flying sessions becoming erratic. Some pupils were far more advanced in the programme than others. Each instructor had two trainees and perhaps it was just 'the luck of the draw' that my flying practice had been very meagre. This was not the fault of the instructor, exercises were frequently abandoned because the Whitleys became unserviceable. We were approaching the time when we would be joining an operational squadron, and were unaware of the increasing extent of crew losses on bombing raids over Germany. The probabilities, or possibilities of survival was not a subject we talked about, we were all eager to complete our training.

At last the Night Flying Orders included my name. I was to fly with another trainee - Sergeant May; the instruction was that we should report to the Flight Office at 23.00 hours. This very late start meant a long evening hanging about, which I spent catching up with my letter writing. It was around 22.00 hours and the numbers in the Mess began to thin out as men started to drift away to their sleeping quarters, leaving the tables covered with empty glasses and ashtrays with wisps of smoke coming from unextinguished cigarette ends. It was time for me to leave and make my way to the 'flights'.

Outside, the frosty night air banished any drowsiness I had felt in the warm Mess. Upon reaching the Flight Office, I found that Sgt May was already there.

"I've been told we have to fly from an airfield near Forres," he informed me. Before I could reply, a Corporal driver came in and announced:

"OK, the van's outside."

Climbing over the tailboard of the two-hundredweight vehicle, we joined an airgunner and navigator who had been detailed to fly with us. This must have been a dreary job for them, flying on circuits and 'bumps' with two sprog pilots.

"What did you do to deserve this?" I asked.

With a shrug of the shoulders, one replied:

"Well, it's a shade better than spud peeling."

"We hope," said the other.

The airfield seemed little bigger than any ordinary field. Just as we climbed out of the van, a Whitley lumbered in for its approach and landing. We all watched intently while it touched down close to the first paraffin flare; the engines spluttered, throwing out a stream of sparks from the red hot exhausts as the pilot throttled back. The initial deafening roar of the engines diminished almost to silence when the aircraft reached the far end of the flare path.

The night seemed almost totally dark; the new moon was just a thin, pale crescent. Stars dusted the sky, with the well-known constellations showing clearly. It was so frosty, we could hear the grass crackling under our feet - a lovely night indeed.

The small Flight hut was dimly lit and thick tobacco smoke accentuated the murkiness of the atmosphere inside. As we entered, Flight Lieutenant Hurry, who had been giving dual instruction to the pilots in the aircraft which had just landed, said: "Well I'm off chaps," and to the Corporal driver who had brought us over:

"OK, Corporal, back to the mess."

Everyone liked Flight-Looey Hurry, he was a swashbuckling character. No one minded his swaggering manner, it suited him and he created an aura of fun and excitement. A few days earlier, his DFC had been promulgated - awarded for the tour of operations he had recently completed. As he disappeared through the hut door, his cap perched on his head at its customary jaunty angle, I felt I wanted to call him back. It was as if some of my earlier confidence had slipped away.

The ground engineer Sergeant pushed the Flight Authorization book across the table for Sergeant May and me to sign.

"The pilot flying the kite now has reported the oil pressure on the port engine a bit low," he told us, rather too casually I felt.

May and I followed a Corporal who took us out to the waiting aircraft. The Whitley which had just landed, taxied slowly back and came to stop near the Flight hut. Together with the navigator and airgunner, we walked to the stationary aircraft. From the cockpit the pilot waved, indicating that he had seen us. A minute later, the door in the rear of the fuselage opened and one by one the crew who had been flying, left the aircraft. Perhaps they were too tired to do more than give a half-hearted grin as they saw us.

Climbing in to the Whitley, I was the first to make my way along the dark tunnel of the fuselage, feeling my way past the various obstructions as I went. The familiar smells of glycol, oil and other odours pervaded the aircraft. The old Whitley was vibrating as the Merlin engines protested noisily at having to 'tick-over' for so long, waiting for our changeover.

It was nearly midnight, and the prospect of having to carry out several hours of circuits and landings was daunting. Sergeant May and I tossed up as to who should be first to pilot the aircraft. Both of us would have preferred the first session, to get it over with. However, May won and was the first to fly. I lifted up the collapsible seat beside him to carry out the second pilot's duties which were minimal.

I had not flown with Sergeant May before and, although not exactly apprehensive, I wondered how good a pilot he would be; like me, it was only his second solo night flying on Whitleys. Our aircraft was the only one flying from the airfield, so our take-offs and landings would not be obstructed by other 'planes. The Sergeant seemed at ease as he taxied the few yards to the beginning of the flare path. Most of his face was obscured by his helmet and face-mask, but I saw that his eyes were alert and confident.

"Ready for take-off?" he called over the intercom.

"Ready, Skipper," replied the navigator.

There was no immediate reply from the rear gunner.

"Are you OK, rear gunner?" asked May.

I was about to suggest that the navigator should go aft to see if the gunner had his intercom plugged in, when we heard his switch click on.

"Sorry, Skipper. Yes, I'm OK.."

I quickly scanned the instrument panel and gave May what I hoped was a reassuring smile for his first take-off that night.

The field was very uneven, making it a bumpy take-off run. Glancing along the length of the wing, the worst bumps caused the wing-tip to waggle up and down a frightening foot or two.

We were half-way round the circuit, when I saw a red light, slightly below our height. I was puzzled at first and then recalled that we had been warned that our circuit would be close to Cluny Hill, which was several hundred feet high and lit with a beacon.

At the back of our minds there was the fear that something might go wrong with these 'clapped out' old machines.

We had been flying for about an hour, when there emerged a reason for this feeling of apprehension. I waited until May had landed before telling him:

"The oil pressure has dropped on the port engine; the temperature seems the same. What do you think?."

"We had better report it," May replied and taxied to the Flight hut. I climbed out of the Whitley and made my way to the small hut. As I entered, I could almost cut the blue haze of tobacco smoke; looking up from a game of Pontoon he was playing with the Corporal, the Sergeant asked:

"Trouble?"

Ignoring his rather grumpy manner, I said:

"There is quite a drop in the oil pressure of the port engine - we don't like it very much."

"What's the temperature?" asked the Sergeant.

"It fluctuates - has gone up to 98 degrees," I told him.

"Well, as I said before, the engine has played up a bit since its last inspection; probably the gauge is a bit out."

"Maybe," I insisted, "but we don't want to lose an engine in flight - this is our first solo night flying."

"It'll be alright," the Sergeant assured me, "unless the temperature goes any higher."

I was not very reassured as I made my way in the darkness, back to the aeroplane. Approaching the box-like shape of the Whitley, I understood how it had been nicknamed 'The Flying Coffin'. Making my way round the rear of the 'plane, I caught a glimpse of the pale face of the tail gunner in his turret. It was difficult to imagine his discomfort in that cramped little perspex bubble, right at the end of the fuselage. I gave him what I hoped would seem like a cheery wave as I passed. Reaching the cockpit, I told the patiently waiting Sergeant May:

"The Sergeant says it's alright to carry on, unless the temperature goes any higher."

May seemed unworried, and continued his flying detail without complaint. After two or three more circuits, he had finished his solo flying. It was now past two in the morning and my turn to take over the controls. I opened up the throttles, the engines roared in response, this made my adrenalin flow and I became instantly more alert. I felt a bit tense but was anxious now to get on with it. Calling the crew on the intercom, I said:

"OK for take-off?"

Each replied in turn, "Navigator ready"..."Rear gunner all set, Skipper."

I glanced at May who gave me the customary all-clear signal. The Whitley started to wander, I corrected the deviation immediately, before it developed into an uncontrollable swing. The speed increased and the flares sped past. I glanced at the Air Speed Indicator - 80 mph - time to start easing the control column back. I felt relief when the Whitley left the bumpy field and became airborne.

Empty blackness was all that appeared ahead, so it was essential now to fly entirely by instruments. I felt 'clammy', realising that any error in the different functions could cause disaster. Correct control of the elevators and ailerons was vital to climb at the right speed - too slow and the 'plane would stall and a crash would be inevitable. A normal circuit consisted of climbing to a height of a thousand feet and flying a rectangular course of four 'legs', approximately three- quarters of a mile from the airfield.

We had now reached the circuit height and I made a ninety-degree turn on the first 'leg'. I could now see the flarepath again which was very comforting. I was looking forward to the challenge of making my first landing a good one.

As I started the final approach, everything seemed to demand priority at the same time - direction, power, height and most of all airspeed; at 105 mph, each second did not seem long enough. I said to myself, "fine; everything's fine; don't fluff it now."

"Twenty-six hundred revs," I said to my second pilot.
He repeated the order and carried it out immediately. I pushed the flap lever fully down; the braking power of the large flaps could be felt right away, causing the nose to dip forward.

"Watch out," I told myself, "we are losing height too fast and there are another two or three hundred yards to the airfield."

I gave the engines more power. As we came over the boundary hedge, the flares now appeared to be racing towards us. Trying to assess our height from the ground, I eased the 'stick' back and closed the throttles. We seemed to float for an interminable time and I had a brief moment of panic as I thought, "God! Have I 'held off' too high?" Then I felt a slight jerk - the wheels had touched the ground. At 70mph there was still a lot of work to do, keeping the Whitley straight and slowing it down with the airbrakes. Each touch of the lever at the top of the control column caused a loud hiss to come from the wheels.

"Good landing, Skipper," a voice said in my headset. I did not know which member of the crew had made this complimentary remark but I was glad to hear it.

I drew back the sliding perspex panel and took a good draught of fresh night air, tinged with the smell of burning paraffin from the flares. It was a strange time to remember - out of the blue - the kitchen in my grandfather's tiny country cottage, where oil was used for lighting and cooking. The memory came and went in a flash. There were more circuits and 'bumps' to be carried out.

After the fourth landing, the Whitley was still travelling at speed as the end of the flare-path approached; a touch on the brakes seemed to make no difference. I applied the brakes more fiercely several times, still with little effect.

"Air pressure has failed," I told May over the intercom. My earlier assurance and energy were drained by a combination of the late hour, dodgy port engine and brake failure.

"I am going to report it," I told my second pilot.

"Yeah, I agree," said May, who must have been equally exhausted by now.

"Don't want to risk running through the hedge."

Once again we had to taxy back to a point near the hut.

I walked across the grass, now almost white with frost. Opening the hut door must have awakened the sleeping Sergeant and Corporal. The playing cards were still on the table. Blinking in surprise, and stifling a yawn, the Sergeant enquired:

"Something wrong; you haven't finished have you?"

"Brakes have failed - no air pressure," I told him wearily.

"Well," said the Sergeant, "we had instructions we must keep you flying and finish the exercise."

I knew that both May and I were behind with our training on the course. The ground Sergeant thought for a moment before saying:

"Do a couple of circuits without landing; that'll build up the air pressure."

"Alright, if you think that will do the trick, I've only two more landings to do.."

I returned to the waiting aircraft, feeling impassive rather than frustrated.

"Told to do a couple of circuits without landing to build up air pressure," I told the weary looking Sergeant May:

"Both engines are getting overheated," observed May.

"So I see - Merlins don't like hanging about on the ground, just ticking over."

I heard a 'mike' switch on and a voice say:

"Christ! Can't we get on with it; I'm freezing to death in the turret."

It was our poor, long-suffering tail gunner. He must have been very cold and bored to death, it was surprising he had not complained before.

"Right - it's shit or bust! Let's go."

I looked at the second pilot:

"Ready for take-off?"

May nodded.

I did as the Sergeant had suggested and flew around for a quarter of an hour to build up air pressure. I did not feel happy about the brakes, but it gave me time to consider the best approach to make. I decided to come in with plenty of power and slightly low, aiming to touch down at the first flare. I did this and was surprised to find that the Sergeant was right - the brakes had fully recovered!

For the last time I taxied the length of the flare-path, looking for the small

DEATH OR DECORATION

Flight hut. In the darkness, I saw the light of a torch being flashed back and forth. Slowly moving towards it, I made out the slight figure of the Corporal who had come out to signal us in. Using the torch quite skilfully, he directed me to the parking spot. Producing a pair of triangular wooden chocks, he jammed them in front of the wheels. Stepping back, he waved his arms in a scissor-like movement, as a signal to shut down the engines.

"Have we really finished, Skip?" enquired the rear gunner.

"Yes, everybody out."

We almost tumbled out of the door in the fuselage, carrying helmets and parachute packs.

Returning in the van to Kinloss, we were all too tired to engage in the usual ribald banter. Before being able to 'turn in', we still had to sign at the Flight Offices and hand in our parachutes. As the Sergeants climbed out of the van on reaching their quarters, I called to them:

"Goodnight, chaps, thanks - sleep well."

"You bet...Goodnight."

There was an atmosphere of total stupor when I entered the officers' mess - not surprising, as it was 4.50 am. A faint smell of ale and tobacco still tainted the atmosphere. In the fireplace only the exhausted ash of the log fire remained in the hearth. All was dead silence. I pushed open the swing doors to enter the kitchen. A duty Corporal and a WAAF looked at me as if I was a spectre.

"Sir!" The Corporal's voice sounded more like an exclamation than an inquiry. He picked up a sheet of paper which he scanned.

"We only had four night flying suppers down. I thought they'd been done hours ago - three of them were."

"Well, I've been flying for over four hours and not had even a cup of coffee. So please make it a good one, Corporal."

"Yes, Sir!"

The best thing about night flying was the rare treat of bacon and egg. The dining room was of course deserted at this hour. Sitting at one of the twelve-foot long tables, I had scarcely waited five minutes when the comfortably built young WAAF came in, carrying a large plate, which she placed on the table in front of me.

"There you are, Sir. Supposed to be only one rasher and one egg really," she announced proudly.

"Thanks -thanks a lot," I said, scarcely sparing time from gazing at the feast of two back rashers, and an almost puchritudinous egg and two deliciously obese sausages, to return the girl's smile. The aroma from the freshly grilled rashers almost made the night's hassle worthwhile. A couple of rounds of toast, marmalade and a cup of strong, hot, sweet tea completed the repast.

That night, a room at the Ritz could not have been more welcome than my small room in the sleeping quarters. I did not even notice that it was only the heat from my body which was warming the freezing-cold linen sheets. I fell quickly into a deep dreamless sleep.

At the end of OTU - the most important flying course - my total piloting of a Whitley had only been 14 hours. I expected to carry out at least one cross-country flight, but there did not seem to have been time for this. I felt that my experience at Operational Training Unit had not really been adequate for the tasks ahead.

The other pilots on my course had been posted to various 4 Group Squadrons. To me, names like Leeming Bar, Dishforth, Topcliffe, Middleton St George and Croft Spa held a legendary magic. THE SQUADRON was where it all happened - raids on the enemy - excitement - the heroes. Until now I had not had time to give it a lot of thought.

On arriving at 'C' Flight Office - for the last time as it turned out- I was told to report to the Adjutant. He was sitting at his desk, with papers and documents oveflowing from the IN tray, OUT tray and PENDING tray - especially the PENDING tray. Looking up , he said:

"Good morning, Pilot Officer Waite?"

"Yes, Sir," I replied, confirming who I was.

"Your posting to the Squadron has come through."

As he fiddled around with the papers, I wished he would get on with it. I could hardly wait for the vital information.

"Ah, yes. Here it is, you're going to number 76 Squadron at Middleton St. George."

"That's fine, Sir, when?.."

"Right away - that is, tomorrow. You can spend today getting clearance from the sections, get packed and collect your travel warrant at 1600 hours."

I saluted smartly and almost fell over the step in my haste to make a start.

The following day was spent in getting 'clearance' from various sections. This was to ensure that I was not holding any equipment which should be returned. Finally, paying my mess bill was all that remained.

I had no one in particular to say farewell to. My friends, Fletcher, McCombe and Johnny Wright had already been posted to their Squadrons. I never heard anything further of 'Fletch', a very upright, rather insular man, or of 'Mac', a young roguish Irishman, whose boyish face hid an underlying toughness. A few weeks later, I received a letter from Johnny's sister, telling me that he had been killed on his fourth operation from Topcliffe. Apart from the sparse training, I had been happy at Kinloss and liked the country and the Scottish people.

CHAPTER 6

76 SQUADRON MIDDLETON ST. GEORGE

The journey at night from Inverness took almost 24 hours. The train was packed and I spent several uncomfortable hours, sitting on my suitcase in the corridor. After several changes of trains, night time came round again and it was almost midnight when the train pulled into the tiny Dinsdale Halt, about five miles from Darlington. The little steam engine, with its three coaches, came to a squeaky stop. I was the only passenger to leave the train. The halt was too small for any night staff, so I stood alone on the platform with my suitcase, while the train puffed away into the distance.

The night was very clear and cold, with frost sparkling on the path. Picking up my case, I walked past the deserted waiting room and crossed a wooden footbridge from where, in the light of the full moon, I could clearly see the fields and hedges receding across the flat landscape. By now the train was out of earshot and the night was silent.

In the total solitude, I stood taking stock of this occasion in my life. It was January 2nd, 1942. During the past year, I had moved from one training course to another, usually travelling in the company of a dozen or so airmen. My present position was quite different. I was on my own and about to join my first operational squadron - 76 Heavy bomber Squadron, 4 Group, Middleton St. George. It somehow made me feel older. With an intuitive awareness, I knew that this was an important threshold for me. Somewhere amongst those fields were the buildings and aircraft hangers of Middleton St. George, locally known as 'Goosepool.'

From a call-box nearby, I rang Middleton and asked for the transport section. A bright-voiced WAAF answered saying she would send transport right away. I was surprised to find the night so silent, as on training airfields there was always the sound of aircraft flying somewhere. The quiet was interrupted by the sound of a vehicle in the distance. I could hear the higher pitch of the 'revs' as the gears were changed to negotiate the narrow country lanes. A few minutes later, a small RAF van drew up. The WAAF driver enquired:

"Pilot Officer Waite?"

As I bent down to reply, she opened the passenger door and I sat beside her. It took about ten minutes to reach the airfield. After a quick check-in at the Guard Room, the WAAF drove confidently round the maze of roads and buildings to the Officers' Mess.

The entrance was the most imposing I had seen since I left Cranwell, with its pillars and lofty, mahogany-framed doors. The time was around

DEATH OR DECORATION

1.00 am. The centrally heated warmth inside was as welcome as it was unexpected. The whole place seemed deep in slumber. The row upon row of black, enamelled coat-hooks in the cloak-room were most empty, apart from a service coat here and there. After hanging up my own coat, I wandered into the ante-room. The large hide armchairs were unoccupied and popular magazines lay on the sturdy square tables. One or two RAF crested bone-china coffee-cups and saucers were left on a side-table.

I wandered around and eventually found the kitchen. The two airmen on duty were surprised to see me appear, but readily produced a brew of rather strong, sweet tea. Beginning to feel very tired after my long journey from Inverness I decided it would be best to curl up in an armchair and wait for the morning.

Shortly after 7 am I heard the sound of crockery coming from the dining hall and, within half-an- hour, the mess started to come alive. From the two corridors which converged on to the main hall, men started to drift in, some wearing uniforms, most in battle dress, and many decorated with flying badges.

After a quick wash, I joined the others in the dining hall. Like the other rooms, this was large, airy and well but simply furnished. As yet, there was only a sprinkling of men seated at the long refectory tables. I collected breakfast from the serving hatch and sat at a table in the middle of the room, where two navigators were chatting over breakfast. I purposely chose the middle of the room, to avoid the 'boob' perhaps, of sitting at the Group Captain's favourite seat. I need not have worried, Group Captain Trail, was not the kind of Station Commander to insist on protocol at the breakfast table. He was a fine C.O., firm, fair, respected and admired by all ranks at Middleton St. George. I did not expect the navigators to include me in their conversation, but the glance each gave me, contained a friendly, welcoming smile.

A room on the first floor was allocated to me, which I was to share with a Canadian navigator.

Leaving the mess, I followed the general direction being taken by the other men. They were nearly all dressed in blue 'battledress', which made any distinction between NCOs and officers less obvious; a unifying factor was the aircrew flying badge.

I had walked only a few yards when a fellow, wearing a different, dark blue uniform with pilot's wings, caught up with me and introduced himself as 'Mac' McIntosh. He was an Australian and his warm, friendly greeting was my first real introduction to the Squadron. We had been walking a while when a staff car drew alongside; it was being driven by Wing Commander Young, 76 Squadron C.O. He was a tall powerfully built man, and his steely blue-grey eyes and close-cut greying hair, stamped him as a man of authority. With a cursory glance at me, he addressed MacIntosh:

"I am going to the Watch Office," and opening the door, added,

"Jump in Mac...let's see what the 'Met' fellows have on offer today."

Mac gave me a slightly apologetic look as he got into the car and they drove off. I would like to have been invited to join the trip to the 'Met' Office but instead, continued in the direction taken by the others, towards the Nissen type Flying Offices on the edge of the vast airfield. The room next to the CO's was that of the Adjutant. My knock on the door was hesitant - I still felt rather overawed at actually being a member of a Squadron.

"Come in," said a muffled voice from inside. Immediately I entered, the Adjutant glanced up from his desk and gave me an enquiring smile. Looking at the small, personable Flight Lieutenant behind the desk, I saluted and said:

"My name's Waite, Sir. I have just been posted from Kinloss."

Turning round to look at a board on the wall behind him, which contained a chart of names, he said:

"Ah, yes, you have been assigned to 'B' Flight; the office is down the corridor on the left."

He interrupted the salute I was about to give on leaving - as much as to say 'we don't overdo the saluting here' - with the words:

"Very glad to have you here; it is a fine Squadron. 'B' Flight Commander is Squadron Leader Packe."

'B' Flight Office was typical - room about twelve- foot square, with brick walls covered in peeling green paint. The one concession to comfort was a strip of red threadbare carpet, which, in its heyday had borne an oriental design. There was an assortment of chairs and two trestle tables, one of which performed the function of office desk. On its well-worn top stood a bottle of red ink, a ruler and the Flight Authorization Book. The red ink was used to enter night flying hours in the aircrew's log books. Two cocoa tin lids, encrusted in grey cigarette ash, served as ashtrays on the other table.

Sitting at the desk, was the 'B' Flight Commander, Squadron Leader Packe, with a dark moustache, his peaked cap perched just far enough back at an angle to stamp him as the typical cinema image of an RAF pilot. He introduced me to the other two in the office.

Flying Officer Bill Kofoed's appearance could not have been less like that of Sqn Ldr Packe. Kofoed was lanky, with a stance which could only be described as a carefree, irreverent stoop. The burr in his voice, with a tinge of the Cockney, fooled me, until I discovered he was a New Zealander. A former sheep farmer, which probably accounted for his quiet fortitude. It was no surprise that he turned out to be a great character, and first-rate operational pilot.

Flight Sergeant Kenny Clack was barely 19 years old. He had unruly, gingery hair and his youthful face still bore adolescent pimples. It seemed

71

impossible that such a youth could be an operational, heavy bomber pilot, with several trips as Captain behind him.

The absence of casual conversation was puzzling me, when the quiet was shattered by a telephone bell.

"Packe here," answered the Squadron Leader and, after a brief pause:

"Yes, Sir, right away." With that, he left the office.

Returning about ten minutes later, he announced casually:

"Nothing on tonight, chaps."

Bill Kofoed and Kenny Clack accepted this news quite impassively.

"Bill, you've got an air test haven't you," which sounded more like an instruction than an enquiry by the Squadron Leader.

"Ah, Waite, what shall we do with you," he mused.

"By the way, what do we call you?"

I wisely discarded the idea of attempting to be facetious by saying,

"Wally, the 'Optic'." This nickname had been given me by my 'best man' and friend Charlie Spilsbury, disrespectfully alluding to my ophthalmic background, and my first name 'Walter' which I never used.

"Ron or Ronnie," I said with a slight feeling of embarrassment; since joining the RAF, I had always been addressed by my surname, except in the company of close friends.

"Right, Ronnie," said the Flight Commander, "Sergeant Stark, one of our 'fresher' pilots, is doing a cross-country; you can fly with him."

I felt a sudden surge of excitement at the prospect of my first experience of a Halifax flight. 76 Squadron was only the second squadron in Bomber Command to have these latest, four-engine aircraft, which were replacing the Whitley bomber.

I found Sergeant Stark with his crew in the locker room; they paid scant attention to my arrival as they were busy getting their flying gear. The Sergeant had a square- shaped face and the solid look of a man who could be relied upon. Approaching him I said:

"I'm Ron Waite, I've just joined 'B' Flight and the Flight Commander has said I can fly with you today."

"Fine," he replied. "I've already filled in the Flight Authorization book, we'll add in your name."

The crew consisted of sergeants. I was the only officer and could have felt uneasy, but they treated me in a friendly way as an equal; which I accepted as a compliment.

With more than a hint of a Yorkshire accent, Stark suggested:

"Why don't you draw a parachute, while I add your name to the Flight Book."

"Where is the Parachute Section?" I asked.

"Gosh, you ARE new, aren't you?" he chaffed good naturedly.

Now equipped with a parachute and flying helmet, I joined Sergeant Stark and his crew in the locker room, while we waited for the crew bus to take us to the aircraft dispersal point. He seemed unsure how to address me so, in a disarming manner, I opened the conversation with:

"By the way, I'm usually called Ron."

This seemed to have broken down any barrier as he said:

"OK, Ron, I'm Dennis; we're doing a short cross-country to Ayr, Stranraer and back to base."

The crew bus arrived - actually an old Napier lorry with the canvas awning half-folded back, exposing the remaining support ribs. The journey took little more than five minutes; the temperature was freezing and we had to beat our arms to keep warm. The lorry stopped near the aircraft. Clambering over the tailboard, I had my first close-up view of a Halifax. I had thought the old Whitley to be rather massive but its fuselage sat close to the ground in an almost docile attitude. The Halifax, however, seemed to have the aggressive attitude of a large, black, stag-horned beetle, squatting on its haunches with its nose pointing skyward, ready to leap. I could not fail to admire the beast!

I followed the rest of the crew through the fuselage and began to feel more at home with them. The pilot had to manoeuvre himself into his seat, after negotiating the undercarriage, flaps and bombdoor levers, and get his left leg round the control column.

I raised and locked the second pilot's seat and took my position beside him. After Sgt Stark had completed the engine run-up check, I turned to him and confessed:

"This is the first time I have been near a Halifax."

"That's OK," he replied, "there isn't much for you to do - lock the throttles after take-off, change the revs when I ask you and check the undercarriage warning light."

I watched intently every move the pilot made, I did not want to miss anything or interrupt with any questions.

Despite it being a cold January day, the sun was brilliant in a clear blue sky. The airfield was covered with several inches of snow, but the runways had been cleared and stood out like long black rulers. The flight took us over the Lake District. The lakes looked still and black, set in a landscape of unblemished snow, making it easy to recognise the shapes of Ullswater, Thirlmere and the other lakes. The beauty and peace of it all made me forget that we were at war. There was scarcely any talk between the crew, as they too, fell under the spell of the Cumberland landscape. The flight had taken just over two hours, and I was pleased to be able to enter in my logbook -

7th January 1942. Halifax 9523. Sgt Stark...pilot...self and crew.

Base - AYR - STRANRAER - base.

During my first ten weeks at Middleton it so happened that the few flights I had taken had been captained by sergeants with all sergeant crews. These young men were like brothers as they flew together, and lived their communal life in the Sergeants' Mess. Many were experienced veterans, and whilst I was never treated as an outsider, it was difficult for them to accept me a 'sprog' officer - into their Non-Commissioned circle. Similarly the officer crews also became a very close-knit band.

Before coming to Middleton, I had not formed any pre-conceived idea about squadron life. I had thought vaguely, that once or twice a week, the squadron would operate against enemy targets. However, during the first two or three weeks there was less activity than I expected. The weather had been fine, with severe frosts at night and daytime temperatures scarcely above freezing, which caused quite a few 'headaches' for the ground engineers, particularly with brake pipeline failures.

My flight with Sergeant Stark had encouraged me to believe that my future as a pilot with the Squadron had taken off, but I found this premature. I was in the situation of being a partly-trained pilot without a crew of his own, and not belonging to any other crew. Every morning I went to 'B' Flight office and listened to the general conversation of the operational pilots, gleaning what information I could. Some mornings, Squadron Leader Packe would disappear for an half-an-hour, when he returned , the previously jocular atmosphere took on a more serious note. He carefully studied the chart on the wall of the pilots' names, and the number of operations they had carried out. It was obvious that an attack was planned for that night. The number of crews required depended upon the strength of the attack planned by 'Bomber' Harris and the Command. Only those crews involved in the night's mission would know the secret information about the target, which would be divulged later at briefing.

I had been on the Squadron for nearly four months without being involved in a single operation; the Squadron Commander tended to keep to the company of one or two selected captains and I felt like a supernumerary. I longed to share the espirit-de-corps of the others, but I had to wait a little longer.

When nothing much was happening, we played baseball or kicked a football about in front of the Flight Offices. One morning, we were told we would be having a clay-pigeon shoot, which pleased me, as I rather fancied myself as a 'good shot' - I had achieved third place at ITW. There was an air of boyish excitement when the clay hurling machine was set up. We gathered around the Flight Sergeant, who had arrived with the 12 bore guns and ammunition. We readily agreed to Sqd Ldr Packe's suggestion that we each put half-a-crown in the kitty for the outright winner. The very cold morning made handling the guns a bit difficult, but when the first clays started zipping through the air, the cold was soon forgotten.

When my turn came, I was over eager - fired early - and missed the first clay. Quickly realising my error, I 'bagged' the next clay with the second barrel. All contestants had six turns at shooting. When the shoot was over and the scores totted up, Mike Renault had the highest score of 10, Bill

Kofoed and I shared second place with 9 each. The morning had been a refreshing change from the normal routine. As the weeks passed, I got to know Mike better, and found that we shared an aptitude for shooting and table-tennis.

I shared a bedroom with a Canadian navigator named Chris; somehow, we did not see very much of each other. On the occasions when we were able to have a chat, I learnt that he came from a small staging-post town called Red Deer, near Calgary in Alberta. One might have expected him to be a lassoing, gun-toting type, on the contrary, he was quiet, aesthetically good looking, with blond hair which lay in rows of waves. A Matinee Idol he may have looked, but in reality had been a trainee school teacher before deciding to throw himself into the fray and join the Royal Canadian Air Force. I liked Chris but had only a short time to get to know him; within a week or so, the Padre and another Officer were sorting out his clothes, papers, photographs and personal letters.

The following day, his next-of-kin would receive an official letter saying..."regret to inform you that...etc." 'Gone for a Burton', was the expression we used with seemingly callous indifference, about aircrew comrades who failed to return from operational missions. It was a term I was to become familiar with during the coming months. It would not have been possible to live with the frequent loss of close friends, without having a protective shell against the 'weakness' of appearing to care.

Returning to my room the following afternoon, I almost fell over a suitcase behind the door. The owner was a navigator I had often seen in the mess. As I entered, he looked up from the chest of drawers where he was neatly stacking away his shirts, saying:

"Hello, I am Frank Collins; I've moved up to share your room."

"Glad to have you share with me, Frank - I haven't too many vices; I don't snore and I haven't smelly feet." Frank smiled,

"That's a good start; you're Ron Waite, the Mess Secretary told me."

"That's right," I replied. "An odd bod at the moment, a crewless skipper."

"Well, that's better than being a clueless skipper," was Frank's rather dry reply.

Frank had been a junior partner in a firm of solicitors before deciding to join the action. He was not tall, probably around five foot six, with dark brown hair parted formally on one side, dark moustache and a complexion which might have been described as sallow. His unruly eyebrows could not conceal an expression of loyalty dwelling in his friendly, brown eyes. I instinctively liked Frank and felt a mutual response. He introduced me to his crew and circle of friends. After four months of feeling isolated, I was very glad to be really involved in the life of the Squadron, and felt grateful to him for this.

DEATH OR DECORATION

* * *

I spent the afternoon of January 29th, practising dinghy drill; upon returning to the mess for tea, the ante-room seemed strangely empty, then I realised that about half the flying personnel were missing. I later discovered they had flown off to somewhere in Scotland, which accounted for the unusual flying activities during the afternoon. My acquaintance with the Operations and Intelligence Officers was not on a close enough footing to ask them directly what was going on. Fishing for information got me nowhere.

The following day, the Intelligence Officer was a little more communicative. Although he was reluctant to have his secretive armour pierced, I was able to glean that a small Squadron unit had flown from Lossiemouth to attack the German battleships sheltering in a Norwegian fjord.

"All safely back, I believe," I heard Flt. Lt. Simpson telling 'Pop' Barrett.

"Yes, thank God," he replied. "Sergeant Harwood had to ditch about five miles off Aberdeen but the crew are safe, if a bit shaken."
I scarcely knew Sgt. Harwood at the time but eventually we became very good friends.

A day or so later, the crews involved in the Norwegian attack returned to Middleton St. George. When dinner was over, with nothing particular to do, I was idly watching one of the WAAF girls going around collecting the empty coffee cups. I had spoken to her once and discovered that she came from a small market town, Midsomer Norton, which was very close to where my farmer friends, the Teek family lived. She was a prim-looking country girl aged about eighteen, and her appearance intrigued me. She used as much make-up as the RAF would allow, which she applied skilfully. Her blonde hair was swept up a little too high, tending to exaggerate her rather thin face. I could not help but admire the care she had taken to make herself look as attractive as possible.

The memory of the Teek family automatically made me think of Mickie and little Diana. They were constantly in my thoughts. If my vision could have subconsciously wandered in a south-westerly direction, somewhere between 190 and 225 degrees, it would have passed over the exact position where they were at that moment. I wondered if they could feel the sudden warmth of my love. Most evenings in the mess, there would be small groups of men chatting or playing cards, while others were silently engaged in writing letters. It was only when I realised that the normal quiet tenor of conversation had become more noisy and voluble, that my reverie was interrupted. There was a drift towards the bar, and the stewards were dashing back and forth with full glasses.

76

There were no operations on this night, and the general feeling of relief was rapidly exploding into a celebration. I had moved up to the bar with an almost full pint, when another one was thrust into my hand.

"Another round...put it down to me," ordered a Flight 'looey.'.

Above the din, a voice with a strong Canadian accent called out:

"Hold it - Hold it."

The tall, blond rear gunner in Frank's crew looked in my direction. Above the hubbub he started singing in a monotone:

"Here's to Ronnie, he's true blue,

He's a drunkard through and through,

He's a drunkard, so they say,

He tried to get to Heaven but he went the other way.

So, drink -JUGALUG, JUGALUG, JUGALUG..."

All those present took up the chant, and continued until I had "downed' my full pint without stopping, in the shortest possible time. I was so 'chuffed' to be the recipient of this singular honour that, in my haste to beat all records, more ale flooded off my chin than down my throat. I managed to finish off the pint in about three and a half seconds and proudly banged the tankard on the bar. I felt overwhelmed by the importance of the occasion, for this was my initiation into 76 Squadron.

By now the party was really swinging; several members had been 'jugalugged' and sobriety had vaporised in an alcoholic haze. Even the most timid was prepared to give vent to his vocal talents.

"Bless 'em all, bless 'em all,

The long and the short and the tall..."

was the first ditty to be sung (?) in its unabridged version.

There was a short respite for tankards to be refilled. The stewards were so busy they had long since discarded their coats. I had never seen the Wingco mixing so freely before and letting his hair down.

"Shilence, please," shouted Mac above the din. 'Mac' McIntosh was the friendly Australian I had met on my first day with the Squadron. He was usually very quiet and more self-effacing than most Aussies I had met, and I understood 'Mac' to be a very competent and confident pilot. So it was rather a surprise to hear him announce:

"Mike will now give his ignitable - ininitiable - inimitable rendering of,

'She thought that she had lost it at the Astor; it was the only one she had..'"

I had never heard this song rendered with such sophisticated insinuation. Mike was a great party man, he had a large repertoire of games and amusing stanzas. His return to the bar was greeted by loud applause.

Owing to the quantity of beer consumed, any remaining inhibitions had been unfettered and everyone joined in the following bawdy song.

The total lack of musical quality was more than compensated by the excess of zeal. It was sung to the well known tune.. 'D'YE KEN JOHN

PEEL..' the vulgarity of the lyrics didn't seem to matter, it went with a swing.

2"Cats on the rooftops, cats on the tiles,
Cats with sore arses and cats with piles,
Cats with their arse-holes wreathed in smiles,
As they revel in the joys of copulation."
2nd verse
"A donkey on a common is a solitary moke..."

Enough! Enough! My binocular vision began to behave in a singular fashion and I had to succumb - I was sloshed. With a slurred 'Goo..night' to my friends, I left the party. As I made my way towards the stairs leading to my room, a powerful jet of foamy spray shot across the corridor. Ducking into the nearest doorway, I realised that a battle with fire extinguishers was taking place. 'A' Flight had taken on 'C' flight, as a member of 'B' Flight, I was pleased I didn't have to defend the honour of my Flight by joining in the fray! As I staggered up the staircase, and despite my neutrality, I received a sharp burst. I was thankful to reach my room reasonably dry, where I couldn't recall flaking out on the bed.

During the next few weeks I was detailed to fly with a crew whose Captain was an Australian named Lloyd-Jones. It would be difficult to describe a typical 'Aussie', but Sergeant Lloyd-Jones seemed to be just that - solidly built, unafraid and not unduly overawed by those in authority. We carried out mostly local flying, during which I followed closely the various manoeuvres made by the pilot, without the opportunity of handling the controls myself.

One night, we were on a cross- country flight which was an exercise in conjunction with searchlight batteries. The task of those manning the searchlights was to attempt to pick out the aircraft in their beams, whilst the bomber pilots were doing their best to avoid being caught. It was good honest fun - providing the 'ack-ack' guns did not decide to join the party! There were many searchlights sweeping the sky with their finger-like beams, but none came within half a mile of us. The whole exercise was becoming rather boring and the sergeant pilot said over the intercom:

"What the hell's the matter with them; if they can't find us, we'll find them." With that he flew straight towards every beam that was close to us, even then we were never caught. Several times, as we approached a searchlight, it made frantic attempts to find us without any success. During our flight, we saw a 'Drem' circle of lights, which indicated that there was an airfield below.

"Let's try out one of the emergency calls, to see if they work," Lloyd-Jones suggested.

"Why not?" replied the Wireless Operator.

The idea of doing this without having a very good reason would have been strictly against the rules; however, a minute later, we heard the Sergeant's voice:

"Hello DARKIE, hello DARKIE, hello DARKIE -OVER."

Without a moment's delay we heard a young girl's voice reply:

"Aircraft calling DARKIE - Aircraft calling DARKIE -this is MILDENHALL, this is MILDENHALL - can we be of assistance - OVER."

Sergeant Lloyd-Jones replied lazily:

"No thanks - just curious."

It was as well for our pilot that our aircraft could not be identified, otherwise he would certainly have been 'on a charge.'

A couple of weeks later, I was surprised to see Lloyd-Jones' navigator, Bobby Fairclough, in the Officers Mess. He had just received his Commission, which gave me the opportunity of getting to know him very much better.

On February 12th, two crews were sent to the Handley Page factory at Radlett, where Halifaxes were built. The duty was to collect two new planes and fly them back to Middleton, for Squadron replacements.

Bad weather had prevented them from taking-off from Radlett. In the meantime, they had spent all their money in London, were out of funds, and anxious to return. We arrived next day and were looking forward to a rare night out in London, and did not share their enthusiasm for an immediate return to Middleton. It was only after a great deal of persuasion, and the offer of an interest free loan, that they were induced to stay a further night.

The crews split up into small parties. I joined Bill Kofoed, the tall New Zealand pilot, my room-mate Frankie Collins, Pete Warner, who was Frankie's captain, and the newly commissioned Bobby Fairclough. Bobby was nineteen; his round boyish face with pink cheeks made him look even younger. His new winter greatcoat and officer's dress cap looked positively pristine compared with our well-worn outfits. His attempt to adopt a 'savoir-faire' attitude could not conceal his obvious excitement.

We had no difficulty in deciding that we would start the evening with a visit to the well-known Mecca of sensual entertainment - the Windmill Theatre. The show was a slightly less splendid version of the 'Moulin Rouge' - there were girls of course - but nothing pornographic. The comedian was excellent - many big 'names' had started there - but he had a tough time raising a laugh. The almost exclusively male audience had come to see the dancing girls.

We arrived during an interval between programmes, and were lucky to get very good seats, about six rows back from the stage. The content of each scene was fairly innocuous but the girls looked gorgeous as they danced in their diaphanous chiffon costumes. The contrast with the blacked-out streets made it seem like a film, suddenly changing from black and white to technicolour. When the hour-and-a-half-long show had ended, we prepared to leave and saw for the first time, the unedifying scramble for better seats - or rather seats as near the stage as possible the moment the curtain came down.

Half the audience it seemed started 'hurdling' over the rows of seats to get near the front. Apart from this incredible spectacle, the noise of the seats banging up and down was unbelievable.

When we emerged from the theatre it was dark. Fortunately there was almost a full moon, which made it easier for us to find our way around the blacked-out streets. Frank was the first to pose the question:

"What shall we do now?"

Bill Kofoed, who had a reputation for the size of his appetite, had no doubt:

"My energy needs stoking up; I suggest we get a meal."

We all agreed and I suggested:

"How about Chinese - the Hong Kong Restaurant in Piccadilly Circus is very good. I'm not quite sure where it is, on a first floor somewhere."

"That sounds fine to me," said Frankie.

We had been standing in a group on the corner of Brewer Street, when Bobby, who had been missing nothing, observed:

"Gosh! Aren't there a lot of girls around here?"

We had forgotten - being so preoccupied with food - that we had been loafing around on the fringe of London's 'red lamp' area.

"We had better move before Bobby falls into the tender trap," said Frankie.

Piccadilly was crowded with people, mostly wearing service uniforms. Not far from the Guinness clock, in a large but dimly-lit hallway, we saw the sign 'Hong Kong Restaurant'. It was, as I had thought, on the first floor and very extensive. A well-dressed Chinese waiter - the head waiter, I presumed - led us to a table. Speaking in Chinese to another waiter, he must have told him to put two tables together to accommodate our party of five. We had to tell the hovering waiter to come back later, as it was obvious we would take some time deciding what to order. Looking around at the other customers, we noticed that several were using chopsticks. Rather fearfully, Bobby asked:

"Do we have to eat with those chopsticks?"

"No." The rest of us chorused.

"This is one of the better Chinese restaurants, I believe. We are certain to have a choice," I added.

We all decided to have the House Special - chicken and fried rice with bean sprouts. Bill said:

"I'll have an extra portion of rice, bamboo shoots and chestnuts."
It was ridiculous of Frank to challenge Bill's ability to consume such a meal, but he could not resist baiting him:

"Bet you 3 to 1 you won't be able to eat it all," challenged Frank.

"You're on," replied Bill with supreme confidence.

When the meals arrived, Bill's was at least twice as large as ours. Even the imperturbable face of the little Chinese waiter showed a flicker of surprise.

We had already finished, when Bill was still struggling through the last third of his mountain of food.

"Don't think you're going to make it," jeered Frankie good-naturedly.

"Oh, yes, I will," said Bill, but his earlier assurance seemed to have faltered. After a most determined effort, it was the first time we had seen our New Zealand friend defeated gastronomically! Very reluctantly he had to leave several tablespoons of fried rice on the plate.

On leaving the restaurant, we decided we could not come to town without savouring the life around Soho - if only metaphorically. In particular, I wanted to wander down Wardour Street where the big film companies had their offices. The next day must have been 'dustbin' day, because large bins were standing on the pavement, awaiting collection. I could not resist lifting the lid off one standing outside the 'Movietone News' office, and to my amazement, it was stuffed to the brim with rejected 35mm Cine film. I would have loved to stuff a few handfuls of film into my pocket to investigate later. Wardour Street had been almost deserted but, in contrast, as we turned into Old Crompton Street, it was difficult to avoid bumping into people.

I paused for a minute to peer into a shop window; as I left to catch up with my friends, a disreputable looking old harpy sidled up to me. She nudged me, then looking first over one shoulder and then the other, said in a loud whisper:

"Would you like to come with me; I could make you happy."
Perhaps she saw the astonishment on my face and, before I could say anything she added:

"I have four lovely girls you could choose from."
I tried to shrug her off as I walked on, but she stuck close to my side. I was tempted to tell her to 'scram' but a feeling of pity prevented me; instead, I said firmly:

"Not tonight, dearie."
She did not persist further. I walked on and thought she must have become totally immune to even the most aggressive rebuff. A little further along the street, I found Bobby, Pete and Bill.

"Come on, Ronnie," said Bill. "We've had several girls offering services already."

"Not me," said Bobby. "No girl has spoken to me yet - worst luck."

81

DEATH OR DECORATION

"You be careful," advised Frank. "You know what the song says, 'Met a little girl in Soho - thought she was on the square -thought she was a shy young maiden - found that I was shy instead'."

A nearby pub beckoned and we were soon inside with a pint of beer each. The beer was less palatable and weaker than the northern beer to which we had become accustomed, but the London's West End atmosphere compensated for this. Our meandering took us up Frith street and down Greek Street, where we paused to look at the 'stills' of the girls in the Revuebar foyer, inviting the lonely or the curious to spend a small fortune on the sleazy show. We looked at each other without voicing an opinion - should we go in, or shouldn't we? Bill was the first to shake his head. We didn't need to say anything and just walked away in mutual agreement.

The Cambridge Arms, in New Crompton Street, seemed to be inviting; looking at my watch, I suggested:

"It's almost ten, fellahs. Shall we pop in here for a final drink?"

"Very good idea," Frankie and Pete agreed. Bobby thought differently:

"I've had enough I think, especially as I'm navigating tomorrow."

We had almost forgotten that we could be flying the next day, although, subconsciously, we were all probably aware of the possibility and had been careful not to overdo the drinking.

"I'll tell you what, Bobby," said Bill. "You stand over there outside while we have a final drink and tell us afterwards how many girls invited you back to their flats."

In the 'Cambridge', the atmosphere was heady. The Victorian bar was divided into mahogany-panelled cubicles, through which a blue tobacco haze was swirling. Small, decorative, cut-glass mirrors were everywhere, refracting the light into rainbow colours. I thought it must have looked just the same eighty years earlier. The hubbub from the voluble customers was so loud, it made conversation difficult.

We had forgotten about Bobby in the street and how he was coping with the filles-de-joie. On leaving the pub, we could just pick out our young navigator amongst the throng, still looking immaculate.

"Hello, Bobby. How have you been getting on?" We were all desperate to ask.

"How many ladies of the town have you had to turn down?" asked Frank.

"HOW MANY? You must be joking. Not one blooming girl has offered ANYTHING." He was obviously disappointed, and we were at a loss to understand it ourselves - his youthful appearance must have brought out a latent, protective instinct in the girls, we decided.

The next morning, we reported to the Handley Page Factory, where the management were very kind and treated us royally. The weather was still murky but, after consulting the Meteorological Office, we decided it was good enough to fly to Middleton. I returned with Sgt Lloyd-Jones, as a member of his crew and during March, on the few occasions when I was airborne, it was with his crew.

At the beginning of April, I was sent to 1652 Conversion Unit at Marston Moor. After a week's dual instruction by Fg Off Turnbull, we moved to the small airfield at Dalton, where I carried out my first day solo flight. It was here that I met a charming Belgian named D'Ursell, who was also a pupil. He was a member of the aristocracy in his own country and held the title of Count. He had been a member of the Belgian Air Force and had flown a fighter to England, from under the noses of the Nazis. He taught me how to play the intriguing game of Liar Dice Poker. It was a very tricky game to master at first, and Count D'Ursell was most patient as he explained the refinements of bluffing one's opponents. Later, I was very sad to hear that he had been killed very early on his operational tour.

I had scarcely embarked on my course of training, when I was recalled to 76 Squadron, my log book being endorsed, 'course incomplete'. Back at Middleton St. George, I was included in the crew of Flt Sgt Kenny Clack.

A few days later, we were briefed to fly to Tain in Scotland. Earlier in the year, the Squadron had operated against the German battle ships sheltering in a Norwegian Fjord. We knew that Tain was to be an advanced base for a similar mission. The previous operations had not been too successful so, this time, we had to wait for ideal conditions; this meant a full moon and Aasen Fjord free of fog. After waiting for several days at Tain, on 27th April, weather conditions were ideal and the operation was ON. I felt calm as I looked forward to my first operation against the enemy. It seemed an awesome responsibility for the nineteen year old Kenny, as Captain on such a mission. My position in the crew was that of 2nd 'Dickie', as the second pilot was called. I was being taken more for the operational experience than the simple duties I had to perform.

It was a perfect evening, as the Halifaxes queued behind each other on the perimeter track, waiting for the take-off signal. The aircraft had a rather odd appearance because, as well as the six 500 pounders on board, a specially designed 4000lb 'block buster' bomb was being carried. This bomb, looking like a huge dustbin, was so large it could not be contained inside the bomb bay with the doors closed - these had to be pumped up by hand until they rested on the belly of the bomb. The armourers had a difficult, sweaty job, winching these monsters on board and one described the Halifax's appearance as that of a pregnant mayfly!

We observed strict radio silence as we waited in the evening sunshine for the green Very light to send us on our way. The atmosphere inside the aircraft was expectant rather than tense; I looked around at the other aeroplanes, with their four propellers gently turning over; they resembled patient gun dogs, awaiting their master's command to go. I glanced at Kenny, his face almost hidden by the oxygen mask; his eyes alert and ready for the operation ahead.

DEATH OR DECORATION

Our CO, Wing Commander Young, was the first to turn onto the runway and take-off. I felt - we probably all did - an inward excitement at the sound of the Merlin engines as they opened to full power. Within a minute our turn came.

"Alright, chaps, here we go," Kenny announced quietly over the intercom.

Soon 'S' for Sugar was pounding down the runway. My only duty was to lock the throttle levers and adjust the 'revs' when instructed by Kenny. The aircraft was performing well and we felt more relaxed, now that we were on course for Norway. The long flight over the North Sea was rather tedious. Way ahead, I could just make out the Wingco's aeroplane, steadily on course; not far behind were three other Halifaxes being flown by Mike Renault, Hank Iveson and Johnny Harwood. The sun was sinking behind us and the full moon, pale as yet, was climbing into the darkening sky. I could no longer see the other aircraft. The four Merlins, with perfect synchronisation, seemed to be purring in the cold air, their exhausts glowing dull red against the dark sky.

As we approached the Norwegian coast, Tommy, our Canadian navigator, was looking for a well-defined island, which was to be our first turning point. From his position in the nose of the aircraft, he called on the intercom:

"Skipper, this is the navigator. I can't be certain of the particular island yet, will you maintain the present course."

"'Roger', Tommy," replied Kenny.

Several minutes later, Tommy called again:

"Hello, Skipper. I can't see the island but have identified Kristiansund, about 30 miles south of our correct turning point; will you steer a new course, 068 degrees."

The pilot made a gentle turn to port, straightening up when the compass heading was precisely on 068 degrees.

"Hello, navigator; on course - NOW," Kenny confirmed.

A brilliant moon lit the snow-capped mountains which rose sheer from the fjords. Although a romantic sight in other circumstances, tonight, the moon-light was ominous for ourselves - the attacking force - and the enemy.

The Norwegians in their isolated farms, and hamlets, hearing the sound of our engines, were aware that British bombers were overhead. Now and again lights appeared from windows; several times we saw curtains being drawn and withdrawn. These brave people were sending us the famous 'V for VICTORY' signal. I wished we could let them know what terrific encouragement it gave us - death would have been the penalty, had they been caught.

The time was approaching 0015 hours. During briefing, we had been instructed not to bomb the Tirpitz a moment later than 0030 hours, because 10 and 35 Squadrons were flying in with a low level attack. Realising we could not meet this deadline, our Captain decided we must bomb the alternative target - the battleships Von Scheer and Prinz Eugen, which were sheltering in a fjord, south of the primary target.

A few miles ahead, the sky was filled with the flashes of exploding 'flak'. Our spot in the sky seemed unnaturally quiet when, with frightening suddenness, searchlights started appearing from nowhere - flashing across the sky, searching for us.

Tommy's voice came over the intercom:

"Skipper, the target is coming up - keep her steady."

Two searchlights flashed across us, lighting the cockpit with a split second's brilliance but were unable to hold us.

"Skipper, I can't see the ships; they are down there in that smoke -keep steady on this course."

"OK, Tommy," replied Kenny, his voice showing only slightly the strain he must have been feeling. As we rapidly approached the mountain side of the fjord, Tommy's voice calmly said:

"Steady, steady...steady. BOMBS GONE."

Immediately Kenny took a violent turn to starboard - to avoid the mountain and the light 'flak' we were flying through. As we were escaping from the target area, Tommy's voice came urgently over the intercom:

"Kenny - that bloody 4000 pounder has hung up!!"

"Right, we'll do another run in. We haven't come this far to drop it in the sea." There was surprising fury in Kenny's boyish voice.

"Skipper, get back on course 080 degrees."

The turn took us temporarily away from the 'flak' guns. A minute of so later, Kenny called the navigator;

"On 080 degrees now."

"OK,Skip," replied Tommy. "A few degrees left...steady - hold that. I'm going to release manually."

"Steady...left a bit...steady...BOMB GONE."

We felt a distinct lurch upwards. Kenny and I looked at each other hopefully - the bomb had probably gone.

For the second time, our pilot took a steep turn away from the target, then straightened up, climbing to clear the mountain. As we did so, a large black fjord appeared below. All Hell was suddenly let loose. The sporadic 'flak' became a barrage - we were flying over the Tirpitz. The rest of the squadrons were almost certainly on their way home and, because we were late, we were now a target for the Nazi's fury.

It was like putting a foot in a hornet's nest. Venomous red jets were flashing from the Tirpitz's guns; shells were exploding all round us. Kenny threw the Halifax all over the place, but there was no evading all the gunfire. He banked so steeply, I thought I would fall on top of him. At times we were flying so low that searchlights appeared to be pointing down on us! Several shells exploded so close that we could hear the pieces of shrapnel puncturing the fuselage.

DEATH OR DECORATION

As we were desperately trying to escape from the fjord, 'Tubby' Lawes, our Flight Engineer, broke in over the intercom:

"Skipper, the port inner temperature is winding itself up -we'll keep it going till we are out of this shit."

"OK, Tubby - bomb door lights are still on, too," said Kenny.

Every second seemed an age, as we gradually left that hellfire behind us.

"Hello, Skipper - Flight Engineer - feather the port inner, the port inner, now."

Almost as he spoke, my hand was moving to throttle back and put the 'prop' in fine pitch.

All gunfire had now ceased; only one or two searchlights fingered the sky in a belated attempt to find us. For a moment, no one in the aircraft spoke; Kenny, our Captain, was the first to break the unnatural silence:

"Well, chaps, what's the situation? I'm maintaining height on three motors."

It was 'Tubby' Lawes who answered:

"A petrol tank has been holed, the fuel gauge is going down rapidly. I will feed the other engines as long as I can on the holed tank."

Tommy Thompson, our Canadian navigator, added to the bad news:

"Bomb doors have been damaged, Skipper. They won't close."

Kenny was still adjusting the rudder trimmer to correct for the loss of the engine as he said:

"We're still over 600 miles from base. Do you think we will have enough fuel, Tubby?"

"It will be a close thing."

"The alternative is to make for Sweden," said Kenny. "We'll put it to the crew."

"There are two destroyers in the North Sea, spaced on our return flight path, in case we're in trouble," I observed.

It was Tommy who put forward the first firm proposal:

"I suggest we make for Scotland."

We all agreed and settled down to face the formidable journey back. Once Kenny had trimmed the Halifax for straight and level flight, his task was to remain awake and alert during the tedious four hours ahead. the Flight Engineer now had the most important task of watching his fuel gauges, working out the best use of the fuel and changing the tank cocks as required. The only thing I could do was to adjust the 'revs' levers to keep the three engines synchronised.

The hours dragged on and fuel was getting dangerously low; we had to face the possibility of ditching in the sea. we were almost resigned to this, when Tubby, who had been peering out from the astrodome above his head, almost yelled;

"Good God - Kenny - I think I can see a light in the distance."

Just a vestige of dawn light was appearing as we all scanned the sky.

"I can see it too," called the wireless operator.

"What do you think it is?" I asked Tommy, who had the best view from the nose of the aircraft.

"It must be - Yes, IT IS -WICK."

We were all babbling with excitement over the intercom, when Kenny cut in:

"Hold on a minute chaps - I'm not sure we can get down at Wick."

In our enthusiasm we had forgotten that it was Kenny's formidable task to put the Halifax down safely on three engines.

"What's the petrol situation now?" Kenny asked the Flight Engineer. "Do you think it will last out to Tain?"

"Just about," replied Tubby, "but with damn all to spare."

It had been nine hours since we took off from Tain. When we spotted the airfield again, no one spoke. We all felt the tension Kenny must have been experiencing as he concentrated on making the landing. There was no room for error - the first attempt had to be the only one. There could be no second chance.

On the approach, Kenny quietly gave me instructions:

"Twenty six fifty revs - undercarriage down - full flap."

I watched tensely as Kenny held the aircraft straight till the final squeal of the tyres indicated that we were safely down. Almost everyone shouted,"Hooray."

"Jesus!" exclaimed one.

"Bloody good, Kenny," said another.

Suddenly, all the emotional relief at having survived this 'baptism of fire' came to the surface.

Shortly after landing, all three engines cut - one after the other - as the last petrol tank became drained. I am not sure whether I felt pride, satisfaction or relief at having completed my first operation.

A few days later, we heard through the 'grapevine' that Kenny Clack had been recommended for an immediate Distinguished Flying Medal for this operation.

The good weather held and the Squadron was ordered to operate against the Tirpitz again on the following night. Our previous aircraft had 58 holes caused by shrapnel, apart from the damage to the bomb doors, so we took the spare machine.

We were in very good spirits as we took off again for Trondheim, and in the back of our minds was the axiom "lightning never strikes twice." This time we avoided losing our position and arrived over the target on time. As we flew over the snow-capped mountains so close below, the fjord came into view. We flew along the north bank, approaching Aavikaunet where the Tirpitz lay, when all the defence opened up. The Germans must have moved in every searchlight and anti-aircraft gun in Norway to defend their prize battleship. The entire sky was swept by powerful beams, leaving no dark space of safety. The shore batteries were pumping up streams of light 'flak', their tracer shells appearing like whiplashes. We could not see the battleship, she was hidden by a smoke screen. As we headed for the centre, Tommy started his instructions;

"Hold straight, Kenny - left a bit- steady -left a bit - steady... STEADY - BOMBS GONE."

Despite the fury of the defence, Kenny held to the bombing run. I saw several other aircraft - some coned in the searchlights. The barrage was intense. Just below, on the starboard side, I saw a tremendous flash grow into a fierce red ball of fire where a Halifax had taken a direct hit. A moment later, another was streaking away, its port wing well alight. This turned out to be the one piloted by Wing Commander Bennett - he later achieved fame as leader of the Pathfinders. He managed to land on the frozen fjord and with four of the crew, escaped into Sweden.

Unlike the previous night, there were more Halifaxes in the sky over the target to share the ferocity of the Huns. We returned to base and felt relieved to have come through the inferno unscathed.

The following day, we were free to do as we wished. Kenny and his all sergeant crew insisted that I should join them for a day out in Tain. I just could not have been more delighted. There was a total absence of rank barrier as we celebrated our survival with unrestrained fervour, all acclaiming nineteen year old Kenny - only lately from Grammar School -as the undoubted hero. The people of Tain were so hospitable and provided food such as we had not seen since the outbreak of war.

Whilst we were celebrating in Tain, our CO, with two or three others, drove into the Highlands. Mike Renault, who was with them, had taken a rifle and shot a deer. We were not too surprised, on returning to Middleton to have quite a lot of venison on the menu.

Back at its home base, the Squadron was required to operate on only eight nights during May. My own flying had been limited to a few flights as a crew member, air-testing aircraft. Flight Sergeant Lloyd-Jones, with whom I had flown earlier, was missing from an attack on Essen in the Ruhr. I was particularly upset, because Bobby Fairclough, my new young friend was navigator in the crew. I was very lucky not to have been included in this trip as Second Pilot. Another Flight Sergeant, with whom I had flown, Flt Sgt Belous, was killed near Yarm on the Yorkshire Moors, upon returning from an operation with engine trouble, his aircraft had crashed after he ordered his crew to bale out.

Following the Tirpitz operations, my status in the Squadron changed; I felt I was no longer a nonentity and began to be included in the operational circle. Frankie Collins my room- mate, became a close friend and, through him, friendships grew with Pete Warner and Bill Kofoed who had previously only been acquaintances. My thoughts returned to those Initial Training Wing days of drill and lectures at Torquay. One had hardly ever seen an

CHAPTER 6   76 SQUADRON MIDDLETON ST. GEORGE

RAF man wearing a flying badge, even in large towns they were a rare breed. I had not imagined then, that such men would become my buddies. We knew very little of each others' personal background and rarely talked about it. Perhaps we did not want religion or social differences to intrude on our bond of friendship.

When the Squadron was not required for night operations, we occasionally went to Stockton-on-Tees or Darlington, where we joined the drinking throng in the Grand Hotel. At Stockton, we liked the Vane Arms Hotel which was lively and comfortable, and where the ale was good. I hasten to add that, although it was nicknamed the 'Prostitutes Parlour', this had nothing to do with such practices. Loose, or more correctly, unattached girls seemed to abound there but, unlike our experiences in Soho, we appeared unworthy, financially or otherwise, to merit their attention.

Some days, operations would be ordered in the morning, and there would be speculation as to what might be the target. In the briefing room, expectant crews eagerly awaited the unveiling of the European map. All eyes followed the red ribbon, stretching from Middleton to where it was pinned down on the target. The various crew members went about their specialist checks - navigation, gunnery and radio. The pilot would take his engineer with him for an air test of the Halifax which he would be flying that night. Then came the long wait for the hour of take-off, all crews mentally and technically ready. If, as quite often happened, a message from Group announced that the operation had been cancelled, one could feel the anger and the frustration.

After the initial let-down, we would return to the mess where the vacuum was filled by drinking, singing and playing boisterous games - the rougher the better. It was a good way of overcoming the anti-climax. Amongst the best table tennis players in the mess was Harry Moorhouse. I frequently played with him, the winner challenging Mike Renault.

During May and June, 1942, 76 Squadron losses had been high, at around eight per cent. Earlier successful attacks on Lubeck and Rostock encouraged Bomber Command to plan an ambitious raid on the Heinkel aircraft plant at Warnemunde on 8th May. The attack was to be made in three waves; it proved to be too complex and the defences were devastating. That night, I was detailed to be duty ACP (Airfield Control Pilot.) I was installed in the Control Caravan, situated near the take-off end of the runway. My equipment was a field telephone to the Control Tower, a Very pistol with red and green cartridges and an Aldis lamp.

Eight Halifaxes queued on the perimeter track, waiting to take off. Amongst the pilots was Harry Moorhouse, who had given me a hard game of table tennis earlier in the evening. The 'phone rang:

"Airfield Control Officer - all clear for take off."

"Roger (message received)," I replied.

Picking up the Aldis lamp, I flashed a 'green' at the first aircraft, which lost no time in turning onto the runway and taking off. From the small perspex cupola in the top of the caravan, I couldn't recognise the pilots' faces but I knew T for Tommy was Harry's machine. As I flashed green at the cockpit, I hoped he could see my encouraging wave.

There was now the long wait of about six hours for the return of the crew. I spent most of the night in the Watch Office with Timmy Tame, the Air Control Officer. Sitting in front of the complicated radio equipment was a chubby little WAAF radio operator, looking very pretty, despite the head-set clamped over her chestnut curls. We engaged in general conversation and spoke little about the crews who were flying steadfastly into...God knows what. Warnemunde being on the Baltic Sea, meant they had to fly over some of the most heavily defended areas in Germany. I took catnaps in an armchair, waiting for 4.30a.m., when they were due back.

Dawn was just beginning to break as I walked over to the caravan. The chilly air outside caused me a brief shiver. There was really little for me to do - just keep a look out so that the runway was clear for each approaching aircraft. At about 4.20 hours, the first of the eight Halifaxes appeared in the early morning light and landed, followed quickly by another. After a break of about ten minutes, two Halifaxes arrived simultaneously on the circuit, and in quick succession, three more. The Officer in the Control Tower gave them their landing instructions over the radio-telephone. 'T' for Tommy had still to arrive. I became anxious for Harry and his crew as the minutes ticked by. The telephone rang:

"Hello, ACP, this is Tame; I don't think you need wait in the caravan any longer, 'T' - Tommy may have diverted to another airfield - over."

"I think I'll give it another ten minutes, I would like to welcome Harry back." I replied.

"Roger - over and out," answered the Controller.

About five minutes later, I heard an aeroplane in the distance. I left the caravan to get a better view. Great! I thought, it looks as if Harry has made it. The Halifax headed towards Middleton. It droned wearily overhead but did not land. Later, we learnt that Harry's aircraft had been found wrecked on the outskirts of the German town, Rostock; the crew were all killed. On the same operation, 158 Squadron at Driffield, incurred the dreadful loss of four aircraft out of the nine Wellingtons sent.

* * *

A member of the Squadron who had received an overseas posting, owned a 1934 Austin Seven Ruby car. He could not take it with him so wanted to sell it for £12. Since there were no ready buyers, he quickly accepted my offer of £10. I was particularly glad to have a car because Mickie was coming to spend a few days at Middleton-On-Row, a tiny village on the Tees. The car seemed to run well, which gave me enough confidence to take her to Darlington. On the return journey the car 'packed up' about a mile from Middleton; with no telephone nearby, we had to walk the rest of the way. Poor Mickie, in high heeled shoes, had a rough time on the country road. It was a shame to have spoiled an otherwise excellent evening spent with friends in Darlington.

This was not the only time 'Old Ruby' let me down. A week later, when returning to the mess at about 11pm, the car lights failed. It was a dark night but as I knew I was only about 30 yards from the mess entrance, I decided I would press on in the darkness, steering from memory. Well, of course, this didn't work. Within seconds, I had completely lost my bearings. With a bang that could have wrecked the springs, I mounted the kerb. Trying to find my way back on to the road again, I ran into soft ground. Eventually I couldn't even turn the steering wheel and became stuck fast. Getting out of the car, I found it had almost 'pranged' the wall of the mess. There was no way I could move the car, now sunk almost up to the hubs in the ground. I left it and went into the mess where a few friends were finishing off their beer. It was late and they didn't appear too willing when I asked:

"My vehicle is stuck in the mud outside. Would any of you chaps be good enough to give me a hand?"

"It'll cost you, Ronnie," said Bill.

"How about it?" he asked the others, "for a round of drinks."

"Agreed," I accepted gladly.

Outside, the darkness made it difficult to see the car. After holding a council of war, we decided it could not be driven or pushed away, but would have to be lifted. We enlisted more help and assembled three men each side of the car. Peter Warner took command:

"One...two...three - UP."

With a 'shloggy', sucking noise, we raised the car - and nearly collapsed under the weight. By making short staggering movements, we got the old Austin back on the road, where we left it.

The following morning we were sitting around in the Flight Office, chatting, smoking and waiting for instructions. I had almost forgotten about the car incident. A sergeant entered who was unknown to me.

"The Adjutant wants to see Flying Officer Waite," he announced.

"That's me," I replied and followed him out.

As I entered the office, the Adjutant said almost jocularly:

"Ah...sorry about your car problem last night."

I thought, "That isn't what he wants to see me about.' Before I could make any remark, he continued:

"The GC isn't too pleased but, if you get the car ruts filled in, nothing further will be said."

"I didn't realise it had caused any damage," I told him, adding, "I will see to it."

DEATH OR DECORATION

I left the office, and since there was no immediate flying programme, returned to the mess. As I approached I was shattered to see the deep ruts weaving across the lawn. I had not previously noticed what a fine lawn it was and that it had recently been re-sown. I went to my room and found L A C Sidney Dunforn busily tidying up. He was the batman I shared with four others -a cheerful lad who enjoyed his work and felt it was an honour to 'do' for the aircrew officers he looked after.

"Sidney," I said. "I'm in a spot of bother with the GC."

"Never, Sir!" was his astonished reply.

"Yep - I drove old 'Ruby' over the lawn in front of the mess last night."

"How can I help?" he asked almost eagerly.

"Do you think you could find another fellow to help fill in the ruts?"
Before he could reply, I added:

"There is five bob each for you."

"Yes, I know just the chap - it's as good as done, Sir."

"That's fine - see you later then."

After spending the rest of the morning practising dinghy drill, I could hardly wait to return to the mess at lunch-time and see how my hired 'gardeners' had been getting on. They had done a fine job and even fiddled in a bit of fresh grass, so that the ruts were quite well camouflaged.

Meeting my friends later, they appeared to be sharing some amusing episode in which I sensed I was the victim. Their chatter ceased as I approached. Grinning mischievously, Bill Kofoed said:

"Sorry, Ronnie, we have played a bit of a joke on you."

"Oh, what's that, Bill?"

"That car business last night and the ..."
Before he could finish, I interrupted:

"I'm having enough problem with that, and I'll be lucky if the Group Captain doesn't have me by the 'short and curlys.'

"That is the point," replied Bill. "We fixed the whole business of the Group Captain with the Adjutant - just as a joke. The GC knows nothing about it."

"You so and so's," I thought, "you would be up to something at my expense."

"Well...have a beer on us," said Frankie, "Cheers."

There was a sequel some two years later, when I was a flying instructor at Riccall, I had to give dual night-flying instruction to a pupil. The long runway there was unserviceable, so I was detailed to carry out the exercise at Middleton instead. This was the first occasion that I had returned there.

It was still light as we flew over the airfield buildings; with nostalgic thoughts, I looked down at the Officers' Mess, some thousand feet below, I had totally forgotten the car incident and could hardly believe that the evidence would still be there. After sending my pupil solo, I went to the mess for coffee and had another surprise. Almost the first person I met was

Allies, my instructor at Cranwell when I was involved in the air collision. He, too, could not have been more surprised.

"You're Waite aren't you?"

"Yes, I remember you, too - Flying Officer Allies."

Then, with mock anger, he told me:

"You - you bugger - and young Acton-Bond, cost me six months' loss of seniority and got me posted to a Stirling Squadron."

"Christopher! How was that?"

"Well, the findings of the court of Enquiry into the air collision stated that the instructor had not taught his pupils sufficiently, to maintain an adequate look out."

"Well, I'll be damned! That was not only unfair, but untrue," was the only consolation I could offer. Of course he didn't really blame me. We both spent a very pleasant hour reminiscing, before I had to return to Riccall.

After the sad loss of Harry Moorhouse, I was relieved to hear that Bobby Fairclough was alive and a P.O.W.; unfortunately the rest of the crew died. Bobby had evaded capture for a week but he was caught on the Dutch border.

*   *   *

It was known that the Air Chief Marshal Harris was anxious to retaliate against Germany with a very strong force of bombers. Rumours got around that he was preparing a thousand bomber raid. Excitement spread like wildfire through the Squadron when, on the morning of 30th May, every available crew had to standby for operations. I was to join Clack's crew again, as second pilot.

We spent the morning checking every item of equipment and I flew with Kenny on an air test of Halifax 'R' Roger. In the afternoon, the crews packed the briefing room as never before - the atmosphere was electric. The operational map was still covered and we speculated on the target amidst the din of excited voices. The chatter suddenly ceased. There was only the sound of scuffling chairs as we all stood to attention when Wing Commander Tait entered. He was not given to smiling much, but could not resist beaming as he revealed the European map, where the red ribbon was pinned on Cologne. A hubbub broke out which he quickly silenced with the announcement:

"There will be 267 aircraft from 1 Group, 218 from 3 Group..."

All were silent until Tait said:

"4 Group will supply 232 aircraft..."

A greet cheer went up -Hooray, Hooray. It was difficult for us to settle down to hear him continue:

"5 Group are sending 236 and OTUs are providing 83 - a grand total of 1053 aeroplanes."

DEATH OR DECORATION

We quietened down to hear the remainder of the briefing. Finally the Wing Commander asserted with grim determination:

"Germany will understand tonight that we mean business. Good luck everyone."

The bomb load was impressive, each Halifax carrying three 1,000 pound bombs and twelve canisters full of incendiaries. Cologne was going to burn. The perimeter track was lined with Halifaxes as we took off at about 10 pm on a cloudless night.

We were still over the North Sea when the port outer engine failed. Our captain had no choice but to feather the engine, drop our bombs in the sea and return to base. We were a very disappointed crew not to be 'in' on this first massive attack. However, we were not disappointed for long. Two days later, we were included in another thousand bomber attack. the target was Essen in the heart of the Ruhr. All went well this time and we were able to identify and bomb the target successfully. During the same week, we operated every other night.

On June 3rd, I flew with Bill Kofoed to Bremen, where the German defences were intense but erratic. Two nights later, I again flew with Bill's crew. The target was Essen, which we had attacked only four nights earlier. As we crossed the enemy coast, many searchlights were criss-crossing the night sky, looking for victims. On several occasions, we saw tracer shells flying in both directions, indicating an aerial battle between enemy fighters and our bombers.

When we approached 'Happy Valley', the name we had given to the Ruhr, things really hotted up. It seemed the Germans had recovered from the earlier shock of these massive attacks and were determined we shouldn't reach our target. The sky was filled with searchlights. There were hundreds of them - long pencils of light moving constantly. When they were directed at us, the slender beam became a great ball of brilliance, flashing past and returning rapidly in its attempt to find us. There were many cones of light holding an unfortunate bomber in their centres. The pilot would throw his aircraft in all directions, trying to escape, like a large silver fish thrashing helplessly. We saw several bombers explode into great red balls of fire, emitting black smoke, as they spiralled downwards.

The next quarter of an hour would be the worst - seeing the inferno ahead and having to fly into it. Bill had worked out a strategy which seemed quite effective. He figured that, if a group of searchlights had an aeroplane in its cone, they wouldn't wander away looking for another, so he flew as close to a cone as possible without getting caught in its beam, and then headed for the next cone. It was terrifying watching at close quarters some other poor devil frantically trying to escape. On such occasions one's own survival was paramount and there was no way of helping the other fellow.

94

The flak barrage was at its worst when the bomb aimer's voice came over the intercom:

"Target in sight, skipper - hold it there - bomb doors open - steady - steady - left a bit - steady -steady."

During these last few seconds, with taut nerves, we just had to ignore the shells exploding all around us. I glanced for a brief moment at Bill Kofoed - all I could read in his eyes and face was quiet determination. Then came a triumphant shout:

"BOMBS GONE," from the bomb aimer.

Bill lost no time in making a steep, rapid turn to port, and we confronted the task of evading the night fighters which were waiting in the 'wings' to pounce. The defence gradually faded behind us, and we felt tremendous relief to be flying over the North Sea, heading for home. We celebrated our survival with thermos flasks of coffee. This was the last of the week's bomber attacks.

My next duty was to take a B.A.T. (Blind Approach Training) Course. This was carried out at Middleton, where my instructor was Flight Lieutenant Roy. The purpose of the course was to learn how to find one's airfield in bad weather conditions, by listening to radio signals and keeping to a figure of eight course, which enabled the pilot to arrive on the approach for landing. The aircraft used for this purpose was an Airspeed Oxford. Each morning, before starting the exercise, Roy would take the controls for about ten minutes and fly hedge-hopping around the countryside. Local farmers had got used to his route. They didn't appear to object to this unofficial low flying and gave us a cheerful wave.

During the summer of 1942, the war in the Western Desert had reached a new peak. General Rommel, the brilliant leader of the German Afrika Corps, had launched a big offensive against the 8th Army. Within a few days, General Auchinlek had to surrender the British garrison at Tobruk. Most of the experienced crews were put on standby for some secret operations. The Halifaxes were having their engines modified and the carburettors fitted with some kind of filter. Rumours were rife - were the filters being fitted against snow or sand conditions.? No one seemed to know, and if they did, their lips were sealed.

Squadron Leader Peter Warner and his crew were amongst those selected. Pete, his navigator Frank and Bob Greenway the rear-gunner, were particularly good friends of mine. Whilst everything was being prepared for what turned out to be a Middle East detachment, all crew members were confined to camp, their mail was censored and 'phone calls were not allowed - such was the secrecy.

Bob, the rear-gunner, had been keeping company with a girl from Darlington. His crew had never been too happy about this, because she had a reputation for being 'hot stuff'. She had previously been going around with members of other crews - all air gunners- and all 'getting the chop' after keeping her company. The girl was regarded as a jinx, the general belief that her appetite for love-making was such as to cause the physical exhaustion of her current boy friend. In the case of a rear- gunner, it could spell disaster. Pete and his crew were convinced of this, and although having the greatest regard for Bob, they threatened to have him taken out of the crew if he did not break with this 'femme fatale'. These threats were more in the nature of banter and not to be taken too seriously. Because of the restriction on using the telephone, frequent calls from this girl asking for Bob became quite embarrassing and difficult to evade without causing suspicion.

"Ronnie...," said Frank after one of these calls, "there is only one thing for it; you will have to arrange to meet her yourself and put her off permanently somehow."

"How can I do that? I have never met the girl and I only know her name is Linda."

"Well, it's the only way," Frankie insisted and the others agreed.

It seemed Linda was a well-educated girl whose father held an important position in Darlington. The next time she 'phoned, I had to answer.

"Hello, my name's Ronnie, I'm a friend of Bob; he isn't in the mess at the moment."

"He never seems to be around these days," she cut in petulantly, "has he got another girl?"

"No, it isn't like that - look - could I meet you, say in Middlesborough?"

"Alright, I am free on Friday evening."

"OK, shall we make it the Grand lounge at eight?"

"Yes...I shall be wearing a grey outfit with a pink blouse," she told me.

"Alright, your name is Linda, isn't it? See you at eight on Friday then."

"Goodbye."

The lounge at the Grand Hotel was very busy. I arrived early and sat with my eyes glued to the swing doors. Presently, a girl came in, wearing a blue or grey costume with a pink blouse. I could tell by the way she looked around that it must be Linda. She was what my mother used to call a 'well-developed' girl, and I was surprised to find she was almost as tall as I was. Her hair was mouse coloured, with gentle waves ending in curls around her neck. As I approached her - still not sure she was the right girl - she looked directly at me.

"Are you Linda?" I asked, not too confidently.

"Yes, and you are Ronnie," she replied quite pertly.

"Yes I am...would you like a drink?" which I thought was a good opener.

Her hazel eyes, almost green in colour, smiled as she accepted. We sat in the lounge, Linda with a gin and tonic, and I with a beer. I expected that she would want to know immediately about Bob; in fact I was the first one to mention the subject.

"Bob's pilot and navigator have to go on a special course. Bob, as a gunner is not involved, but because of the nature of their work, he is not allowed to leave camp."

I almost convinced myself that this 'cock and bull' story was true. She just shrugged her shoulders and continued chatting quite freely about this and that. I never had to look for a topic of conversation. We had two or three drinks and the time went quickly enough.

The local train we caught to Middleton to return was very small - only four carriages behind a tank-shaped engine. Each carriage had eight fusty compartments furnished in hard, drab coloured moquette, as old as the hills. There were no corridors.

A number of people caught the train at the same time but at Stockton, only about three minutes away, most of the passengers disembarked. Linda and I sat in corners facing each other. Daylight was fading as the engine chugged out of the station. The next stop would be a Halt, with a single wooden platform, used by airmen returning to Middleton St. George airfield, the journey taking about a quarter of an hour.

As soon as the train had left the station, Linda came over and snuggled up to me. Bending closer, she offered her face for a kiss - little harm in this, I thought, and responded to her unspoken request. The harmless kiss suddenly exploded into a very passionate one. I was even more astonished when she took my right hand and placed it inside her blouse. Trying to appear cool and suave, I withdrew from the clinch.

"What about a cigarette?" I asked, putting my hand in my pocket. She replied in haste and rather impatiently:

"Not now," obviously wanting to continue the embrace.

"What about Bob?" I enquired, "after all, you are his girl."

"WAS his girl, it seems," she replied, again putting an arm around my neck and at the same time, groping for my fly buttons with the other hand! There seemed to be no escape from this strapping nymphomaniac. What had started as a harmless kiss soon developed into a very embarrassing predicament. I thought 'come on Middleton Halt, it can't be far now.'

The moment the train started to slow down, I disentangled myself and lowered the window. Despite having avoided any climax in the affair, I barely had the strength to turn the brass door handle! Leaping onto the wooden platform, and slamming the carriage door shut, I looked into the still open window and called:

"Goodbye, Linda...it's been quite an evening."

I felt somehow it was unnecessary to add, "Shall I give Bob your love?"

Phew! Apparently it was no idle threat of Pete Warner's to throw Bob off the crew if he did not disengage from this Darlington hussy.

Whilst the crews were waiting to go to the Middle East, the Squadron suffered several very bad accidents. The first was a terrible 'prang.' An Oxford from the 1516 Beam Approach course, flew head-on into a 76

DEATH OR DECORATION

Squadron Halifax. The Oxford fell to the ground in a mass of pieces. The Halifax spun into the ground just outside the airfield. Pilot Officer Bingham died with his crew, as did the pilot of the Oxford. I never discovered if he was my instructor on the course I had taken only a month earlier.

During the afternoon on the following day, Sergeant Ashton was carrying out an air test with his crew when, shortly after take-off, both port engines cut out. There was not a thing the unfortunate pilot could do about it. At such a low height, it would have been impossible to climb or correct the swing to the left. The Halifax banked steeper and steeper, finally diving into the ground. The ambulance and crash tender raced to the scene. Flight Lieutenant Peter Dobson, who was in the Watch Tower at the time, dashed down the concrete stairs and into the flight van. He tore straight across the grass to the crashed Halifax and arrived before the other vehicles, which had to go via the perimeter track. The pilot and four of his crew were already dead. The rear-gunner, Pilot Officer Higgins, DFM, was trapped in his turret, severely injured. A member of the fire-crew who was there at the time, related to me afterwards what he had found. When he entered the burning aeroplane, he saw Flt Lt Dobson - 'Dobbie' as we knew him - gently supporting 'Higgie'. He was paying no heed to the flames close behind him, which could have engulfed the Halifax at any moment, had the petrol tanks blown up, his only concern was to comfort the unfortunate rear- gunner.

As the months and years passed, I got to know Dobbie very well. There were other occasions when his courage was an example to everyone, and he was unquestionably one of the most accomplished Halifax pilots in Bomber Command.

Until the mass attack upon Cologne, I had been in the habit of making a short prayer to God, before going on operations. It usually took the form of a brief request that I should return safely. If the mission was expected to be particularly hazardous, I sometimes made my supplication on bended knee at the iron bedstead in my room. On one such occasion, I had difficulty in finding the best form of words. I had tried one or two versions which did not sound too unctuous, the best I came up with was "Please God give me the skill to fly safely back to base." It was then that I realised, that, no matter how it was phrased, I was still asking for a privilege.

It was to be expected that from an average Operation, 5% of the airmen would not return. I could not expect the Almighty to be selective and felt it was infra dig to ask for preferential treatment. From then, I worked on a better premise - God helps those who help themselves and relied upon double checking that the red safety thread on my parachute was intact.

CHAPTER 7

CAPTAINCY

July 1942 was the month when most of the experienced operational pilots of 76 Squadron were sent on detachment to the Middle East. Wing Commander Young left Middleton with sixteen Captains and crews. There could have been scarcely a handful of trained men left when Squadron Leader 'Jock' Calder hastily took command of the now decimated 'home' 76 Squadron.

I had shared instruction with two other pupils - Sergeants Butt and Nicholson - and had no idea what had been their previous experience. As far as I was concerned, I had not completed a course since SFTS at Cranwell. The total of my night flying to date had been one and three-quarter hours solo at Cranwell and six and three-quarter hours at Kinloss on Whitleys - all of which had been circuits and landings.

During the week commencing July 20th, after receiving dual instruction from Sdn Ldr Calder, I carried out six solo landings in the Halifax. Now, my night flying had reached the incredible grand total of 10 hours and 20 minutes since I had joined the RAF!

This was the situation when, after breakfast on 26th July, I sauntered up to the DRO Notice Board. Looking casually at the Operational List for that night, it was in almost disbelief that I saw, heading the list:-

Captain .... Fg Off Waite
2nd Pilot .... Sgt Moir
Navigator .... Sgt Pool
Flt Engineer... Sgt Greenwood
BombAimer .... Sgt White
MU/Gunner .... Sgt McCauley
R/Gunner .... Plt Off Glasgow

Two other crews were on the list, captained by Sergeant Butt and Sergeant Nicholson.

At first I thought there must be some mistake, because my Conversion Course had been interrupted and my Pilots log book endorsed - 'course not complete'.

My crew were unknown to me although they knew each other well, having trained together as a crew since OTU. For me, it was the first time I had been Captain of a full crew. Had they known that their pilot, on this,

99

their first operational mission, had never carried out even one night cross-country flight, they would no doubt have been very uneasy - if not terrified! From this period of the war onward, replacement crews for the squadrons, arrived already as a crew flying together and better trained, largely due to the Empire Flying Training and American Arnold schemes, which were working very successfully.

To return to the 26th. Later in the morning I met my crew when I airtested 'B' for Bertie - the Halifax II I was to take that night. I had to overcome my earlier trepidation and was too occupied with the preparations to feel scared. After I had given the machine a thorough test flight, only minor adjustments were needed. It was fortunate that I made quite a good landing, as this probably gave the second-pilot a sense of confidence that they had a very experienced skipper!

Briefing was held in the Operations Room at 14.30 hours and we waited - as calmly as we could - the arrival of the CO. The large map of Europe on the wall did not have the usual red ribbon stretched across it and pinned to the target, so we could only speculate where it might be. The general opinion was that it would be a fairly 'soft' target such as Calais, Dunkirk or St. Nazaire.

As the Commanding Officer entered we jumped to our feet. His voice was decisive as he said:

"Alright...sit down fellows...I won't keep you in suspense...the target for tonight is HAMBURG."

We remained silent for a moment and one could almost hear the sharp intake of breath. We were not expecting a heavily defended German city and would have been much happier with St. Nazaire. During the briefing, airgunners and pilots were warned that Nazi Fighters could be expected to be very active along the River Elbe estuary and that around Hamburg, the anti-aircraft barrage would be concentrated. The weather was expected to be good for the entire trip and take-off time was 21.30. I cannot recall that I found the waiting period too nerve-racking, but I experienced a tremendous inner excitement. Sam Glasgow, an American and the only other Officer in the crew, joined me in the Mess for the traditional supper of bacon and eggs.

Dusk was falling as we arrived at the Flight Office. There was much to do as we got into our flying suits, checked parachutes, stowed away our Thermos flasks of hot coffee, sandwiches and packets of raisins. There was little chatter, we were too busy and new to the game, to indulge in the ribaldry usually displayed by the veteran crews. Finally, we turned out every single personal item from our pockets and handed them to the Officer-in-charge Pockets. Even a bus or cinema ticket could be of value to the enemy, should we be captured. They might indicate the area from which we came, perhaps, even the number of our squadron. It was only necessary - by international law - for us to give our name, rank and service number, if captured, the Germans invariably tried every trick they knew, to extract information.

Now we were ready, we climbed aboard the aircrew bus which took us to the dispersal point, where our aeroplane, bombed up was waiting for us. Sergeant Butt and his crew were the first to be dropped, then came our turn. We climbed out, calling good-luck wishes to Nicholson and his crew, who were at the furthest point.

The ground crew were standing around the dark shape of our Halifax, and the large starter battery trolley was at the ready as we approached. After a final word with the ground Sergeant in charge, the Pitot head cover was removed. Before climbing into the fuselage, I headed the queue for a final pee on the tail wheel. I was never sure whether this ritual was a matter of need, or just for luck!

It helped my confidence that Sergeant Moir seemed quite at ease as he sat beside me in the second pilot's seat. When I had completed my cockpit drill and called the crew on the intercom, to check that they were all OK, I commenced the taxi run around the perimeter track to the take-off point. The green light flashed at me from the ACP and we were on our way. The Rolls Royce Merlin engines responded thunderously as we sped down the runway, carrying our 7000 pound bomb-load. At a height of 1000 feet over the airfield, the navigator called:

"Hello, pilot...course one-one-zero...repeat one-one- zero."

"Pilot to navigator...on course one-one zero...now." I replied.

Below, I saw the circle of Drem lights drifting away and the thought crossed my mind that this was the first time that I had flown further than ten miles from my base at night - it made the thousand mile round trip to Hamburg quite a challenge.

We had been flying uneventfully for an hour or so, when a voice came over the intercom:

"Rear-gunner to Captain...there is an aircraft about one thousand yards astern...could be a fighter...will keep you posted."

About half a minute later, Sam Glasgow called again:

"Aircraft closing rapidly...evasion action Captain."

Without replying, I started a corkscrew movement, which I continued for several minutes. As nothing seemed to be happening, I called:

"Rear- gunner...any sign of the fighter?"

"No," replied the gunner, "I think we have lost him."

Some five minutes later, I heard the 'click' of a microphone:

"Hello skipper...Flight Engineer...the port inner is going U/S, the temperature is normal but the pressure has dropped and it is losing power." Looking at the gauges, I saw a distinct fall on the port- inner engine boost gauge.

"What do you suggest?" I asked the engineer.

"Looks very dodgy...better feather it," was his reply.

Turning to Al Moir, I said:

"OK, Second Pilot, feather the port inner."

Almost as I spoke, Sergeant Moir was carrying out the instruction. Despite this being my first flying with a failed engine, I was surprised to find I could easily correct the swing to port, using the trimming tabs, I could fly straight quite comfortably. It was frustrating to have to jettison the bombs and return to base. The long flight back was uneventful.

It was the middle of the night and still dark when we arrived over Middleton St. George. Because the hydraulics were operated from the port inner engine, I could only make one attempt at landing. Once the undercarriage and flaps were lowered, they could not be raised for a second attempt - I had to keep my nerve and concentrate. The Airfield Control Officer in the Watch Office switched on the airfield Drem lights which could be seen clearly from 1000 feet.

On the first circuit, I overshot the funnel lights leading on to the runway and decided to go round again. The next attempt, I commenced my turn earlier, and the approach looked good. I delayed lowering the undercarriage as long as possible, just in case it was necessary to over-shoot. As I reduced power to lose height, the Halifax swung suddenly to port and straight towards a hanger.

Because of my inexperience with the loss of an engine, I was taken completely by surprise. Sheer fright must have brought my adrenalin to the rescue. I pushed hard on the rudder bar with my right foot, to correct the swing which seemed about to bring us to disaster. My forehead felt moist and cold under my leather helmet, and my hands clammy as they gripped the controls. I think it was my sense of survival which helped me to react instinctively. We were now very close to the ground when I was able to line up with the flare path. I called to Moir:

"Full flap." The ground was approaching so rapidly I almost shouted the instruction..."CLOSE THROTTLES."

Moir hauled the throttle levers as I eased the control column back for the landing. The tyres squealed as they scuffed on the runway- we were down and safe.

"Thank Christ!" I exclaimed with sheer relief.

I never really discovered how the crew felt, they must have thought their 'number was up'. However, I felt their attitude 'warmed' towards me afterwards - gratitude for having survived, I guessed.

Sergeant Nicholson successfully completed his mission to Hamburg. The third Captain - Sergeant Butt - failed to return. It was later discovered that his aircraft had been shot down and crashed, just before midnight, on the outskirts of Hamburg.

One of the 'perks' of being an Operational Station was the high standard of entertainment we were offered. There was a mood of happy anticipation on this particular evening because we were to be given a Grade 1 ENSA show. At the top of the bill was Renee Houston and the comedian duo - Jewell and Warriss. The camp Cinema was packed with airmen of all ranks.

The audience was warmed-up from the start, when Jewell and Warriss made a lively entrance from the back of the theatre. The lowest ranks were in the back seats - the AC 'plonks' - who were greeted by Warriss with "Ullow mates...ow are yuh?" As he approached the NCOs, his voice became more deferential, "Good evening...Flight Sergeant," and addressing the Station Warrant Officer, "Nice of you to come, Sir." Upon reaching the front row, where Group Captain Traill was sitting, both comedians fell to their knees in homage. "Your slaves...O Mighty One," quoth Warriss, which brought the house down.

An attractive chorus-line gave a toe-tapping number to open the show. The house lights went down, the orchestra started to play and as the curtains parted, Renee Houston - appearing like a dream stepped into the spotlight. Her lively personality came over the footlights before she had said a word, and her renowned lovely figure, clothed in a gown of gold and scarlet diagonal stripes, drew grasps and cheers from an appreciative audience. After her first number, about two dozen airmen eased themselves from their seats and quietly left. This was not lost on Renee who, realising they were about to leave on a mission, waved to them and wished them luck.

At the end of the show, we waited in the Mess to entertain the cast to supper. Had I known beforehand that, quite by chance, I would be sitting next to the 'star', I would have been a nervous wreck. I need not have worried, Renee was a charming supper companion. She was totally without affectation and kept me entertained with anecdotes - told in her lilting Scottish accent - she was also a good listener. At the end of the evening, she asked if she could have a tunic button - to keep as a memento. Before you could say, 'brasso', she was holding my top tunic button in her hand! However, I held no illusions, I was sure she had a box-full, from equally enchanted airmen.

At breakfast the next morning, Squadron Leader 'Jock' Calder told me that he had been entertaining one of the girls of the Company who had a huge Teddy-bear which she took everywhere with her. The company had given shows at many different air stations and the Teddy - complete with log-book, had flown in a variety of aeroplanes. Jock had agreed to fly it in a Halifax, to a country house somewhere near Bridlington and bale it out, after entering the flight in it's log book. In the cold light of day, I rather think he rued his generous offer of the previous evening.

Halifax 'G...George' needed an air-test so, with Sdn Ldr Calder at the controls. We took off with only a vague idea where the house was situated. It did not take long to reach the area when we spotted a large country house. We reduced height and started to circle. In no time, several people came out on to the drive waving excitedly. This was the house - used regularly to accommodate ENSA performers. Over the intercom I heard Jock tell me:

"Go to the rear door Ronnie...when you think it is about right...drop the cargo."

Holding the large Teddy in my arms, with its log-book duly endorsed tied tightly to it, I made my way aft. Jock had reduced height to only 50 feet; I found it quite difficult to thrust the Teddy against the slip-stream when unloading it at what I thought to be the right moment. Returning to the cockpit, I saw that my aiming point had been quite good - the bear had landed about sixty yards away in an adjoining field. The last we saw of it, or the Company, was two members of the party hurrying to recover it.

On July 29th, Sergeant Nicholson and I were briefed to attack Saarbrucken in the Ruhr. It was a clear night with a bright moon, and we had been warned that enemy fighters would almost certainly be very active.

The Halifax I had taken on the previous raid on Hamburg, was having an engine replacement for the one which failed, and I took a different machine - 'C' for Charlie. In view of the brightness of the night, and the risk from Nazi fighters, I decided to push the Halifax to the maximum height when over enemy territory. We reached almost 24,000 feet, which turned out to be good tactics. I saw several of our bombers flying below, where they were clearly silhouetted against a bank of white cloud, which made them easy prey for the German JU88s and Messerschmitt 110s. My crew saw several aerial battles going on and two of our bombers go down like giant flaming torches. We carried out our attack on the target and returned without any problems.

On July 31st, we were sent to attack Dusseldorf. The Halifax I had to take was 'B' for Bertie, the plane I took to Hamburg and now appeared serviceable again.

The night was dark but a rising moon took the edge off the darkness as we waited on the perimeter track to take-off. When the green light flashed from the ACP caravan, I made a final check with my crew as I called over the intercom:

"OK, let's go."

Harry Greenwood, my flight engineer, was sitting beside me, ready to lock the throttles after I had pushed them fully open. Gathering speed, the runway lights sped passed as we rapidly approached the end of the runway. The speed was almost 100 miles per hour when I gently eased the control column back to lift the aircraft off the ground - nothing happened as the twenty-eight tons of aeroplane raced on. We were nearly at the end of the runway before 'B' for Bertie became 'unstuck', clearing the airfield boundary with precious little to spare. My sigh of relief was brief, the Halifax was very reluctant to climb.

CHAPTER 7   CAPTAINCY

During the next quarter of an hour, Yorkshire farmers, accustomed to the nightly roar of outward bound bombers, must have been shattered by the noise of our aircraft just above their rooftops. We were crossing the English coast at about 5,000 feet when I realised the machine was not performing properly. Calling Harry, I asked:

"Our rate of climb is very poor for the boost and revs; what is wrong do you think?"

"I don't know, Skipper. All engine temperatures and pressures are normal," was his reply.

"I will maintain present power and revs and hope it will improve," I said with little optimism.

We were about half way across the North Sea and had reached a height of 8,000 feet. It was normal to put in the supercharger at about 12,000 feet, but our climb had been so sluggish I called the flight engineer again to ask if I should put the 'blower' in now.

"Yes, Captain," he agreed.

I did not want to abort the mission, so operated the supercharger and pressed on.

The moon - now high in the sky - lit the night, with its eerie, bluish light, as we approached the Dutch coast; ahead searchlights were criss-crossing the sky. We could not coax the Halifax any higher than 8,000 feet - less than half the usual height for crossing the enemy coast.

We had avoided the searchlights. I was about to tell the crew we would probably be unable to bomb Dusseldorf and would attack the alternative target, when there was a 'click' in my headphones - it was Sam Glasgow, my rear gunner:

"Captain, there's an aircraft about 1,000 yards - port quarter - probably a fighter."

I called my mid-upper gunner, McAuley.

"Mac., leave the fighter to Sam - you search the skies for any others."

A moment later, McAuley called to say that another fighter was coming in on the starboard beam. Sam called again:

"Fighter closing in, get ready TURN TO PORT - GO - GO - GO!"

As I pushed the aeroplane into a diving turn, yellow tracer shells streamed over the cockpit. The mid gunner's voice came over the intercom:

"Skipper - THEY'RE FIRING AT US!"

A split second later, all hell was let loose as shells exploded around us. I was looking at the instrument panel when a shell burst close behind it, filling the cockpit with smoke and the acrid smell of cordite. Death seemed certain and the thought flooded into my mind, how will Mickie and baby Diana cope without me?

I had lost two or three hundred feet in the dive and it needed considerable strength to pull the Halifax into a climbing turn to starboard. The firing seemed to have stopped, so I straightened out into level flight. The realisation that I had survived gave me a fierce, instinctive determination to stay alive.

First, I had to determine the state we were in. Thank God the engines were still running, their defiant roar was music to my ears. I switched on the intercom to talk to the crew and found it was dead; this was a serious blow. The smoke cleared from the cockpit to reveal that several of my instruments were out of action - the directional compass, climb and glide indicator and, by far the most serious, the airspeed indicator.

The first crew member to appear was Sergeant Miller, the bomb-aimer. We had to remove our helmets and shout into each other's ears - above the noise of the engines - now our only means of communication. He said:

"Bob is badly hurt and bleeding from wounds to his wrists; I have put on a rough bandage."

Bob Pool, the navigator, had been in the forward compartment with the bomb-aimer during the attacks.

"Alright," I replied to Miller. "Will you see how the gunners are?"

He returned immediately to tell me that the flight engineer had closed the the bulkhead, protective, steel door and this had been jammed by a shell. Both gunners were to the rear of this door, also beyond, were the fuel cocks on which our petrol supply depended. Harry was working frantically to free the door, with his limited tools.

We were still flying towards Germany with our bomb-load when Miller saw what he thought was an airfield below. We opened the bomb doors and released our load - hopefully on the enemy airfield. As I turned the aircraft on to a reciprocal course for England, I found that the rudder and elevator controls were not responding normally - they weren't positive and had a 'sloshy' feel.

The task of flying the crippled bomber back to England seemed insurmountable but I dismissed any idea of baling out over Holland. My crew were a fine and competetent 'bunch' - I could depend on them. Harry had succeeded in freeing the jammed door and came to report on the scene in the back of the aircraft. Sam, our stalwart American rear-gunner, was uninjured and very wide awake in his turret, which had probably been damaged. He said later, "there was a hellava lot of ayer gettin'in!" The report on Mac was grim. Harry and John Miller had not obtained any response from Mac, still in his turret on top of the fuselage. They had managed to cut away his harness and lower his body on to the floor. What they saw almost sickened them; half his head was missing. It was fortunate for the rest of us that a bullet, or shell, had spent itself on the bullet-proof glass fitted behind the pilot's head! By this time, Bob Pool, his wrists swathed in bandages, was sitting with ashen face on the step to the forward compartment.

The flight back, over the North Sea, now seems like some dream sequence. Without the air-speed indicator, I could only fly by 'feel'. Several times the plane became unstable, and it was only by pushing the stick forward to increase speed that I managed to avoid stalling the aircraft.

Bob, who had been kept primed with hot coffee, refused morphine to relieve the pain, so he could keep a check on the position of Polaris in the sky - about the only means of helping me to stay on course.

Eventually I saw a thin line of surf shining in the moonlight, indicating the English coast. At this stage of our homeward flight the IFF - Identification Friend or Foe equipment would have been switched on. This was not working, so it came as no surprise when searchlights popped up, probing the sky suspiciously. In the distance we saw a German raid in progress, probably on London.

Our radio was out of action so we were unable to transmit a distress call, and could not expect any assistance from the ground; even if an airfield had put lights on, an attempt at landing with this crippled Halifax would have been not just hazardous, but suicidal. We had not survived the night to perish in a field or wood. I made the decision - there was no other option - jump for it. One member of the crew told me that they might be able to put a parachute on McAuley and push his body out; I decided against this, fearing that perhaps it might land in a populated area.

John and Harry assured me that Bob would be able to bale out and, if necessary, would pull his ripcord for him. I instructed Harry to go aft and tell the rear- gunner that he was to come forward and jump from the front escape hatch; in other circumstances, he would just have rotated his turret and baled out backwards. Being unable to communicate with him, I wanted to be certain that he had left the aircraft before I jumped myself.

I gave the order "ABANDON AIRCRAFT". As soon as the escape hatch was opened, a colossal rush of air took me by surprise - dust and papers blew all over the place. I could not see the other fellows leave the plane. I was still struggling to keep the Halifax as straight and level as possible, directed towards the sea, when Sammy Glasgow came from the tail - the broad grin he was wearing, and his cheerful thumbs-up gesture, gave my spirits a big lift. He disappeared forward, down the step. It gave me a strange feeling, now that I was alone; it wasn't fear of baling out, but my brain seemed to be frantically trying to think of some way of saving the Halifax, despite the fact that she had been a bitch of an aeroplane!

Harry had clipped the parachute to my harness before he left. I removed my hands and feet from the controls and jumped down the step to the escape hatch. The roar of the engines and the rush of air was quite deafening as I sat on the edge of the hatch. I wasted no time dropping out. The plane passed overhead and I pulled my ripcord.

As I fell free, it seemed a long while before the canopy opened with a big jolt on my shoulders and an even bigger one in my crutch. Dangling in the sky, the thing that struck me most, was the absolute silence. Even in the dead of night on the ground, there is always a slight sound - up here, only

DEATH OR DECORATION

Baling Out

utter silence. I could just make out the vague shapes of fields and here and there, what appeared to be woods.

At first my descent was so slow it seemed as if I was suspended indefinitely in space. After several minutes spent swinging gently on the silken cords, the ground suddenly rushed up at me. After hitting it with an almighty thump, I gathered up the large silk canopy. I had landed in a field with a crop of yellow mustard. A little way off I saw the roofs of a couple of cottages. It was about three o'clock in the morning when I knocked on the door of one of them. The upstairs window opened and the face of an elderly lady appeared. I called:

"Don't be afraid; I'm a British airman and I have just baled out."

"Oh! Oh!" she said. "Just a minute, I'll come down."

The door was opened by a diminutive lady wrapped in a dressing gown.

"Oh, do come in," she said without hesitation.

"I could tell you were English and not German by your voice."

As soon as we were inside, another little old lady joined us. I soon discovered they were sisters - Misses Edith and Hannah Cox. They were marvellous - restraining their excitement in their anxiety to care for an airman who had 'dropped' in on them in the middle of the night.

They insisted that I should have at least a boiled egg and a pot of tea. I was most surprised when Miss Hannah asked:

"Would you like a cigarette? We don't smoke very often."

"Thank you very much," I replied - gosh how I needed that cigarette.

Hannah produced a packet of 'Tenners' - I almost coughed at the thought. Tenners were considered to be about the worst wartime cigarette made. I accepted with grateful thanks.

108

CHAPTER 7   CAPTAINCY

The cottage, called 'Bacon's End' was rather aptly named, I thought. The ladies managed to get a message to the nearby village of Great Canfield and I was collected by the RAF soon afterwards.

The other members of my crew were rounded up and we were taken to North Weald fighter aerodrome. We were very worried because one member - Bob Pool- was missing. I took a very dim view of the casual attitude shown by some of those 'in charge', and insisted that they pulled out all the stops to find him. As a result, I believe, the Home Guard and police made a thorough search. I discovered later that Bob had landed in the garden of a magistrate's house. His hosts had done everything to make him comfortable; they had re-dressed his wounds and informed an RAF Station, but the telephone operator failed to pass on the message!

We looked a very dishevelled bunch as we started our rail journey back to Middleton. We were tired, without caps, and needing a shave. I was minus a flying boot - lost in the slip-stream when I baled out. The whistles, which we carried on 'ops' in case we had to ditch in the sea, dangled from our lapels, swinging to the movement of the underground train as we travelled to Kings Cross. In our crowded compartment was a very immaculate Group Captain. The gold 'marmalade' decorating his cap seemed to highlight our scruffiness; his expression manifestly disapproved of our appearance - a disgrace to the Air Force!

There was an epilogue to the night's adventure, which I thought quite astonishing. Miss Cox sent me the tear-off calender sheet in her kitchen for that day:

1st August 1942.
'When any calamity has befallen, the first thing to remember is, how much has been escaped.'

Dr. Samuel Johnson (1709-1784).

Back at the Squadron, we had to attend the customary de-briefing. During our interrogation, the story of our two night fighters was met with incredulity. We were told quite bluntly that German fighters never hunted in pairs. Despite official disbelief, the episode was considered worthy of considerable publicity. The same day, the story of our air battle was included in the BBC's News Bulletins and a Press Officer arrived at Middleton to cover the story. During the interview, I told him that after being driven away from Miss Cox's cottage, we were about to pass a country pub when I suggested that we stop and have a drink. As I walked into the public bar of the 'Blacksmith's Arms,' to my astonishment, I found two members of my crew were already there! The next day, amongst the 'dailies' headlines, was one in the Daily Mirror:

"BOMBER CREW BALE OUT - MEET IN THE VILLAGE PUB."
None of my family in Bristol were aware of the episode of course, but

Mickie's sister - Winnie, saw the headline and rang her immediately, saying:

"Have you seen the papers - bomber crew bale out and meet in the village pub - sounds just like our Ron!"

Little did she know how right she was, and how well acquainted she was with her brother-in-laws partiality to a celebratory glass of beer.

Two weeks later, five caterpillar badges arrived. These were given to aircrew who had baled out to save their lives, and gave them automatic membership of the Caterpillar Club, which had been initiated by the Irvin Parachute Company. It was intended to be worn as a lapel or tiepin and was in no sense a decoration. So, I was mystified at the remark of W/Cdr. David Young, when he said:

"The best place to wear the badge is in the navel."

There were frequent occasions when the Wing Commander's remarks or decisions were difficult to understand.

Mike Renault related how once, he was rebuked by David Young for disagreeing with him over a very vital issue. Mike was flying Halifax 'L' for London, carrying 8000 lbs of high explosives on a raid on Germany. During the take-off, the plane swung viciously to the left unexpectedly, and Mike had to use all his skill to get airborne. Later, he reported the problem to Young who insisted it was Mike's piloting error and not a faulty aeroplane.

A few nights later - when Mike was not operating - another pilot was given the same Halifax to fly on a bombing raid. Renault warned the pilot about the swing, but was so concerned that, instead of going to bed, he went to the airfield to watch the take-off. He saw 'L' for London swing badly to port and heard the hiss of brakes being fiercely applied as the pilot vainly attempted to overcome the swing. The aircraft became airborne, but only after it had crashed into a crane near the end of the runway, leaving a trail of broken propellers and other parts. The now, crippled, bomb-laden Halifax flew low over Yorkshire - in real trouble. Mike told how he went to the Watch Tower where he found the Wing Commander, quite calm and giving instructions over the R/T to the crew of the stricken plane. They were told to fly out to sea, jettison the bombs, then return over the coast and bale out.

One is bound to wonder why the Commanding Officer, Wg Cdr Young had allowed another pilot to take this Halifax after the experienced Mike Renault had reported it not to be airworthy.

The past few weeks had been fairly traumatic and it was a relief to be granted leave. I made the journey from Darlington to Bristol during the night. When the train was a few miles from Birmingham, for no apparent reason, it came to a halt. Half-an-hour later the journey resumed and it was past one o'clock in the morning when we pulled into New Street Station, Birmingham; an air raid had caused the delay. The smell of steam hung in the air as I stepped on to the platform, glad to be able to stretch my legs. Despite the usual aroma of a railway station, the air seemed fresh and cool after the long spell in a smokey train compartment. I saw a ticket collector and asked him:

"How long does this train stop in Birmingham?"

"About twenty-five minutes, but we are running late - it can't leave before 3.10," he replied.

Satisfied that I had plenty of time, I went to the canteen. I was served promptly and leisurely drank a cup of coffee. After placing the cup on a table littered with empties, I returned across the footbridge to the platform. As I descended the stairs, I realised that the train was no longer standing on Platform 4. I checked it was the correct platform, then enquired of a porter what had happened to the train.

"Bristol train left about five minutes ago." I was told.

With mixed feelings of disappointment and anger, I tracked down an inspector who informed me that services had been disrupted and the next train to Bristol was not due until 7.20 am. I told him all my gear was on the earlier train; he was very apologetic and said the only thing he could do was to telephone Bristol and arrange for my kit to be retrieved.

Returning to the platform, I saw what appeared to be a goods train pulling in. A porter told me it was the 'fish special' from Crewe - destination Bristol. Walking up to the engine cab, where the driver and fireman were chatting, I explained what had happened and asked if I could travel with them.

"Not a chance!" they told me and, although I said I would be most unobtrusive, they seemed genuinely sorry but could only add:

"More than our job's worth."

Feeling cold and dejected, I walked the length of the train. Half-way along, a large van had its sliding doors two feet ajar. Glancing quickly inside, I saw it was filled almost to the roof with large, dirty, grey sacks, containing assorted packages.

"Right," I said to myself, "this is going to be my transport to Bristol."

Making sure I wasn't seen, I hopped inside and scrambled over the mountain of sacks. This proved to be more difficult than I had expected, the sacks shifted with my weight, and I eventually slithered to the floor on the opposite side of the doors, well hidden from the platform. When I had adjusted my body to the shaped of the packages, my resting place was not too uncomfortable. It was now a matter of waiting for the doors to close and the train to start its journey - with a bit of luck I might arrive only an hour late.

Within a few moments, I heard the doors move but, instead of closing, they were being opened. I thought, if they throw any more sacks in, I shall find it hard to breathe. I heard muffled voices outside on the platform, and suddenly, a couple of sacks from the top of the pile disappeared. Lord!

DEATH OR DECORATION

Wrong Male

Someone was removing the sacks. The pile was diminishing at an alarming rate, I realised that the van was being emptied. Discovery was imminent - there was no escape - so I decided to reveal myself. When I stood up, the effect upon the two men who had been unloading was devastating.

"Good God!" exclaimed one. "Christ!" said the other.

I really think they were calling on the Almighty to explain the RAF apparition suddenly before them. They decided the situation demanded the attention of the guard. He duly arrived and after hearing the brief details, instructed the men to continue unloading. He appeared to be only vaguely listening to my story, as he stared at the 'wings' on my left breast. I sensed that RAF pilots were high on his 'honours list'.

The guard was a thick-set, tough looking individual, more like a farmer than a railwayman. He studied my face intently then, with a hint of cunning said:

"Come along wi' me."

I followed him to the guard's van at the rear of the train. He looked carefully up and down the platform before saying:

"Quick - hop in."

Without wasting a second, I found myself in an old van, with a small observation platform at each end and a large horizontal wheel which I assumed was some kind of brake. A partition divided the compartment. On a small bench seat was a cushion covered with a good quality moquette, now ingrained with soot and grime, giving it an appearance of shiny, black leather.

The guard waved his flag, then jumped aboard the moving train with confidence attained by years of practice. After placing his blue enamelled

112

canister of tea on the little coke stove, he carefully wrote in his log book, showing no concern that I was an unofficial passenger. He then chatted amiably about his young nephew who had recently joined the RAF, hoping to become an RAF gunner. I soon learnt that a vegetable allotment was his main interest. After a while, he asked:

"Do you play cards?"

"Poker, occasionally."

"How about pontoon?" he enquired.

"Well yes - I think everyone can play pontoon."

From a shelf he took a packet of cards, which had been so well thumbed that the edges had become 'furry'. There were frequent intervals during the card-playing whilst Harold - as he was called - made observations and notes in his book. The journey passed remarkably quickly and in no time at all, we were drawing into Temple Meads Station.

Harold told me to wait for a signal from him before leaving the train. As soon as the train stopped, he jumped on to the platform and quickly beckoned me. I wanted to thank and reward him, but there was only time for a brief, "Many, many thanks", before seeing the last of my good friend.

My earlier anxiety about my belongings vanished when I collected them from the Manager's Office, and I was now relaxed, ready to enjoy my week's leave.

The first evening I spent with Mickie, visiting my parents in Keynsham. We left quite late, taking a short cut via a country road. We were approaching the tiny village of Queen Charlton, when I saw a light flashing ahead. A row of cottages, hidden by a bend in the road, came into view. From the upstairs window of one of them, I saw a hurricane lamp being moved across the uncurtained window. I watched for a while and concluded it must be some form of signalling. Returning to the car, we decided to report what I had seen to the nearest police station.

The Duty Sergeant, dubious at first, decided it was worthy of investigation. After he had recorded my name, address and telephone number, we continued our journey home. I felt certain I had discovered an enemy agent and with an active imagination, considered the possibility of having discovered a whole network of spies!

When my week's leave was nearing its end, I felt disappointed that I had received no message from the police. Curiosity forced me to return to Whitchurch Police Station to enquire about the mystery.

"Ah...Yes, Mr. Waite - the lamp-in-the-window business. We did watch the premises. You were right, someone was making signals."

I was all agog to know the answer, but the Sergeant was stretching the matter out - savouring the news he was about to give.

"It was a young farm labourer in the cottage, he had a sweetheart who lived along the lane. After he'd left her at night, he sent her messages with his lamp...one flash for a kiss...two flashes, 'I love you'...three flashes - I would have to blue pencil that one!" He chuckled.

I found the climax as amusing as he did, although I was rather disappointed that I had not stumbled upon a spy ring. The week's leave had passed all too quickly. It had been wonderful to have Mickie's loving companionship again. My farmer friend had generously found me two gallons of precious petrol, so that I was able to do more visiting than I had expected.

*　*　*

On the 5th August, 1942, Wing Commander Cheshire took command of what remained of 76 Squadron after the Middle East detachment had left. It was a daunting task to rebuild the unit into a front-line Squadron. The Wing Commander had already been awarded the DSO, DFC and b⌒r, and was renowned in Bomber Command.

His arrival stimulated our enthusiasm like a breath of fresh air. Without impairing his position as C.O. and avoiding any cliques, he had the ability to be friendly with those under his command. When there was a quiet evening, he sometimes gathered a few fellows around for a game of cards or a modest gamble. I suspected it was not so much the gambling he enjoyed, as being able to make use of one of the luxury wedding gifts he had brought back from America. This consisted of a magnificent pigskin case containing every gambling game imaginable - roulette, chemin-de-fer, poker dice, etcetera - which just had to be used.

It would have been a mistake to assume, because of his youth and camaraderie, that he lacked resolution. He was a fair and firm disciplinarian, always looking for the highest standards of efficiency.

During August, the Squadron only carried out three night operations. On the 11th, 'Chesh' joined the main force of 150 aircraft to attack Mainz. During the morning of the 20th, I was told I would be required for a mission that night. My crew - whom I had not flown with before - were all NCO's. (The Dusseldorf crew had returned to their own captain - Sgt Moir.)

The mission was what was called a 'Nickel' sortie - a leaflet dropping operation. The target was Dijon in France; the trip would be fairly long one of approximately 1,300 miles.

We discovered at the briefing that the main purpose of the operation was to test the efficiency of a new electronic navigational aid for long distances from base, called 'Gee', which was regarded as an almost magical piece of equipment for navigation and target identification. The Navigation Officer, who gave the briefing, firmly warned the navigators not to rely entirely on 'Gee' but keep their normal 'dead reckoning' navigation going throughout the entire operation, in case the 'Gee' equipment failed.

114

CHAPTER 7   CAPTAINCY

We were the only crew operating that night. At precisely 10.30 pm we took off on our mission. Because we would not be flying close to any heavily defended areas, the flight was expected to be fairly trouble free. Long hours of flying straight courses would be tedious for me. Had I known my crew better, I could have had an occasional chat with them but, realising how important it was for the navigators, I only called the navigators when necessary.

One or two searchlights appeared near the French coast, but their attempt to find us seemed half-hearted and they were soon extinguished.

I had been flying a steady course for about half-an-hour and we were now well into France. It seemed a long time to be flying the same course, so I called on the intercom:

"Pilot calling navigators; aren't we due for a change of course yet? Over."

"We will give you a new course in about five minutes, captain."

I disengaged 'George', the automatic pilot, which had been keeping the aircraft on course. Ten minutes passed and still no message came from the navigators. We were flying at a height of 3,000 feet and, as I peered into the blackness ahead, I perceived some light patches in the sky. Keeping a watch on them, I realised they were snow-capped mountains. I knew that our route should not take us nearer than eighty or ninety miles from a mountainous region and called the navigators with considerable urgency:

"Captain calling navigators - what the hell is going on down there - I can see the bloody Alps ahead."

"It's OK, skipper..." was the reply.

"It doesn't look alright to me - take your heads out of the 'office' and have a look."

Within two minutes I received the instruction:

"Alter course to zero-three-zero - now."

This was a massive alteration to the previous course, which indicated that the navigation had gone badly astray. After one or two further small changes of course, we arrived over the target and unloaded the leaflets.

We now had the long haul back to England which we expected would not be too hazardous. There was little improvement in the navigation: long spells of silence gave me an ominous feeling that all was not well. Even if I could have helped with the navigation, without a second pilot, I would not leave the flying controls to the dubious efficiency of 'George'. I told my navigators over the intercom of my dissatisfaction, but felt that if I badgered them too much, it would only make matters worse. Eventually, they told me we were over the English Channel, and the wireless operator was getting a QDM (radio fix). Actually, we were not over the Channel at all, but about sixty miles west of Paris.

"Navigator to pilot - alter course to three-five-zero, repeat three-five-zero."

Wearily, I replied:

"On course three-five-zero- now."

Dawn was breaking as we approached Le Harve, and I could plainly see the scattered farms of Normandy. At 3,000 feet and in daylight, the Halifax was a 'sitting duck' for any Hun fighter.

I called:

"Pilot to rear-gunner."

There was no immediate response and I suspected that he might have fallen asleep - he could hardly have been blamed. It must have been a miserable trip for him.

"Pilot to rear-gunner - wake up for God's sake - keep a look out for fighters."

"Yes, skipper - very good, skipper." His voice sounded quite alert.

Every second I expected the worst but, thankfully, there was still no sign of a fighter. The previous day, a strong force of Canadian Commandos had landed at Dieppe. The raid had been valiant but not successful. Our Spits and Hurricanes had inflicted heavy losses on the German fighters - they were probably grounded and licking their wounds.

Our fuel was running very low and as we crossed the English coast near Selsey Bill; the flight engineer advised me to land and refuel. It was almost 7 a.m. when I landed at Sutton Harcourt in Oxfordshire.

The runway was very short - less than 1,000 yards - so, in order to keep the all-up weight as low as possible for take-off, I requested that only tanks one and three should be refilled. Whilst the re- fueling was going on, we had breakfast and discovered, on returning to the Halifax, that they had filled all the tanks! The village church, surrounded by tress, was close to the end of the runway. I had it in mind to make the stupid so-and-so's drain the surplus fuel. The rough ground in front of the tarmac runway was firm, so I decided to use this as an extension to the runway take-off.

Sutton Harcourt was a flying training station. By the time we were ready, hundreds of trainees had finished breakfast and were lined up, waiting to see this 'giant' bomber - that they themselves might soon be flying - demonstrate its take-off. Eagerness shone from their young faces as they watched. In order to make use of every inch, I swung the aircraft as close to the boundary hedge as possible. This brought a protest from my rear-gunner:

"Christ, skipper - you've put me right in the bleeding hedge - I feel like a perishing sparrer!"

'Well, don't lay any bloody eggs," I heard an unknown member of the crew remark.

As the Halifax roared towards the end of the runway and lifted off, I took a rather steepish turn to starboard, which must have looked quite spectacular. I expect the onlookers thought I was showing off - actually it was necessary to avoid the church. Flying back to Middleton was uneventful, the operation taking nine hours twenty minutes altogether.

The Squadron did not operate during the next week, which was uneventful. I only carried out a little local flying.

One morning, waiting in the Flight Office for instructions, the 'phone rang. It was the Wing Commander who wanted to see me in his office. I walked down the corridor jauntily enough and knocked on his door.

"Come in."

I entered and saluted. 'Chesh' smiled and asked me to sit down. I wondered why he wanted to see me but did not have any feeling of apprehension - I had not put up any 'black' as far as I knew. He looked directly at me, very intently, before asking:

"Ronnie - what went wrong on the Dijon operation?"

The suddenness of the question took me by surprise.

"We got completely lost, sir."

"You were Captain and, as Captain, you are responsible for the success of an operation."

"Yes, that is true, Sir, but the problem was one of navigation."

During the interview, the Wing Commander was never hostile. I sensed that he felt in sympathy with my position. Despite my argument that I had not been trained as a navigator, he returned to my responsibility as Captain. I left the office rather dispirited with a feeling of being hard done by.

Later, when I was brooding on the matter, I wondered if the Wingco had been aware that I had not previously flown with that crew. Also, my failure to denounce the two navigators for incompetence at de-briefing could have been a reason for criticism.

Within a few days, I was again called to the Wing Commander's Office, and told that I was being recommended to fly twin- engined aircraft. I felt a great sense of disappointment; I would not be continuing my tour with 76 Squadron. This was hard to accept, particularly after serving a rather tough apprenticeship and beginning to get into my stride.

My thoughts were preoccupied with wondering what type of twin-engined aircraft I would soon be flying - hopefully the new wonder aeroplane Mosquito, a dream of a plane. At it turned out, I stayed with the 'heavies'.

CHAPTER 8

1658 HEAVY CONVERSION UNIT - RICALL

Whilst I was awaiting a posting to twin-engined aircraft, I was asked to give check-dual flying to one or two newly arrived pilots. Then, early in September, 1942, a new training unit was formed - 1658 Heavy Conversion Unit at Riccall, close to a hamlet between Selby and York.

On the 13th September, with Squadron Leaders Dobson and Calder, we opened the new Station. Everyone had to make several ferrying trips from Middleton, filling the Halifaxes with necessary equipment and items such as 'bone-shaker' service bicycles and two palm trees to decorate the mess - 'mess' it certainly was, with airmen, NCO's and officers crowded into a communal, newly built, damp concrete building.

The airfield itself had been built on marshy land so it was not very surprising that, not long after our arrival, the end of the runway and part of the perimeter track disappeared into a bog! The surrounding landscape was rather beautiful and remote, with several small lakes dotted amongst woods. We found the lakes very useful as landmarks when coming in to land in bad visibility.

One of my early pupils, David Thomas, had a lyrical voice which stamped him unmistakably as a man from the Welsh valleys. He had a quiet, imperturbable nature and I expected him to be an easy pupil. Thomas sat quietly attentive during the preliminary exercise, whilst I demonstrated the flying characteristics of the Halifax. Some pupils, at first, were slightly in awe of the aeroplane's size, but he did not appear to be intimidated.

Thomas made normal progress under dual instruction and his landings were quite good, however he seemed incapable of controlling the height of the aircraft on approach. Circuit after circuit, I told him:

'Thomas, start reducing the height...now."

He would make a token movement of the throttles but had no idea how much adjustment was required. After several hours of instruction, I decided that we would make one more circuit without my saying a word to him. All went well until the approach; he lowered the undercarriage, turned towards the runway, but made no attempt to lose height. I said nothing...we floated over the airfield boundary at about 500 feet. I wondered if he had decided to land in the market square at Selby! He just carried on regardless, so I had to say:

"Raise the undercarriage, Thomas, and do another circuit."

After we had landed, I went to the Flight Commander - Squadron Leader Dobson.

"I have given Thomas over five hours dual and I still can't safely send him solo."

"That's alright, Ronnie. I will take him on."

I was very relieved.

It was customary, when instructors had sent a pupil on his first solo flight, to go to the control tower and watch their fledgling's performance. Several days later, I met 'Dobbie' in the tower and asked him:

'Have you got someone going solo?

"Yes," said Dobbie, "our mutual friend, Thomas."

"How about his approach?"

"He still comes in a bit high, but, on his own, he will do better - he is safe enough," Dobbie asserted, giving me a wry smile.

We appeared unconcerned, as we watched in silence, underneath there lurked a little bit of tension. As usual, Thomas came in high and had to lose height rapidly. This made his final approach more difficult, but, in the end, he made a good landing. We looked at each other and grinned with relief. This was only the beginning of the 'Thomas saga.'

Ten days later, we were carrying out night flying training. Dobbie and I found ourselves in a similar situation, both with pupils making their first solo night flight. We stood in the Watch Office, peering into the darkness at the navigation lights of the Halifaxes as they taxied around the perimeter track. In the stillness we could hear the Merlin engines - quiet at first - then roar into full power as an aircraft took off.

"That will be Thomas," said Dobbie, as a Halifax disappeared quickly into the dark. The average time taken to complete a circuit was about ten minutes: because it was Thomas, we allowed an extra five minutes 'deliberation time'.

After fifteen minutes, we went on to the balcony to look for him. There was no sound nor sight of an aeroplane on the circuit. A few minutes later we heard aircraft engines but could see nothing. Other flying instructors became interested and joined us. We all stood, quiet and intent, as we listened.

"Doesn't sound like a 'Hali'; what do you think, Dobbie?" asked MacAgutter.

"No, it doesn't, but the engines may be out of sync."

The sound came nearer and we all joined in the guessing game.

"Sounds a bit like an Anson," was my offering.

"I don't think it's a Lanc," remarked another; then an aircraft just became visible. As the plane came in to land, the engines still had a very unfamiliar sound. At the end of the runway we heard the engines switched off and a voice came over the RT in the Watch Office. The Welsh accent betrayed its owner:

"Calling Control...this is 'S' for Sugar...could you send a tender, we need a tow."

Dobbie dashed down the concrete stairs, jumped into the Flight van and drove off to the end of the runway. Later the story unfolded. A large branch of a tree was protruding from the nose of the Halifax - propellers were almost missing from one engine and badly damaged on another. After take-off, Thomas must have decided to roost in a small wood in Escrick Park, about a mile from the runway! Somehow, he had managed to keep the Halifax airborne and 'stagger' around the circuit. Any other pilot would have been as shattered as the aeroplane, but Thomas seemed quite calm, only very apologetic for the damage caused.

Four days later, we had three trainee crews carrying out night cross-country flights, which consisted of flying a triangular course over England and Wales, lasting four hours. Thomas and his crew were one of them. The three crews took off from Riccall within a few minutes of each other and were expected back at 3 am. Three o'clock came and two aircraft appeared on the circuit almost together, both making safe landings. The officer in charge decided to allow Thomas an extra fifteen minutes before taking any action. The quarter of an hour passed with no sign of Thomas, so it was decided to call the Royal Observer Corps.

"This is 1658 Heavy Conversion Unit, Riccall...We have a Halifax trainee crew overdue; have you a plot of him in your territory?"

"We had a plot on a Halifax at two-thirty hours and the only information we can give you is that he was on a bearing somewhere between Flamborough Head and Stavanger in Norway."

"That will be Thomas!" said Dobbie with conviction.
However, he did return safely, albeit thirty minutes late.

Bomber Command's training tactics appeared to change as the war progressed; they had to I supposed. The intensive bombing of Germany caused very high crew losses and squadrons were in urgent need of replacements. I felt that pilots were often passed out before they were competent.

During October and November, new flying instructors were arriving from the squadrons. They were pilots of the crews who had defied the odds of three-to-two against surviving a tour of operations. It seemed that the Air Ministry had a policy of awarding a DFC or a DFM to captains of crews on completing thirty missions. The nightly losses of five per cent of the bomber force made the outlook at the beginning of a tour, either DEATH or DECORATION!

Johnny Harwood, 'Bunny' Bunclark, Val 'Mac' Agutter, Kenny Clack and Peter Gaskell were amongst the first arrivals at 1658 Heavy Conversion Unit. Within a week or two, their distinguished flying awards were promulgated, and each recipient of a 'gong' was celebrated with a good party in the Mess. A great camaraderie developed between all the instructors - perhaps less close than that on the Squadron, but with the same feeling of comradeship.

DEATH OR DECORATION

The next batch of pupils presented less of a problem than David Thomas. I felt I was able to send them on their first solo, after a normal amount of dual instruction. One morning, on the list of new pupils, I saw the name Fletcher. As soon as he entered, we recognised each other. John Fletcher had been my night flying instructor at Cranwell in 1941. The tables were now turned, as I was to be his instructor. He had completed his tour on Whitleys during the early days of the war and was about to undertake a second tour.

Fletcher was a natural pilot. During the first dual exercise, I had only to demonstrate any manoeuvre once and he was able to execute it perfectly. John completed his Halifax training and was posted to 76 Squadron as Flight Commander, with the rank of Squadron Leader. Less than three months later, he fell victim to a Hun night-fighter, and was killed over Belgium. Despite his outstanding ability as a pilot and Captain, he could not overcome the odds stacked so heavily against him.

At about the same time, other ex-pupils also failed to return; Flight Sergeant Thom, a New Zealander, became a P.O.W. in Italy. Sergeant Gold and Flying Officer Black were killed over Berlin. Squadron Leader Barrett was brought down by 'flak' over Essen. New trainees were arriving - fresh, eager and optimistic. This was not the time to indulge in sentiment. I was reminded of the valiant pilots of the Great War, and their defiant, "Here's a toast to the dead already, and Here's to the next man to die!"

Living conditions at Riccall were improving; we now had separate Messes, but the food was very basic, which was not the fault of the Catering Officer. The Station was new and there had been no opportunity to establish any beneficial relations with local farmers. The main entertainment in the Officer's Mess was the large, old but efficient HMV radiogram. It was decided to grant ten pounds from the Mess funds for the purchase of new records, and 'Mac' and I were given the pleasant task of buying a selection.

The weather was bad, making flying impossible. Mac and I took a day off and went to Leeds. We planned to buy the records first, then have a meal and visit a show in the evening. We were lucky to be able to book rooms at the Queens Hotel, which was almost filled with guests. The shop assistants were very helpful, gladly demonstrating the records of our choice, mainly featuring the big bands -Dorsey, Bigard, Ellington and Grappelli. Glen Miller was not yet on the 'scene'. The variety programme at the Empire theatre looked inviting, with Ann Shelton topping the bill, so we booked seats early. The show was excellent, with plenty of topical humour, magic and music.

Leeds, inexplicably, had suffered little from German bombing, unlike many other cities of similar size. At 11 pm, the residents' lounge was comfortably filled with guests. The profusion of chatter and laughter made the war seem a distant unreality. We sat with our drinks, enjoying our temporary escape from Riccall, when a girl with blond hair passed by.

"Mac - I believe I have just seen Ann Shelton - perhaps she is staying here."

"Well, don't just sit there, Ronnie - go and find her," said Mac.

It did not take long. I found her sitting with an older lady and a younger girl. Using my best possible approach, I told them my friend and I had been to the theatre and we thought Ann was superb. We would be delighted if they could join us for just one good-night drink. It was Ann's mother who, at first, gave me a dubious look and I felt certain she would not accept the invitation. Mac walked over to join me. Her eyes seemed to smile approval at the 'blue-eyed' boys of the Royal Air Force, wearing 'wings', with the addition of Mac's recently acquired DFC ribbon, so she consented - not too readily, though.

"Just one, then," Mrs Shelton stipulated. "Ann has a matinee, as well as the evening performance tomorrow."

Ann's mother was a nice, quiet lady. She kept a watchful eye on Ann, and her other daughter, Joy. Mac, using his not inconsiderable charm, failed to impress Joy, who made it clear that, of the three Services, she distinctly preferred the Royal Navy. We were both guilty of 'shooting a line' on a grand scale, whilst trying to convince them that it was the RAF which was having most of the war action. These tactics must have been successful, as Ann even asked us for our autographs! We, in turn, invited her to Riccall, if she could possibly come, to entertain us, explaining that we were only a small Station. She was charming and agreed readily, which was very generous for someone with a 'star' rating. We returned to Riccall early next morning in the best of spirits.

The weather improved considerably, making it possible to maintain a full flying programme. Christmas was approaching. I had not been on leave for some time, so Mickie and I made arrangements for her to visit me. My sister, Doris, was delighted to have the opportunity of looking after Diana for a few days.

It was about 9 pm when I met Mickie at Leeds Station. She came along the platform through clouds of steam - as though in a dream. She was wearing an attractive winter coat with her head tucked cosily into the large fur collar - she looked stunning. The slow, stopping train journey to Selby passed quickly enough, as we had so much to chat about. We went straight to the Londesborough Arms Hotel, where I had booked a room for three nights. The huge log fire in the lounge-bar was not only welcoming but seemed a good omen for the next few exciting days.

I had to carry out normal flying duties and paid more than usual attention to the daily flying programme. I was rather fed up to find that I was down for night flying on the very first night of Mickie's visit, however I was pleased to have the first duty from 1800 to 2000 hours. I had already given daytime dual instruction to my pupil, Flight Sergeant MacQuarrie, whom I found to be a competent pilot. With a bit of luck I would be able to send him solo after a few dual circuits, enabling me to finish early.

The conditions were sharp and frosty, with excellent visibility, as we clambered into the Halifax - ideal for night flying. It was only necessary for me to keep a careful watch while MacQuarrie operated the controls. He handled the infamous take-off swing perfectly, keeping the aircraft on a straight course between the row of runway glim lights.

Just after lift off, the last of the lights flashed passed and we commenced the first circuit. I was unworried as I watched, waiting for the undercarriage lights to change to red - indicating that it had retracted. Instead, suddenly, the bomb-door warning lights appeared on the flight panel.

"Jesus!" I almost screamed at MacQuarrie, "The bomb-doors are open". In the darkness, he had grabbed the wrong lever and pushed the flaps lever down. The first intimation I had of this, was when I saw the flaps indicator needle falling on the dial. I felt an icy chill as I realised our plight - scarcely two hundred feet on the altimeter and, even with full power, a perilously low airspeed. The Halifax could only lose height under such conditions.

"I've got her.." I called to MacQuarrie.

The flying controls felt soggy - split-second decisions were required - fate had to be on our side. I pressed the bomb-door lever to 'closed', at the same time raising the flaps in small jumps 50 degrees...40 degrees...30 degrees...stopping at 20 degrees. I was relying on intuition. It was necessary to increase the dangerously low airspeed by easing the control stick forward. The Halifax started losing height. God! We were going to 'buy it' I felt with certainty.

Thoughts flashed across my mind like lightning - the town of Selby, with its lofty Minster, was almost on our flight-path and only about a mile away. Tucked under the shadow of the Minster was the Londesborough Arms Hotel.

I was beginning to lose hope; our height was falling and I could already see individual trees passing below. Then - as suddenly as they had flashed on - the bomb-door warning lights went out and the undercarriage lights flickered, indicating that it was retracting. Thank God! There was now a good chance we would make it. The aircraft started to gain speed and I was able to increase height. Our impending disaster had probably lasted only a matter of two or three minutes - it seemed like a lifetime.

Once the flight was on its normal course, I felt rather 'drained' and thankfully called Mac Quarrie on the intercom;

"Alright, Flight Sergeant, you take over and complete the circuit."

"Right, Sir - Whew! That was close."

Another voice came over the intercom. It was the rear-gunner:

"Does that mean we have permission to breathe again, Sir?."

"Captain to crew - make sure all the drinks in the bar, tonight, are on Mac."

For the reader to understand what happened during the take-off with Flight Sergeant MacQuarrie, it is necessary to explain that, in the Halifax, the undercarriage, flaps and bomb-door levers were located on the right-hand side of the pilot, at seat level. The levers could be identified by 'feel' - the undercarriage lever was the longest and about the thickness of a walking stick. Alongside were the other two levers, each about eight inches long; they were distinguished by the flaps lever having a knob at the end, the bomb-door lever, a projecting dowel. The undercarriage and flaps levers worked in the normal sense - down for 'lower' - up for 'raise'. The bomb-door lever worked in reverse. I had many pupils during my time as a flying instructor and this was the only occasion on which such a mistake was made.

We carried out three more circuits and landings without any further problems. My pupil seemed calm and unaffected by the experience. As we taxied round for the fifth take-off, I said to the Flight Sergeant:

"One more good circuit - then, would you like to go solo?"

"Sure, Sir," was his eager reply.

He flew competently and confidently so, after landing, I told him:

"OK, MacQuarrie - carry out four solo circuits, then call the Watch Office to send out the next detail."

Returning to the control tower, I found Peter Gaskell in charge of night flying.

"Hello, Peter. I have sent my pupil solo."

"He's flying 'C' for Charlie, isn't he," Peter replied. "You have your wife up for a few days, haven't you, Ronnie?"

"Yes. She is staying at the Londesborough Arms."

"Why don't you push off now?" Peter offered, "I will keep an eye on your pupil."

"Thanks Peter," I said gratefully, "I will just watch MacQuarrie do one circuit and then go."

When I arrived at the Londesborough, I found Mickie encircled by a group of my friends. Being the only girl in the party, she was obviously enjoying the attention being lavished upon her.

Haggarty -a pupil - had a double reason for celebrating; it was his birthday and he had completed the flying course. He had invited Bunny, Mac, Dobbie and Johnny Harwood for a meal. 'Haggie', a nationally known rugby player, was popular with everyone. His warm Irish brogue accentuated his sense of fun and zest for life. When he found we were staying at the Londesborough, he insisted we should join the party. Conversation, stories and banter flowed easily around the table, leaving little time for eating; it was an hilarious evening.

DEATH OR DECORATION

The following morning, we didn't surface very early and I had to race around to get Mickie to Selby station in time to catch her train to Bristol. In one way, this was an advantage - we had less time to spend on unhappy farewells. My short journey back to Riccall was miserable, as I realised that time was steadily increasing the distance between us.

The weather remained very good and I was averaging three flying training sessions a day with my pupils. It was nearing Christmas, so we decided to hold a party to entertain wives and selected local residents. A Friday was the chosen day, and we all looked forward with enthusiasm to this - our first official party at Riccall. Two days before the event we were invited to collect as much holly as we liked for decorating the Mess, from the Escrick Estate; our Transport Section supplied a 10 hundred-weight van with WAAF driver and I was detailed to fetch the holly. The morning was really cold - frost sparkled on the ground and the chilly air caught one's breath. The van with its driver arrived.

"I think I will drive," I said to the girl. She had a look of surprise as she replied:

"It is my job, Sir. I don't mind driving."

"I know, and you are very good too, but I think I would like to drive."

We indulged in a little idle chatter on the way, both enjoying the break from normal routine. Just beyond the village, on the second of a double bend, we suddenly met a sheet of black ice covering the road. I daren't brake and tried to steer out of trouble. The van started to spin and my attempt to correct it was unsuccessful; after two complete revolutions, the van finished up facing the opposite direction. Was my face red! I felt a complete idiot - particularly after insisting on driving.

"Jeepers! - Lucky we didn't land up in the ditch," I said shakily.

She didn't reply - just grimaced philosophically, probably thinking that all officers were big-headed chumps, anyway. Not wished to 'lose face', I continued the drive to Escrick Hall. The gardener helped us to load the van with ivy and holly, lush with large red berries. Standing beside the van, neither the WAAF nor I made any move towards the driver's seat. With a rather shame-faced smile, I gestured for her to drive. As to be expected, she drove faultlessly but, having advanced knowledge of the icy double bend, she took it slowly without skidding.

We had a Polish Officer on the Station, who had been laboriously trying to improve his halting English. Pestering his friends for coaching met with scant response. His dominant need, it seemed, was the ability to say the right thing to the girls he happened to meet.

Excitement smouldered beneath the savoir-faire atmosphere of the Mess as Friday party night approached. Riccall was not large enough to be entitled to a full dance orchestra from Group, but a quintet kept the floor crowded with their lively music. Group Captain Ward was there, with his wife, she was an attractive lady - dainty features and soft wavy hair accentuated her femininity. She also had a way of putting junior officers at their ease.

Jan, the Pole, was delighted when, encouraged by his friends, he had his invitation to dance accepted by Mrs Ward. They danced a waltz. Jan's footwork was impeccable, although having a certain stiffness associated with continental military men. Feeling that he should make use of the valuable phrases he had learnt from his friends, he made a cautious opening with:

"Meesis Vard, you arr ay glamoorous beetch."

Mrs Ward, at first astounded, and then thinking she must have heard incorrectly, drew back from Jan and smiling said:

"What did you say?"

After some encouragement, Jan repeated, with added confidence and fervour:

"You arr..ay glamoorous beetch."

"Who told you to say that?" she asked him.

"Oh, my Ingleesh frenz, they tell me vot to say to pleese Eenglish ladies," he replied with pride.

"I will have something to say to your English friends when I see them," said Mrs Ward, trying to conceal her amusement.

The Squadron's appetite for replacement crews was as demanding as ever, and our flying programme could only be halted very briefly to celebrate Christmas. On the 24th December, I had one flying session which was intended to give a demonstration flight and familiarisation to a pupil, Sergeant Beuchler. In order to save waiting time on the ground, instructors were allowed to use their judgement as to when it was safe to take-off, without requiring permission by radio.

I taxied the Halifax to a point close to the end of the runway, which was clear at the time. Looking around the sky, I saw another aircraft commencing its approach. There was sufficient time for me to take-off, but thinking it might be a pupil making his first landing, I delayed, allowing the other plane to land first. When it had cleared the runway, I opened the engines to full power. We had moved a short distance down the runway when there was an almighty explosion. I closed the engines down immediately, without having a clue as to what had happened until I saw the starboard outer propeller, complete with its boss and reduction gear, hurtling erratically through the air to crash beside the runway. Later I reflected that, had I been impatient and the failure occurred during a critical point in taking-off, our sudden demise would have been certain.

It was a dodgy business flying those ex-squadron aircraft, many of which were really 'clapped out'. The same day, this point was proved once again. Johnny Harwood was making his final approach to land, when he not only heard a loud bang, but a blade from one of the propellers came off, cut through the fuselage and sliced down between his back and the seat. He was very lucky only to suffer a stiff back, and, as he put it, 'a bum as sore as a bear's backside.'

Near misses and painful posteriors were soon forgotten as we prepared to enjoy Christmas Day. Wartime Christmases were an odd mixture. The freedom from duties and above average food were most welcome. We revelled in a kind of phoney euphoria which concealed true feelings of separation from loved ones at such a time.

It was customary in the Service, for the Officers to act as waiters and serve the airmen their Christmas dinner. The attitude of officers to this custom varied - some hated it, whilst others, including myself, enjoyed it very much.

On the stroke of one o'clock, we arrived - well primed - at the Airmen' Mess. As we entered, a loud cheer went up - mixed with a few good-natured boos from the rows of airmen sitting at the long tables. In the manner of professional waiters, we jostled each other at the servery in our attempts to be the first to be served - we didn't want to keep our clients waiting! One officer went round the tables with a great jug of beer, topping up each glass the moment it fell below the 'plimsoll line'. The fellows were in fine form, seizing this yearly opportunity to 'take the mickey' out of the officers. I was serving in my best deferential manner, to be met with remarks like:

"More roast potatoes my man - and be sharp about it!"

Christmas dinner in our own Mess seemed a rather restrained affair after the lively hour with the airmen. On Boxing Day morning, an invitation was sent to the staff senior NCOs and Warrant Officers to join us for informal drinks. As we waited at the bar, a party of about a dozen arrived together. We lost no time ensuring that each had a drink in his hand. There was an atmosphere of 'stiffness' at first, which was difficult to break down - perhaps we were trying too hard to avoid any appearance of rank barrier - absent when working alongside one another. It could not have been due to the presence of our rather portly Station CO Group Captain Ward a very experienced commander, who was able to combine respect for his rank with a friendly but uncondescending manner. However, it was not long before inhibitions waned and we enjoyed a very rewarding get-together with our non- commissioned colleagues.

My first detail one fine January morning, was to take one of our advanced pupils - Flying Officer Holmes - for a check dual flight. After completing the exercise, there was still a half an hour's flying time left. A few miles away, I knew of an Italian prisoner of war camp; what better way of rounding off the session than taking a close look at it? Turning to Holmes, I suggested:

"How about giving these EYETIES a close inspection?"
Holmes agreed with enthusiasm, I then called the crew.

"Hold on fellows, we are going to show these Italians a close view of a Halibag."

The camp was situated in a flat and isolated area, ideal for low flying. I reduced height to tree-top level. Flying a large aeroplane at this height is very exhilarating, enhanced by the hint of danger and the accurate judgement demanded. As we roared over the enclosure fence, groups of men scattered in all directions like frightened sheep. Flying at about 200 miles an hour, we only had a brief look at the men, who were mostly short and thick-set, which did not seem to impede their dive for cover. The rear-gunner had the best view and showed his appreciation with the remark:

"Bloody good show, Captain...how about another circuit?"

"'Fraid not," I replied, "they might get our aircraft letter and report us."

The last we saw of the camp was when I banked steeply away over buildings which were probably the HQ.

Chatting in the Mess one evening, Dobbie said he had seen an advert in a flight magazine, offering white, one-piece flying suits for sale, and voiced an idea:

"Mac - Ronnie - how about it, shall we send away for some, they are under a fiver each?"

"They are not permitted gear, old chap...but who cares," said Mac.

"We could say they save wear on aircrew dress," I suggested.

Then and there we ordered half-a-dozen - one for each flying instructor in 'B' flight. We agreed to start wearing them together on the same morning. Dobbie, Mac, Bunny and I, all turned up at the Flight Office wearing the new white suits. We must have looked as if we had stepped out of an American film set! We were the subject of much good natured ridicule, which we put down to understandable envy.

Returning to the office one morning after completing an exercise, Max was talking to a strange Flight Lieutenant, they were poring over the Flight Authorization book.

"What goes on 'Mac?'" I asked.

He raised his brows in a frown, and I realised something was wrong.

"Someone in 'B' Flight has been carrying out some very naughty low flying," he told me.

I felt apprehensive as I quickly remembered my P.O.W. Camp low flying spree. My aircraft must have been traced.

"Which aircraft was it?" I asked, fearing the worst.

"'G' for George, last Thursday afternoon."

I breathed again as I recalled that I had flown 'U' for Uncle that day. It was soon discovered that the pilot was one of our pupils - Flight Sergeant Gilpin. His face wore a guileless expression and I would not have thought he was the type to indulge in such an escapade - and what an escapade! He had been instructed to carry out solo flying practice, but had taken the opportunity to do a flying visit to his home town - Ashby-de-la-Zouche. Several eye witnesses gave graphic evidence of the extremely low flight of the Halifax over the town. One eye-witness gave an almost humorous description:

"I saw the plane come across the Market Place, turn left down the High Street, and make a sharp turn at St. Saviour's Church.." or similar words, as if describing the path of a cyclist. Gilpin had flown so low approaching the town, that his tail wheel caught an overhead powerline, plunging half the town into darkness. Mac then recalled the occasion:

"Do you remember, Ronnie?...Last Tuesday 'G' for George landed with a missing tail-wheel."

"That's right," I replied, "Dobbie, you and I searched the runway, couldn't find it and were completely baffled."

The Flight Lieutenant enlightened us:

"The tail-wheel was found in a field, torn off when the Halifax struck the power cable."

The Flight Sergeant was Court Martialled and received what I thought was a fairly lenient punishment - some loss of pay and seniority. He was allowed to resume training at a different Heavy Conversion Unit.

The weather in Yorkshire during the winter of 1942/3 was very variable, but there were few days when we were unable to fly at all. Often, thick fog shrouded the airfield which lifted by mid-morning. The sequence changed one day, when, after a clear start, fog descended during the morning. We became concerned for one of our pupils who was flying solo.

Ivo Thompson, our senior Airfield Control Officer, suggested we should fire Very lights from the end of the runway if we heard an aeroplane. We agreed that this was a good idea and after a few minutes, heard the sound of engines. Peering through the fog we could see nothing and the sound went away. Ivo fired a green light and we heard the engine again. An aircraft appeared out of the mist, and after a zig-zag approach to the runway made a bumpy landing. It was not our Halifax but an Airspeed Oxford. A few minutes later, engines were heard again, this time, the sound was of a larger plane. Ivo continued his St Bernard act - firing off greens and rescuing the lost - when a Lancaster lumbered in. The Lanc had scarcely taxied clear of the runway when we heard engines over-head. Ivo fired a succession of greens. We heard the engines change to fine pitch; it was our Halifax this time, which came through the mist to make a safe landing. Ivo, with his Very pistol had collected four, a pretty good 'bag' for a foggy morning.

*　*　*

Riccall airfield was in the 'back of beyond' - not so much because of its distance from civilisation, as its lack of access. The hamlet of Skipworth provided the nearest pub, which could only be reached by a lane of almost two miles. In winter this was ankle deep in mud. Once I tried to cycle there, the wheels slithered from one track to another, making balancing the old 'bone-shaker' quite a feat. Imbibing strong Yorkshire bitter had increased my confidence, but played hell with my bike control, making the journey back a disaster.

RAF Riccall did not rate even a Grade IV ENSA entertainment. Our main diversion - apart from our beloved radiogram - was the excellent game of Liar Dice. There were no complicated rules, and once Poker calls had been memorised, the only requirements were to be bold, skilful at bluffing and have a sense of fun. With a kitty of three pence, and threepence for the 'cat's life', no fortunes were to be made or lost.

The isolated life we lead, made a visit to York very welcome. It is a wonderful city, the names of its fifteen gates are evidence of its antiquity, names like - Stonegate, Goodram Gate, Coppergate and Fishergate.

A complete stand-down was very unusual. When it happened, we cadged a lift on whatever transport we could find and headed for York. The party would include my flying-instructor friends, Johnny, Joe, Mac, Bunny and Peter. We usually lost Peter early in the evening, he never missed calling at the Old Castle Inn. The landlady was beautiful, tall and in a class all her own. We were sure that the elegant Peter was attracted but he never admitted to any romantic attachment. The rest of us made our way along the medieval Shambles towards Blake Street where the Half Moon was the Mecca of the aircrew. Customers were packed shoulder to shoulder in the small bars...with a dozen 'Excuse me...Excuse me'...it was possible to shove one's way through the blue smoke haze to the bar. It was necessary to shout the order for drinks, above the noise of the happy, jabbering throng. The welcome from the smiling popular landlord Fred, was always heart warming. If you had been around long enough for the comely barmaid to use your Christian name, you could consider yourself a veteran.

There were joyful reunions with old squadron friends - those who had survived - sadly there were many more on the other list: "Remember Tommy?...Went for a burton on Cologne." "How's Lofty Gregory getting on?...He must be near the end of his tour" .."Oh, he got the 'chop' on that Essen trip...God knows how many we lost that night." Head-shaking was brief...the loss of friends was commonplace. "Fill 'em up Betty and one for your gorgeous self." We were determined - perhaps too determined to have a good time.

When we had quaffed sufficient ale, some of us made our way to the De Grey Rooms. The evening dances held there were well conducted, under the vigilant eyes of the manager who stood for no horse-play. The colonnaded entrance and lofty rooms, bore evidence of its former Regency glory. The building still retained a certain grandeur but had become tatty, and - rather unfairly - we renamed it the 'Disgrace Rooms.'

DEATH OR DECORATION

Three of us went there - Joe, the strong silent type Yorkshireman with a permanent ingenuous smile, his twinkling eyes leisurely scanned the room for the most attractive girl. Mac was entirely different - tall, aesthetic and a man of irresistible charm. He was gifted with the use of words and often trotted out old English expressions with a natural gallantry which totally bemused the girls and amused those of us who knew his Don Juan ways. His only interest in the De Grey Rooms was the hope that he would meet a certain red-headed Amazon of a nurse from the Purey Cust Nursing Home - she was a fine-looking girl but she would have frightened the life out of me! I was motivated because I was fond of dancing. Good dancers were in great demand and one had to be quick. Having spotted a girl with talent in her feet, my technique was to amble over in her direction as soon as a dance ended, then pounce with my request as soon as the music recommenced. Success was not always mine and after one or two rebuffs, "I'm sitting this one out, thank you" or "I have a partner," I hastened back to the 'Half Moon.'

It was a luxury to have a free morning or afternoon, finding one day I had both, I decided for a complete change, to go to Leeds. I felt lucky when I saw that the film 'Orchestra Wives' - which I had hoped to see - was showing at the major Cinema. The film did not disappoint me, the story and music took me into another world for a while. I wanted to make the most of my day out, so after having a meal, I went to the first performance at the old Theatre of Varieties. It was one of the oldest music halls in the country - unchanged for more than half a century. The plush upholstery was grey, but in the folds it could be seen that it had been bright blue. An illusive odour tainted the atmosphere which I later discovered came from small flickering gas lights, fixed high in the walls of the corridors. It must have been my imagination that I could smell the aroma of quality Havana cigars in the auditorium.

Behind the balcony was the bar, where it was possible to watch the stage whilst enjoying a drink. The names of the artists performing were either unknown, or had long since fallen from the top of the bill, which made the notice hanging in the bar rather sad:
"MEET THE STARS IN THE BAR"

I sat alone at a round bar table, fitted with a brass rail, having a drink, when several men popped in, took a quick look around and then popped out again. Their faces seemed familiar and then I realised they were some of the performers. It was not so much a matter of 'meeting the stars in the bars', as the stars looking for a patron who would buy them a beer. It would only be fair to say that on the whole, the artists' performances were very good. I enjoyed the unique experience of seeing such a genuine old time music hall.

132

I caught the last train to Hull which stopped at Selby and within a few minutes the rocking of the train had sent me to sleep. After a short snooze, I awoke and peering out of the window, saw only the passing scenery and would have to wait until the next station to find out where we were. Staying awake, I saw that we were now passing through a dense urban area and I knew that I had slept through the stop at Selby. The train was slowing down to enter Hull station. It was late and few travellers left the train. I enquired from a porter:

"When is the next train to Selby?"

His reply came as no surprise:

"Not until the 6.40 in the morning'

Well, that was it; not wishing to kip down on a cold station all night, I went in search of a pub or hotel. Everywhere was closed, so I made for the police station - they would know of a place. The station sergeant was sympathetic as he told me:

"Sorry Sir, we don't know of anywhere, especially this late at night."

"Well, what about here," I asked. "Couldn't I stay here until my train leaves in the morning?"

"Not very well Sir," then, after dubious look at the other officer, suggested:

"You could sleep in a cell, I suppose."

"Excellent," I said before they could have second thoughts, "that will suit me fine."

"Alright," said the sergeant, "we've just brewed up - a nice cup of tea will clear your head."

"I haven't been drunk," I replied, "but I would love a nice cup of tea."

Exchanging knowing and disbelieving glances, they handed me a mug of steaming tea.

"Right, follow me," said the sergeant, as he led me down corridors to one which was fitted with iron doors, which were ajar.

"The best we can offer - it is a woman's cell though," left me pondering what could be the difference.

There was a ventilator near the ceiling, but without a window, it was stuffily warm. The cell was empty, except for the wooden bunk against the wall, glazed cream tiles which covered the walls to the ceiling, gave the cell the desired punitive appearance. The pillow was a 'horror', being an oval shaped drum, probably made of plywood and covered with brown leatherette. The inmate didn't sleep on it - but was concussed on it! With the pillow wrapped in my greatcoat and covering myself with a blanket, I slept astonishingly well. I was awakened in the morning with another cup of tea and after showing my gratitude to the police by contributing a ten shilling note to the 'Police Widows and Orphans Fund' box, I left to return to Selby.

DEATH OR DECORATION

A few days later, I was granted my quarterly leave. My thoughts were so filled with anticipation of a week's leave, that I found it difficult to get to sleep; my leave pass made out for 'after duty' on 18th March 1943. The Flight Commander gave me the first morning duty, so that I could get away by lunchtime. My duty was to give dual instruction and familiarisation to a new pupil - Sergeant Fisher. I dressed in my best blue and had my case packed ready to collect from the Mess, as soon as my detail was completed. The aircraft I had to fly was 'T' for Tommy, a machine which had no vices and which I had flown often.

I described the functions and characteristics of the Halifax to my pupil, signed Form 700 and we took off promptly at 8.30 from the short north-south runway. This was in use because the long main runway was unserviceable. The strong south-westerly wind blowing would make the landing in a crosswind rather tricky. After I had finished my prepared demonstration, I throttled the engines back to plus two boost. The port outer throttle lever suddenly became very stiff; I paid scant attention to this at first as everything else was behaving normally, and I continued the exercise.

Nearing the end of the flight, the lever still felt 'odd' and unaccountably 'springy'. With thoughts of landing in mind, I wished the long runway had been in use - just in case...It crossed my mind that perhaps I should seek another airfield, with its runway into wind. My second thought was that the problem did not seem too serious, and after all, my bags were packed and waiting below. I prepared for the landing.

It seemed strange on looking down, to see the runway we rarely used with the Selby-York road running alongside. All was going well on the approach, but as we got nearer the ground, the crosswind caused the Halifax to drift. When the aircraft was about ten feet from the ground, I commenced the 'hold-off' and with my left hand grasped the four levers, to reduce power to the engines. Instantly, the port outer lever sprang forward out of my hand to the full power position. I pulled back on the lever but it would not budge. Although we had landed, the outer engine was going full bore, causing the Halifax to swing violently to starboard and leave the runway. The impetus almost threw me off my seat, making it difficult to reach the control panel to switch off the engines. The starboard undercarriage collapsed and the wing dug into the ground, bringing the Halifax to an abrupt stop. The fire and crash tenders arrived and we were taken, unhurt, back to the flight office.

When I reported to the Chief Flying Instructor, he naturally wanted to know all that had happened. As I recounted how the throttle lever shot out of my hand, as if by magic, he was mystified to the point of disbelief.

The interview about the costly prang being over, I wondered how I dared broach the sensitive question of leave. Mustering my nerve, I said:

"By the way, Sir, I was due to go on leave after this exercise.."
As the Winco gave me an incredulous look at my gall, I thought...I've had it...then he replied:

"Oh, I don't think you need cancel it - make a full report, then off you go." As I left the office - hotfoot to collect my ready-labelled case, I wondered how sanguine Sergeant Fisher felt at the prospect of flying Halifaxes.

I had a wonderful leave, despite some rather disquieting news about my optical business. Pop - Mickie's father, had been attending to the financial side of the business since I joined the RAF. He obviously disliked having to tell me anything which would mar the joy of being with Mickie and Diana for a few days. It seemed that the manager I had employed, was terrified of the air raids on Bristol and lived some fifteen miles away in the country. Each day, he left the business at about 3.30 pm to avoid the black-out, and arrived quite late in the mornings, with almost ruinous results to the business.

On returning from leave I was eager to know the outcome of the crash enquiry. When the port outer engine was stripped down for inspection, a two inch bolt was found jammed inside the carburettor: it was never discovered how it came to be there. As I moved the throttle in the cockpit, the bolt must have shifted position, until it finally jammed the butterfly in the wide open position, inside the carburettor.

After lunch one day, most of us were sitting in the anteroom reading the periodicals, when Jackie Newcombe said:

"Have you seen this month's 'Flight' magazine?...the centre spread had a photo of a Lanc flying on two engines, saying what a superb aircraft it is."

"What a lineshoot.." I said, "we have been doing that for months."
Peter Dobson, in a nonchalant manner said:

"I'll tell you what, let's go up and fly a Hali on one engine."
Had it been anyone else but Dobbie, we would not have taken it seriously. Someone asked: 'Who's going to do it?

"I will," said Dobbie; we all enthusiastically agreed, and it was set up for the next day. Dobbie said he would fly Halifax 'U' R9430, whilst Jackie and I would take 'Z' and fly in loose formation, taking a cameraman with us.

Dobbie was a first class Halifax pilot and we were not apprehensive as we watched him stop and feather three engines - not content with that, he then flew on each engine in sequence, from the port outer to the starboard outer. It was expected that the plane would lose height fairly rapidly but he proved the Halifax could be flown on a single engine.

The following month a photo of the event appeared in 'Flight'. Later, I heard that as a result of the publication of the picture, several bold, but less talented pilots had crashed through attempting this, and an order was promulgated forbidding any further single-engine flying.

Aviation books have often printed the photograph, sometimes accompanied with a technical explanation for the flight...I have recounted how the flight took place from Riccall on 22 June 1943.

('Dobbie' later became Wing Commander Dobson, DSO, DFC, AFC, and commanded No 158 Squadron at Lissett during 1944- 5.)

* * *

The hard-working engineering section was under constant pressure to maintain the ex-squadron machines in serviceable condition. Sometimes they fought a losing battle, as in the case of 'J' for 'Johnny'. This clapped-out old Halifax invariably developed some fault shortly after becoming airborne. Towards the end of June, an officer arrived, wearing a dark blue uniform of the Air Transport Auxiliary, on his shoulder the two and a half gold bands of his rank. He came to fly 'J' away for disposal. After running-up the engines and thoroughly inspecting the old war horse, he decided it was not fit for the flight. The aeroplane had to be disposed of somehow, and it was 'put about' amongst the crews that it had to be flown to Staverton in Gloucestershire. I quickly realised this was within 'hitching' distance of Bristol and started to look for others who would be interested in crewing with me. I found three others, together we volunteered for the flight.

The Halifax had been stripped of every surplus piece of equipment, even the radio. June 26 was a beautiful day, which made us feel more assured about the venture. During the pre-flight cockpit check, two engines had a rather large mag drop, otherwise everything else was normal. The engines crackled and roared as I gave them full power for take-off. I held my breath as we climbed away from the airfield; if we reached even a thousand feet and something 'packed up', I would still have a good chance of a safe landing. The Merlins 'purred' as with increasing confidence we reached 3000 feet - we could hardly believe how well 'J' for Johnny was behaving. The distance of 170 miles to Staverton was rather long, without the benefit of proper navigation or radio. Pilot Officer Bailey acted as my second pilot and navigated - mainly by 'Bradshaw' (following the railway lines). We avoided the major towns and after flying for an hour saw a sizeable town ahead, which we thought might be Goucester. Plt Off Bailey returned from his position in the nose to ask:

"Can you come down a bit, so that we can have a closer look?"

I reduced height to about 800 feet and circled the town. There were many elegant Georgian buildings, this, with the absence of industries, made us feel certain it was Cheltenham. To the port side, we saw below a beautiful green area, where a game of cricket was in progress. As I carried out a 45 degree turn around the perimeter of the ground, the white clad figures stopped play and turned their faces upwards. It could have been the immaculate creased white trousers and the ladies college spectators which prompted Bailey, to say:

"Definitely Cheltenham, I think!"

As they gazed up at the Halifax's intrusion on their game, I wondered whether they were curious, furious or just thought we were 'swanning' around: they had no idea it was the old aeroplane's swansong.

Within a few minutes we found Staverton airfield and carried out a reconnaissance circuit. We saw below, the hangars and many twin-engined aircraft. I was uneasy when I saw that the shorter of the two runways was in use, particularly when I discovered there was a hillock with a small barrage balloon flying from it, almost in line with the approach. Without the benefit of radio, I was unable to contact Flying Control. Having an aircraft as large as a Halifax landing in a fairly small airfield, I assumed that a message would have been sent to them, advising them of our estimated time of arrival. I flew low over the long runway, hoping to indicate that I wished to land on it. There was no response from the ground, so I had no alternative, than to prepare to land on the short runway. In order to avoid the hill with the balloon, I had to almost dive on the approach, so that I could use the whole length of the runway after landing. I touched down at the beginning of the runway and had to use the brakes fiercely throughout the whole length. The brake air pressures became exhausted, the plane ran off the end of the runway, coming to stop only yards from the main Gloucester-Cheltenham road! The aeroplane had flown perfectly and we were lucky that it was only near the end of the flight that two engines developed glycol leaks with soaring temperatures.

The Airfield Controller logged our arrival and referred us to the Chief Engineers office. We staggered under the weight of the engine and airframe log books which we had brought with us. In the office, I was greeted with a rather casual:

"Yes?"

"I have just delivered Halifax R9366, and here are the log books," I announced.

"Right," said the engineer officer.."any engines?"

"ANY ENGINES!" I almost choked out.."I've just flown the bloody thing in."

With an almost disbelieving look, he said:

"I thought you had brought it down on a 'Queen Mary' (a road transporter)."

"You weren't expecting it then?" I asked.

"I don't think so...but the fuselage will be most useful for training...I will give you a receipt for the log books."

Without thinking about his superior rank, I said:

DEATH OR DECORATION

"Bugger the log books, Sir... I would appreciate a receipt for the Halifax."

Almost reluctantly I was given a piece of paper -

"Received from Flt Off W R Waite, Halifax Mk.I R9366...26 June 1943."

Later I reflected - with so little interest taken in the aeroplane, I could have landed it on Weston-Super-Mare's vast sands, and set up as an ice-cream parlour after the war.

As with all training units, 1658 HCU had its share of accidents. An unusual one occurred when a pupil was flying at Burn. This was an operational airfield, with its eastern boundary so close to the main York-London railway line, that the telegraph wires had been lowered to avoid aircraft flying into them on landing. The pupil was making a good approach, when a lorry loaded with gravel crossed his path. The pilot did not see the lorry, and the undercarriage struck the vehicle, overturning it. Sadly, the lorry driver was killed. The pupil was instructed to fly his damaged Halifax back to Riccall. Jock Calder and I were at Burn at the time, with Jock at the wheel of his car, we raced back in time to see the pilot make a competent crash landing.

This was the beginning of a spate of accidents, culminating in an unusual non-flying one. 'C' Flight office was close to the marshes to the east of the airfield and frequently muddy. There had been torrential downpours on this day, which had turned the dispersal into a quagmire. It was only four in the afternoon when the CFI ordered a stand down - not entirely due to the weather - there were hardly any serviceable machines to fly. I was in 'B' flight office when Jackie Newcombe phoned:

"Is that you Ronnie?...This goddam weather has made our dispersal into a bog, do you think you could collect me?"

"Certainly Jackie," I replied, "I will come over right away."

The office was housed in a corrugated Nissan hut, with a small vertical hut close by. The path had almost disappeared in the morass. Steering was difficult as I backed the small van down the path; the wheels slithered in all directions, spraying mud at the same time. From my restricted view, I tried to keep an eye on the office door when there was a sharp BANG, followed by what sounded like a tiled roof collapsing.

Wondering what the blazes could have happened, I got out of the van, at the same time as Jackie and a sergeant appeared at the door. What had been a small, tall hut, was now a shattered heap on the floor. In the middle of the wreckage there stood a tin dustbin-like canister. Still sitting defiantly on top, was a scrubbed, white lavatory seat - it was the outside 'bog'. It was because the hut was made of hard asbestos, that the slight tap from the van had shattered it to pieces.

138

All the instructors returned to the Mess for tea, and knew about the 'pranged bog', except the CO, who was still in his office - brooding no doubt about the parlous state of the training programme.

I decided it was not the most opportune moment to confess to my transgression. The steward who had answered the Mess telephone called out:

"Flying Officer Waite is wanted in the CO's office."

"God, you're for it," said Mac. Peter joined in the general derision with:

"I wouldn't be in your shoes, Ronnie."

I had not seen the 'blighters' so cheerful all day. As I made my way to the office, I tried to bolster up my feelings that the C O could not possibly have found out so soon. After knocking and entering, the normally soft-spoken South African CO, barked:

"What the bloody hell have you been playing at this afternoon, Waite?"

He usually called me Ronnie, so I knew this was big trouble - stalling for time, I asked innocently:

"What do you mean, Sir?"

"You know bloody well what I mean...and I want to know what happened." I started to explain in detail - the rain - the mud - the good turn I was doing Jackie, when he interrupted:

"So...just to save Newcombe getting a bit of mud on his shoes, YOU had to go and knock the shit-house down."

With all the hassle he had suffered lately, it was not surprising he saw no humour in the situation.

"RIGHT...I have had enough.." he said, "you are going to be charged with it...hand in your Flying Clothing Card to the Adjutant right away." (This card, issued to aircrew, listed expensive items of flying clothing which would be charged for if lost carelessly.)

The card was duly endorsed:-

LAVATORY...portable...Mark? No? airmen for the use of...I felt a perverse sense of pride, probably to be the only airman to have a lavatory on his Flying Clothing Card!

Those who flew Halifaxes, knew they were strong aeroplanes but apart from the notorious swing to starboard on take-off, early models had many shortcomings. Even when the aircraft was serviceable, the flying performance was often unpredictable. The Air Staff and A and AEE, appeared less concerned with the serious problem of rudder over-balance, which we were experiencing, than the less important matter of exhaust flame dampening. Many accidents could not be explained, and, as one eminent aeronautical engineer put it - nor could the pilots complain, with aircraft spattered over the countryside.

One day in June, a group of us were casually watching the flying, when a Halifax on the circuit started a turn, which to our horror, developed into a spin. Almost together we said, "Christ...what's gone wrong?" We could

DEATH OR DECORATION

'C' 'Looless'.

only watch helplessly, as the Halifax spun slowly into the ground close to the airfield. The earth-shaking explosion was followed by the usual mushroom of dense black smoke and red flames - like some ghastly cauldron.

We walked silently into the office to discover that the plane had been captained by Flying Officer Canning; he had been giving two-engine flying instruction, but we never discovered if this had contributed to the crash. Mercifully, the crew must have died instantly.

Towards the end of July, Bomber Command's main effort was directed to nightly attacks on Hamburg. During the daytime, the American Flying Fortresses were also hammering the city; this went on nonstop for almost a week, and must have been hell for the population - the Nazis were certainly reaping the harvest they had sown against Britain. Many of the planes - British and American, could not make it back to their bases. In the vastness of the North Sea, many crews, cramped in their little dinghies, were praying for rescue. Non-operational stations sent their training crews, with a qualified captain, to search for them.

On 29th July I was sent with a crew of eight, to search a defined area on the North Sea, about 100 miles east of The Wash. We had been patrolling for about two hours when a crew member sighted something in the sea. I changed course towards what appeared to be an upturned boat. After reducing height to almost sea level, we saw that it was a large dead whale. The creature was inverted, which gave its ribbed underside the appearance of the planks of a boat. Whilst we were looking at it, the wireless operator's voice came over the intercom:

140

"Hey...Skipper...we're so bloody low, I've lost the trailing aerial in the sea!" This shook me into realising how close we were to the waves and if I did not climb quickly, we might be amongst those needing rescue! Scanning the sea for hours was a weary job, but no one could relax whilst our comrades were so desperately in need of help. We were disappointed to return 'empty handed'.

We once again had the opportunity for a night out in York, and made the famous Betty's Bar our rendezvous. In the lounge bar, a very large tinted mirror almost covered the end wall. A few months before, some 'clot' had scratched his signature prominently in the middle of the mirror - ruining it.

The proprietors, who were very pro the RAF - instead of taking umbrage - provided an industrial diamond pencil, so that signatures could be properly inscribed. By now, the bottom six inches of the mirror was covered with names. Mac, Johnny and I decided it would enhance the historical importance, if we added ours. During the evening we had been quaffing beer, as a result, I facetiously added to my signature...Ronnie the Rotter!

Almost forty year later, Betty's Bar was modernised. The owners - as a tribute to the wartime bomber crews - made a centrepiece feature of the mirror...now covered with names, together with a large-scale map of the airfields surrounding York. My youngest son Paul, who was not even a 'twinkle in the eye' when I etched my signature, found it on the mirror when he visited the City in 1979.

At the end of the evening, we made our way to the railway station approach, to wait for a taxi. Close by, and almost as well known to us as Betty's Bar, was another establishment - not as sumptuous - but held in high esteem. It was literally a 'hole in the wall', consisting of a large room with a tiny window. The bare wooden floors were on two levels - reminiscent of an early Wesleyan chapel. Eight plain wooden tables, with bench seats either side were the only furnishings. The attraction was not the decor but the delicious aroma of sizzling pork sausages and fried onions, waiting to satisfy the ravenous appetites. The dugout cafe was run by a charming woman - always dressed in a simple black dress. She was affectionately known as Auntie to the airmen who feasted at her simple table. One member of the party had to be posted outside, ready to grab the elusive taxi.

A break from the daily routine came when a half a dozen of us were invited to a rook shoot, on a nearby estate. The secluded parkland was beautiful and peaceful. As we approached two large thickets, the peace was shattered by the strident cawing of hundreds of rooks. We were handed twelve-bore guns by the bailiff and given our positions to shoot: it was assumed we knew the dos and don'ts of gun drill.

I eagerly pushed cartridges into both barrels and at the first opportunity, opened fire, I believe I bagged a bird with my second shot. A few yards beyond a stile, there seemed a better shooting position, so, with the haversack of cartridges over my shoulder and the gun under my right arm, I climbed the stile. As my foot touched the ground on the other side a terrific explosion lifted me off my feet. I could not imagine the cause until I saw a hole in the ground, beside my right foot, large enough to take a baby's bath. Despite having used guns on several occasions at the Manor Farm and knowing the drill, I had failed to 'break' the gun. I looked around thankful that no one had witnessed my folly.

Towards the end of January, a party had been arranged in the Mess, to entertain wives and friends. I had a night flying detail, to give dual circuits and landing instruction to a Sergeant Mercer. I looked forward to joining the party later, when I had completed my duty.

My sergeant pupil's flying was quite satisfactory and I had expected to be able to send him solo after I had given him one dual circuit. During the next take-off, as the Halifax was approaching 100 miles per hour, Mercer, quite correctly, eased the column back and the plane became airborne. Immediately after he had lifted the undercarriage lever, I felt a slight jolt, which Mercer must have noticed too, as he gave me a brief glance. I did not feel concerned, until the undercarriage warning lights flickered between red and green, then I suspected that the slight bump we felt, was due to Mercer having allowed the Halifax to 'kiss' the ground after the undercarriage had started to retract. I was unsure if damage had been sustained, until we were flying on the cross-wind leg, preparatory to landing. Upon selecting undercarriage down, the warning lights continued to flicker. I called the Watch Office on the radio:

"Calling Control - this is 'S' Sugar - the undercarriage won't lock down, I am carrying out another circuit - over."

A WAAF radio operator's voice replied:

"Flying Control to 'S' Sugar, your message received."

On the next circuit, the flight engineer operated the first emergency system but this was ineffective. After I had attempted to 'shake the under-cart down' - without any luck - I instructed the engineer to use the final air emergency, but this too was unsuccessful. Now, feeling more concern, I again called the Flying Control tower:

"'S' Sugar to Control - emergencies haven't worked - we are coming in with a damaged undercarriage - over."

This time, the Airfield Control Officer himself replied:

"Control to 'S' Sugar - all clear for landing, services standing by, listening out."

I had been too busy to give a thought to the party in the Mess, which was in full swing. A radio, on the bar counter, had been tuned-in to the radio-telephone frequency and friends were listening very casually. When it was realised that there was going to be a crash-landing, the party was interrupted almost en bloc - guests included - they came to the Control Tower, to watch the 'cabaret' Halifax 'S' for Sugar was about to provide!

The night was dark but clear, and from one thousand feet I could clearly see the runway glim lights. The landing itself would be straight forward, but there was a risk that sparks, caused by the undercarriage scraping the runway, might set the aircraft's fuel alight. I called the crew over the intercom:

"Captain to crew - take up crash positions."

The replies came back from the various crew members:

"OK., Captain."

Night landings were not my strongest point - but this had to be good - I could not afford the slightest misjudgment. Sergeant Mercer raised the revs to 2850 and I lowered 'full flaps' only when I was certain to make a landing. My concentration did not waver during the next vital seconds as we were approaching the runway lights at about 110 mph. The touch-down was almost perfect and I held the starboard wing high as long as possible. When the speed had fallen to approximately 80 mph., the right undercarriage collapsed, causing the Halifax to swing to the right. After bumping off the runway, it slewed across the grass, coming to rest when the wing dug into the ground, with the propellers broken.

The ambulance and fire tender arrived as we were clambering out of the plane. No one was injured, and there was plenty of time for me to join the guests in the Mess, where the party continued with renewed vigour.

It was at this party that one of our Gunnery Officers put up a slight 'black'. He was the Riccall bard and had composed a new bit of doggerel. He buttonholed one or two of the male guests in the bar, to try out his latest poem on them; it went,

Bloody HellThis bloody town's a bloody cuss,No bloody train, no bloody bus,Nobody cares for bloody us,Bloody

Riccall.All bloody clouds, all bloody rains,No bloody roads, no bloody drains,The Council's got no bloody brains,Bloody

Riccall.The bloody films are bloody old,The bloody seats are

bloody cold,You can't get in for bloody gold,Bloody Riccall.The bloody pub is bloody queer,A bloody bob for bloody beer,And

is it good, no bloody fear,Bloody Riccall.The bloody dances make you smile,The bloody band is bloody vile,It only cramps

your bloody style,Bloody Riccall.Best bloody place is bloody bed,With bloody ice on bloody head,You might as well be

bloody dead,Bloody Riccall.Most of his listeners

appreciated the wry humour, the one exception - none other than the local Parish Councillor.

Bunny Bunclark was typical of the young men, who had not long left school when they volunteered to fly. The excitement of Squadron life, with its challenge to their skill and courage, was the summit of their youthful aspirations. It never occurred to them that their names could be amongst the missing. They did not think about dying.

During a short stand-down, Bunny invited Mac and me to his home in Wakefield for the weekend. Mrs Bunclark gave us a royal welcome. During the evening, we were feted with the warmth and hospitality of their friends; an endless number of houses had to be visited - only for a few minutes - to meet so and so. At each stop we were treated lavishly, and it was not surprising, the next morning we viewed the world through a haze of over-indulgence.

We decided a walk up the hill to the town centre would clear our heads. The exercise and fresh air helped, and a visit to Boots would complete the cure. The store was full of Saturday morning shoppers - mainly women - we were conspicuous in our uniforms. Wakefield was mainly an industrial town, most of the male population were probably away at the war, or engaged in weapon making.

Acting as our spokesman, Mac enquired at the pharmacy:

"Look, old chap...we were a bit pie-eyed last night...consumed too much 'grog'...have you anything more potent than an aspirin?"

The tall, angular pharmacist studied our faces in turn, noting the pallor, then without a word, disappeared behind a frosted glass screen, above which stood three large glass jars, containing sinister looking red, blue and green liquids. He returned a few minutes later, carrying three glasses which contained a cloudy liquid. We were not expecting to take our medicine on the spot. The spectacle of three embarrassed RAF pilots, 'downing' the obnoxious potion, provided the shoppers with unexpected Saturday morning entertainment.

The news I was receiving from Bristol about the Optician business was not encouraging. Pop was becoming so worried about it, he phoned me one evening to say that funds were running very low and that I would have to take some action. I dismissed the unsatisfactory manager and advertised for a replacement. I had only one reply from an older optician, who was nearing retirement. He had his own business at Westcliffe-on-Sea, but its proximity to London had made life difficult for him. He closed down his own business and was happy to come to the West Country. He was conscientious but had a rather officious manner - which did not go down well with the clientele - despite this, the business improved and got out of the 'red'. The net profit was negligible, but I no longer had to subsidise the business from my Air Force pay.

*   *   *

A small vital component on an aeroplane is the pitot head. This small right angled pipe, situated outside and under the fuselage, provides the information to the Airspeed Indicator in the cockpit. When the aircraft is on the ground, it is covered with a canvas bag, to keep it clear of water or dirt. Before a flight, it was part of the drill for the ground crew sergeant to remove the cover and inform the pilot.

Halifax 'U' for Uncle had come into service, after an inspection and required an air test. I was asked if I would take two or three ground personnel and two WAAFs, who had not flown before. Strictly according to regulations, this required the CO's authorization but as it was only a fifteen minute flight, I agreed to take them.

My pre-flight check showed that all the engines and controls were performing normally, so, with my unofficial 'crew' stowed comfortably - we were ready. I turned the Halifax onto the runway and commenced the take-off. It was unnecessary for me to look continually at the Airspeed indicator - experience gave me the 'feel' for the moment of lift-off. we were well down the runway, when I gave a quick glance at the ASI...at this point, we would have been travelling between 90 and 100 miles per hour. I was unprepared for the shock - the ASI was reading ZERO. It was too late to abort the take-off, so I had no choice but to climb the Halifax into the sky without knowing the airspeed. The thought flashed across my mind that the cover had been left on the pitot head - I could not recall the sergeant telling me it had been removed. Only the second pilot was aware of the problem, and I made a sign to him to keep silent - the last thing I wanted was to alarm the passengers.

I made a wide circuit of the airfield - climbing gently, whilst the passengers were happily looking down on Selby and the surrounding countryside. My mind was fully engaged on the crucial landing approach. Erring on the safe side, I brought the plane in fast, aiming to land at the beginning of the runway. I gave the order to the second pilot:

"Full flap' He complied immediately.

The flaps took longer than usual to come down, which confirmed that I had speed to spare. The moment we crossed the airfield boundary I closed the throttles; the Halifax floated a long way before touching down safely. I looked involuntarily heavenwards in gratitude! After taxying to the dispersal point, my passengers disembarked.

"Thank you Sir, that was smashing," said one smiling WAAF.

"I must write and tell my mother," said the other.

"Glad you enjoyed the flight," I said nonchalantly - as I removed my sweat- soaked helmet.

Yes...the pitot head cover had been left on!

In common with many of the other younger pilots, Bunny disliked being an instructor and wanted to be back on operations. At a Mess party, when several Group HQ officers were guests, Bunny cornered one of them and begged him to use his influence; within a few days, his wish was granted and he returned to 78 Squadron. After a short while on the squadron, he paid a visit to Riccall to meet his old friends. He extolled the benefits of being back on ops:

"It's great to be back on the Squadron," he told me.

Those who knew him well, noticed that there was a change in him. The old spontaneous boyish laughter was missing, replaced by a feigned exuberance. His eyes appeared restless, as though afraid of what we might read in them. It was a sign we had sometimes seen in others, when the realisation had dawned that the odds were too great - inevitably - one night, the enemy would claim another victim. An expression generally used was that so and so...had the 'mark'.

Not long after this visit, Bunny 'failed to return'. I was very sad. Three of my Riccall friends - veterans in their early twenties, died with their crews. Flight Sergeant Kenny Clack, who won the DFM, the night I was his second pilot, on the Tirpitz raid, had received a Commission and risen four ranks to that of Squadron Leader in less than eighteen months. He returned to 76 Squadron, as 'C' Flight Commander, for a second tour.

On the night of the disastrous operation to Nuremburg, his Halifax exploded just as he had called for his crew to 'abandon aircraft.' The mid-upper gunner was the only survivor, who was able to say that they fell victim to a German night-fighter, using the latest tactics of firing upwards, from beneath the bomber. Kenny was still only twenty years of age. The Bomber Command casualties were the greatest of the war - over one hundred bombers lost in one night.

Jackie Newcombe and I had become very good friends, while we were at Riccall. He was twenty two years old, tall with film-star good looks and easy charm. It was no wonder that he was very popular in his Devon town of Torrington. On a weekend pass, we travelled down to Farrington Gurney, where we joined Mickie and her friends; we spent a very happy lively time at the Manor Farm.

Jackie had already completed a tour with 78 Squadron when he was posted to 76 Squadron for a second operational tour. The railway marshalling yards at Hasselt in Belgium would have been considered an easy target, especially to Jackie and his crew - amongst the most experienced on the Squadron. Jackie died with four of this crew; two members had been able to bale out - one became a prisoner of war, the other succeeded in escaping.

An amusing incident happened one evening after dinner, as most of us were sitting around quietly reading or writing letters. Harry Drummond placed the book he was reading on the table, walked over to the radiogram and put on a record. There would be no prize for guessing the record he chose - it would be his favourite- Purcell's Trumpet Voluntary. Even those of us who enjoyed this kind of music had become very weary of this over-played classic. Harry reverently lowered the needle on to the record, closed the lid and sauntered over to his armchair to relish his beloved Voluntary. The trumpeting of Purcell's work filled the anteroom, making it impossible to concentrate on anything else. Harry, a tough but warm-hearted man from Tyneside, sat with an expression of contentment on his rugged countenance.

Flight Lieutenant Peter Gaskell, slowly left his chair and walked to the radiogram. Without a word, he lifted the needle from the record. Purcell's trumpet suddenly stopped. Henry looked up from his book in sheer disbelief at the abrupt termination of his beloved music; the rest of us just watched for the next move - Harry was speechless. Peter then removed the record and walked leisurely to where Harry was sitting. Peter raised the record high and brought it down sharply on Harry's head, shattering it into pieces. Still not a word was spoken as Peter went to the bar, ordered a pint of beer which he offered to Harry, who by this time had recovered from the shock. Harry accepted the drink with remarkably good grace, to the accompaniment of cheers and laughter all round. The incident acted like a starting gun, the music was changed to Barney Bigard's 'Big Fat Mama with the Boogie Beat', and the serious drinking of the evening began. Purcell's Trumpet Voluntary was replaced from the Mess Contingency Fund!

One afternoon early in August, I was waiting to fly my next detail, when Mac Agutter came in; he lacked his usual buoyancy and his face was ashen.

"What's up Mac?" I asked, "You look awful."

"Ronnie...I have had a shattering experience," he replied, obviously shaken.

"I was giving a two-engined flying demonstration and had feathered the starboard outer engine; as soon as I had stopped the starboard inner, the rudder slammed over to starboard." He then described in detail what happened. The Halifax turned sharply to starboard and started to sideslip. Then, using all the strength in his left leg, with his pupil joining in, they could not shift the rudder bar. The aircraft continued to spiral downwards. I interrupted his story to ask:

"What was your airspeed, Mac?"

"155...160...more than adequate," was his reply.

"How did you get out of it?"

"I tried everything, Ronnie...I thought my number was up...in desperation, for no logical reason, I tried the trimming tabs..blow me down, the machine started to recover and level out.

"At what height were you then?"

"Little more than a thousand feet."

"Well...congratulations Mac...it sounds as though you narrowly escaped 'the chop'".

147

DEATH OR DECORATION

For a long time, it had been known that the Halifax had serious design faults with the tail unit. The A and AEE had been experimenting with variations to the rudder, in the meantime, we still had to fly these Mark I and II aeroplanes.

It was shortly after Mac's frightening experience, that I faced a tricky situation. I was giving dual instruction and had to demonstrate two-engine only flying. The weather was fine, the blue sky being broken by a few large cumulous clouds. When we reached five thousand feet, I explained the procedure - stopped and feathered, first the starboard outer and then the starboard inner engines. Whilst I was taking action to correct the large swing to starboard, I had not noticed the large cumulous cloud which was rapidly approaching. Within seconds, we were enveloped in grey, swirling fog - blotting out visibility and the horizon. As we entered the cloud, the Halifax shuddered and felt unstable. Normally, this would have just been uncomfortable - with two 'dead' engines on the same side - rather worrying. When I glanced at the 'turn and bank' indicator the needles appeared to have gone 'haywire'; the aeroplane's flying attitude felt wrong, appearing to be sideslipping. As I remembered Mac's experience, a cold sweat gripped me. The fog swirled outside causing me to lose the natural 'feel' of the controls. My attempts to adjust the rudder and ailerons to overcome the sideslip, seemed only to make matters worse - I felt quite desperate. I had not spoken to the crew, they must have realised something was amiss - heaven knows what anxiety they were experiencing.

As suddenly as we had entered the cloud, we emerged into clear skies, the Halifax was flying more or less straight, if not level. I was soon able to get the aircraft on an 'even keel' and wasted no time in restarting the two engines and flying back to Riccall.

Halifaxes Mk. I and II could not maintain height flying on two engines only and to attempt an emergency landing would almost certainly be disastrous. The only purpose of the exercise could have been to attempt to hold the aircraft level long enough to abandon the plane in case of need.

After this experience, I hated having to give two engine flying instruction, partly due to the strain of keeping up an appearance of confidence in front of the pupil - no matter what. Pupils had an unswerving belief that their instructor was infallible. However, when I was detailed for this exercise, I suffered from bouts of diarrhoea.

The accumulated effect of business problems, and the loss of so many close friends, made me heartily sick of the war. I tried to shake off the depression which overwhelmed me for days on end.

One day, a relatively small matter triggered of my dejection. I was in Leeds one afternoon, when I found myself short of cash, I had my cheque book with me but the banks were closed. I was certain a fellow optician would cash a small cheque for me - three pounds was the amount I believe. Calling upon an optician with the same qualifications as mine, I asked for this favour, suggesting he could refer to the General Ophthalmic Register for confirmation. To my amazement he refused, treating me as an imposter. Bitterness welled up inside me, as I reflected that I too, could have enjoyed the security of our reserved occupation; Mickie also, was under continual strain, experienced by all the wives of bomber crews.

It was about this time that I was called to the CO's office. Looking up from his desk as I entered, he said:

"Ronnie, you are to be posted to a Squadron for operations, not sure yet just when, a crew will be found for you."

This was the last thing I could have wished for, and no doubt my expression spoke for me. The Wing Commander continued:

"You don't look too happy at the prospect."

I should not have found the news so unexpected, I was following in the wake of John, Bunny, Kenny, Jackie and the others. I cannot recall much of the interview, except being asked personal questions and if I was physically well. I replied that I was well enough, except for bouts of the 'squitters'. He asked:

"Have you seen the doctor?"

Replying that I had not, the CO told me to see him right away, and that he would give him a ring.

Returning to the Wing Commander's office, he said that I was to take 48 hours leave - not specifying that it was to be sick leave.

After phoning Mickie to tell her, we decided to make it 'special' and booked to stay at the Old Ship Inn at Thornbury. Full of happy anticipation I met her at the Hotel on the Friday evening. The leave started wonderfully, with a romantic, candlelight dinner in a quiet corner of the old beamed dining room. Afterwards, we took a leisurely walk along a country road until it was time to 'turn in'. She was wearing her favourite scarlet and black dress, which set off her blonde hair and I felt proud of her as we entered the bar. We chatted over a night-cap; carefully avoiding any subject which would mar the joy of being together, but I could not throw off my despondency. When we retired to our room, the romantic sequel to our evening never materialised. Now the spectre of impotency added to my misery.

Upon returning to Riccall, I found the pupils I had been instructing before I went on leave, now had other instructors and Wing Commander Harry Drummond, DFC, DFM., had replaced Wg Cdr Thompson DFC, as Chief Flying Instructor.

One morning I was asked to give three-engined landings to a pupil whose instructor was away. It was good to have something positive to do, but in the evening, my spirits fell again. I walked to the village of Little Skipwith and had a couple of beers in the local pub. Returning along the country lane I tried thinking of other things, but my mind obstinately returned to the uncertain future. The change in Bunny's demeanour when I last saw him, just before he was killed on ops, haunted me and my own sense of doom was inescapable.

If I could have arrived at a Squadron without delay, with a crew to work with, I would have felt better. I was no longer part of the team of instructors and I felt completely alone. Eighteen months earlier, when I commenced ops, I was enthusiastic, eager to fly against Germany. On the Squadron, the brotherhood of the aircrew, their strength and support made you feel invulnerable. As the months and years passed, it became increasing obvious that this feeling only mollified the true situation. Bomber Command were certainly pounding the Nazis but at an enormous and almost intolerable cost in aircrew casualties.

I had resigned myself to the unknown future with as much stoicism as possible, when, next day I received a posting. I was to join the Gunnery Flight at Leconfield, where No 466 Royal Australian Squadron was based.

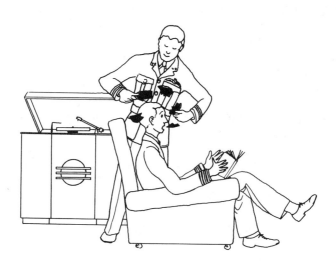

Breaking the Record

150

CHAPTER 9

GUNNERY FLIGHT - LECONFIELD

Johnny Harwood flew me to Leconfield and after being allocated accommodation in the Officers' quarters, I reported to the Gunnery Flight, where I met the CO - Squadron Leader Webb. He told me that I would be carrying out 'fighter affiliation' exercises, which I was familiar with at Riccall; where Spitfires were used as 'attacking' aircraft in the training of pilots and air-gunners in the use of evasive tactics against enemy fighter attack. Sqn Ldr Webb told me that the aircraft I would be flying, were Boulton-Paul Defiants - aircraft which earlier in the war had achieved considerable success as a night-fighter, and had similarities to the Hurricane, with the addition of a gun-turret. I remarked to the Squadron Leader:

"I haven't flown a single-engine aeroplane since my Tiger Moth days."

"That's OK," he replied cheerfully, "here is a Pilot's Flying Manual, it is all in there."

I was introduced to the only other Defiant pilot - a slim, good-looking young Flying Officer - Johnny Easton DFM.

Then next morning, having studied avidly the Flying Manual the previous night, I met Easton again, who 'genned' me on the 'Defies' two rather unpleasant characteristics - its tendency to swing viciously to port on take-off, and 'dropping' a wing if approaching to land with too little airspeed.

I felt very exhilarated as I climbed into the close-fitting cockpit for my flight. The cockpit drill received my closest attention - 2 pumps on the KI gas, 20 degree flap - full starboard trim and so on. After giving the engine run-up check - it was important not to forget the ground airman, who had been lying across the tail plane to keep it down. There was a true story of a fighter pilot who had taken- off with a young WAAF ground crew girl, still hanging over the tail- plane. He carried out a complete circuit and landed without knowing that he had carried a very unwilling and petrified passenger!

As I gave full power to the Rolls-Royce Merlin Engine for take-off, I was very thankful for Johnny's warning about the swing. Compared with the rather cumbersome four-engine Halifax, it was a tremendous thrill to feel the flexibility of this little fighter. The disenchantment I felt about flying, during my last days at Riccall, vanished instantly, as I threw this seemingly tiny aeroplane in the clear sky. My fascination with the 'Defie' was shaken somewhat as I flew over the airfield, preparatory to landing. The engine suddenly had a nasty coughing attack. Searching rapidly for

151

the cause, I realised I had not changed over to another fuel tank, as laid down in the manual, consequently the engine was starved of octane. Looking ahead, I was alarmed to see the propeller judder and almost come to a stop. I pushed the nose down and the engine picked-up again - it was appropriate to thank God that I did not have to look for a field somewhere to force land in! My approach to the landing was a little faster than was recommended, to avoid any chance of stalling. Nipping over the airfield boundary at about 130 MPH, I 'held off' just right, to make a very good landing.

With the first flight 'under my belt', I was quite ready for the duties ahead. The Whitleys and Defiants carried camera guns so that the successes or failures could be assessed later in the cine projection room. There was always a great amount of friendly rivalry and argument, as to who had shot down who! I have to say - in all modesty - the 'Defies' could usually claim the victories.

On my first exercise, I climbed to 6000 feet but could not see the Whitley anywhere. I thought, 'Blast it! I shall look a right fool if I have to return without even having seen my victim. Then, as I banked steeply to port, I saw the long black shape of the bomber as it passed over a field of corn, someway ahead and below. I put the Defiant into a dive, to make an attack on the Whitley's starboard quarter. At a range of about 600 yards, I expected the bomber to start 'weaving' but it continued on a straight and level course. Closing rapidly, I found it difficult to assess the range. At what I estimated to be about 300 yards from my target, I pressed the firing button; as I did so, I was surprised that it gave me an instant thrill - for a moment I realised how the Battle of Britain pilots must have felt, when doing it for real. As I broke away from the attack, the Whitley started to weave, making it much more difficult for me to get a 'bead' on it for the next attack. Later, in the projection room, we were able to watch the film and analyze the evasive tactics.

At this time, I had no idea how long I would be stationed at Leconfield. There were no night flying duties; I thought it would be an excellent opportunity to 'live out' and have Mickie and Diana stay with me.

Opposite the main entrance to the airfield, was a very large house - the Castle Farm, which flanked the main Beverley road. There must be many rooms there, I thought, and called to enquire. My knock on the door was answered by a sturdy good-looking man of about forty-eight. His dark brown hair had receded evenly, which gave him the look of a benevolent monk, at the same time, his eyes gave me a very suspicious look.

"Yes?" was his brief greeting.

"You have such a beautiful, large house - I wonder if you have any accommodation you could spare?" I asked, diffidently.

"I have let rooms, but I am not any longer," was his terse reply.
I was to discover the reason for his suspicion later. As he was about to close the door, I pressed on with:

"I would be most grateful, my wife and I have been separated for three years now, and this is the first chance we have to be together."
He was still about to close the door when I added hastily:

"We wouldn't be the slightest trouble -I promise you."
He studied me for some moments before saying, with his Yorkshire accent:

"Well - you may as well come in a minute."
I heaved a deep breath as I felt there was now a vestige of a chance. He repeated that he had decided not to take in any more RAF personnel, still without giving his reason. I discovered his name was Judson, and assumed he must be a bachelor as no mention was made of any family.

My powers of persuasion were successful when he agreed - still showing some reluctance - to allow me the use of two rooms. Having got thus far, I broached the thousand dollar question:

"Would it be alright to bring our little girl - she is only three?"
He didn't actually say, 'You crafty devil,' but his look said it!

When the time came and Mickie arrived with Diana, our excitement was restrained, as we could hardly believe that after all this time, we would be together again. It was quite a cold October day and the long and tedious journey with Diana had almost exhausted Mickie.

Arriving at Castle Farm, we found that Mr Judson had a roaring log fire going in our sitting room to greet us. We could hardly believe our good fortune when he showed us the little adjoining bedroom he had allocated for Diana. A large, flagstoned kitchen also, was for our exclusive use - this too, had a fire going in the old kitchen range. All of this was more surprising when I learnt that his earlier reluctance to accept RAF people, was because his wife had run off with an RAF Officer - leaving him with his ten year old daughter, whom he had to send to boarding school. During our early conversation with him, we heard of his rather unusual hobbies - he was a keen photographer and had a large miniature railway lay-out up in the attic, running his trains to a strict timetable.

The first morning at the farm, Diana had discovered a 35mm cassette of film lying on the kitchen table, left there inadvertently by Mr Judson. Like lightning and before I could reach her, Diana's enquiring little fingers had found the tab and pulled out the entire roll of precious unexposed film. During wartime film was almost unobtainable and I was shattered at what had happened - especially after Mr Judson's kindness to us. Johnny Easton agreed to stand in for my afternoon duty, whilst I went hot foot into Beverley, to try and replace the film. I visited every photographic shop and chemist in my search. Luckily I found one - not quite the same type - Agfa instead of Kodak, but I was thankful to get hold of that.

DEATH OR DECORATION

A big party and dance had been planned to be held in the Officers Mess. When Mr Judson - we never got around to using Christian names - heard about it, he said:

"You must take my car to go to the dance."

"I can't do that," I replied, "the Mess in only a couple of hundred yards from the farm."

"You can't let Mrs Waite walk to the dance in her party frock - I insist you take my car and go in style."

Needless to say, I accepted his generous offer.

The farm dog named 'Spot', was an unfriendly little terrier who growled a threat at everyone. One night, quite late, there was a scratching at the door. Sitting pitifully outside was Spot, his chest covered with blood. Aware of his bad tempered nature, I was hesitant before gently handling him. However, he submitted quietly as I washed his chest which had a frightful wound, which really needed stitches. I spoke to him gently as I tended his injuries, his eyes normally suspicious - seemed full of gratitude. We believe that he had fought a fox, there were many in the area. He slept for days and ate little, but made a full recovery.

When I was chatting about photography with Judson one day, he told me:

"A funny thing happened one winter night. Another RAF chap was staying here with his wife - well I suppose it was his wife - when he knocked on my door and asked if I would take a picture of his missus." I was all ears as he continued:

"I thought to myself - funny time of day for a photograph - but went along to their room with my camera." My curiosity was now thoroughly aroused as he continued:

"When I entered the room, there was the lady, sitting stark naked, in the round bath tub." I could scarcely believe his yarn.

"It's true," said Judson, "I took the picture and left without saying a word."

Some days later, when I was using his enlarger, which he allowed me to use, I came across a print of a plain, plump woman sitting naked in a bath tub. She wore a bland expression and possessed a bosom which could be best described as bulbous - the most unpromising subject for a 'pin-up' was my impression, but it proved the truth of Judson's story.

There were many rooms in the rambling farmhouse, and Mr Judson was hard put to it to know who was staying there at times. He told us that one morning, as he was going to the bathroom, he saw a tall stranger, dressed in a smart bathrobe, coming towards him. As they passed each other in the passage, the stranger, grinning broadly and without 'batting an eye' said, "Hello there - fine morning!", without the slightest idea he was addressing the owner!

154

CHAPTER 9   GUNNERY FLIGHT - LECONFIELD

Mr Judson had been out for the evening and it was late when he came to our sitting room, without speaking, he beckoned us to follow him. We followed him to his bedroom, which we had never seen before. The room contained the largest double bed I have ever seen. The bed was covered with a highly coloured woollen horse blanket. As we tiptoed to the edge of the bed, an almost imperceptible little hump revealed Diana, curled up sound asleep, cuddling her favourite dolly. To make herself really at home for the night, she had placed her little personal 'potty' under the bed. Diana must have wandered into his room and been so enamoured with the colourful blanket that she decided she would spend the night there.

She wasn't a mischievous little girl but very adventurous and on another occasion had us really worried. It was getting dark one evening and her bedtime was due. There was no sign of Diana and a search of the house did not disclose her whereabouts. It was decided to look around the out-buildings and if she was not there, we should have to notify the police. All was quiet as we passed the enclosure where the turkeys were kept but as we approached the large hen house, the birds were noisy and had not settled down for the night.

"She will never be in there," said Mr Judson, but Mickie, knowing her better added, "I think we had better take a look."

Sure enough, in amongst the roosters, we found our little girl, preparing to spend the night with them and not the least afraid. We were very relieved when we got her tucked up in her own bed.

"Good morning," Mr Judson addressed us brightly one morning, there was a look in his eye that suggested everything was not as usual.

"Good morning," we replied.

"You slept well last night?" he enquired.

"Why, yes, any reason why not?" I asked him.

"Only that there was a German raid on the airfield," was his laconic reply.

"I didn't think it was worth disturbing you; there isn't a shelter anyway." The airfield was only across the road but the bombs falling from a low-level attack had not made enough noise to disturb us. Later in the morning, we heard vivid stories of how the German Dorniers had attempted to destroy Leconfield as a bomber base. High explosives had damaged some of the aeroplanes, but on the whole, the Station had escaped lightly. The worst aspect was the dropping of anti-personnel 'butterfly bombs'. It transpired that two WAAF only were slightly injured. The Squadron Commander was very lucky, when driving around the perimeter a 'butterfly' fell behind his car, which was almost blown-up, but he escaped uninjured.

A diversion from the normal farm routine occurred one day, when Judson decided to remove the remains of a haystack, located at the bottom of the farmyard entrance. 'Spot' was in attendance to deal with any rats or mice which were certain to be at the foot of the stack. Several half-wild cats had drifted in for the sport and were crouching at a respectable distance, too shy to come very close. When only a foot or so of hay remained, one or two mice started to scurry from the stack - the number quickly swelling to dozens. 'Spot' was having a field day; with one quick snap of his vice- like little jaws, the mouse died instantly. He quickly tossed it over his shoulder as he wasted no time in looking for the next victim. Despite 'Spot's' frantic efforts, and the cats, who were doing their utmost, the quantity of mice grew till they must have numbered hundreds. Like a fast moving river, they all streamed in the same direction - under the yard double doors, leading on to the road.

Judson rushed upstairs to see the direction the mice were taking; they were scampering across the road in one narrow stream. The middle cottage of a row of cottages across the road, had it's door slightly ajar. They were scrambling and tumbling all over one another in their urgent need to find safety. A few seconds later, an upstairs window in the cottage, was flung open by a women who had almost gone berserk. Her threatening gestures towards the farm made the farmer chortle heartily. He had a mischievous sense of humour, but of course, apologised later to the distraught lady.

On the morning of the 20th October, I was detailed to fly Defiant 'P' and carry out all types of air attack against the bomber, whilst it took full evasive action. The weather was perfect with a clear blue sky. I looked forward to the exercise, determined to make it very realistic, so the gunners could feel that a real Nazi fighter was after them.

As I levelled out at 7000 feet, the 'Defie' - quite unaccountably - turned almost upside-down. It took only a moment for me to discover the cause. From the middle of the port wing, a piece of material, eight or ten feet long and about six inches wide was trailing. I righted the aircraft, but had to use considerable rudder and aileron to keep the plane level. Then the Defiant suddenly started to vibrate. Looking along the wing, I saw the material lengthen and then tear away from the wing altogether. I re-trimmed the aeroplane and flew back to base, making the approach to land faster than normal, to avoid stalling prematurely.

After making a safe landing, it was discovered that a wide band of rubber, which covered the two main wing sections had broken away. This had exposed a large gap in the wing, which had caused all the turbulence. Apart from this 'minor' incident, the next few weeks went smoothly. I thoroughly enjoyed flying the Defies, despite their dubious reputation, and the joy of being able to live out with Mickie, made me wish I could spend the rest of the war at Leconfield.

CHAPTER 10

1663 HEAVY CONVERSION UNIT - RUFFORTH

In the middle of November Wing Commander Dobson, who was the Chief Flying Instructor at Rufforth, had occasion to telephone. When he discovered I was at Leconfield and what I was doing, he said they were short of Halifax instructors at Rufforth and that he would arrange for me to be posted there. I told him that I would much rather stay at Leconfield, but he insisted and before the end of the month I found myself at Rufforth flying Halifaxes.

An officer who had been 'living out' was posted away. I lost no time in meeting the owners of the house in Acomb Green, where he had been staying. I was able to take over the rooms which he had vacated and move Mickie and Diana in right away. Mr and Mrs Barton and the family with whom we were staying were lovely people and made us feel really at home.

The flying skill of their previous tenant - a Flight 'Looey' Pilot - was extolled rather more frequently perhaps than I would have wished. One Sunday morning, I was the first instructor detailed to fly. The weather appeared rather duff, so I was asked to carry out a weather test. After take off, I had scarcely reached circuit height when I flew into cloud: What an opportunity I thought to give the Bartons a low-flying demonstration. The land formation to the south of Acomb Green had a wide deep bowl.

Approaching from the south, I was able to fly at house height. At the last moment I pulled the stick back, to do a steep climbing turn over the house. If the Bartons were sitting up in bed reading the Sunday newspapers, it must have come as a bit of a shock to see through their window, a Halifax approaching. When I arrived home in the evening, I said nothing of my low flying escapade. Mickie greeted me coolly and asked:

"Did you fly that Halifax over the house this morning?" The tone in her voice left no doubt about her displeasure. I had to confess,

"Yes, but I did..." She interrupted me before I could make my excuse, saying:

"Well don't ever do that again - I thought the plane was coming down the chimney - frightened little Diana and me to death." With a final irrefutable remark she concluded:

"It wasn't a bit clever, just stupid." She was entirely right of course, however, I never heard again of the flying prowess of the former tenant!

Our rooms were on the third floor, at the top of the house. When Bomber Command was carrying out a maximum effort attack, we could

157

hear the drone of bombers most nights. The sound of hundreds of Merlins coming down the chimney to reverberate around the room. Looking out, we could see the Halifaxes of 4 Group passing over, like flocks of migrating birds. As each group flew over, I could identify most of the Squadrons, by the direction from which they came - 76 from Holme, 78 from Breighton and so on. The fleets of bombers, silhouetted against the darkening sky, made a fantastic but formidable sight.

We were expecting another baby sometime in August. Mickie decided that she would return to Bristol, which she did in February 1944.

It was fortunate for me that the sleeping accommodation in the Mess was full, because I was able to stay in Rufforth Hall, a splendid mansion, a mile or so from the airfield. I shared a room with Joe Ward, the lack of privacy did not matter, as we were good friends. I had the use of a bicycle, but Joe, who was now a Flight Commander, was entitled to a Matchless motorcycle. Most of the journeys in the mornings I made sitting precariously behind Joe on the pillion. It was pretty dodgy, hanging on round the many bends, which he never took at less than 40 mph with 45 degrees of bank. Joe was an inveterate pipe smoker, which made the journey rather like sticking one's head outside of a railway carriage window behind an old steam puffer.

Since Mickie had returned to Bristol, I spent more free evenings in York. One evening, I was on my own, propping up the bar in the Half Moon, when Connolly, an Australian navigator I knew, came in. He was a typical Aussie - friendly, generous and with that rather likable trait of having a certain disregard for authority, particularly if it was pompous. 'Conn' was smaller than the average Australian, his casual, relaxed manner made him a pleasant companion. As we shared a drink he enquired:

"What are you doing the rest of the evening?"

"Oh...I don't know...mooch down to the Old Castle Inn, have one there, then return to Rufforth," I replied.

"I think I might try 'hoofing it' round at the De Grey Rooms later...why don't you come along?" Conn suggested, adding: 'I've booked a room at the Royal Station...it's a murky night - you could 'pig in' with me if you like."

"Thanks Conn...that's fine, I will do that."

"The room number is 27...look for the key on the board in the foyer, if it's gone, go on up...if it's there, you can claim it and I'll know you are already in."

At the Old Castle there was no one that I knew, so I went on to the Royal Station Hotel, arriving about 10.30. Scanning the key board, I saw that No.27 was still on it's hook. The night porter was on duty, so I asked him:

"Could I have room 27 key please?" He handed it to me without hesitation. The bedroom was a standard type room and had a long narrow window looking out to a blank wall. The bed, which was larger than a single, but hardly a double, was pushed against the wall. After having a quick wash, I left the door unlocked and went to bed, putting myself close to the wall.

My first deep sleep was disturbed when the door opened and someone entered. It wasn't Connolly, but a wireless operator who was unknown to me.

"Who the hell are you?" I asked. Without telling me his name, he replied:

"I met 'Conn' he told me I could use his room."

"Well, you will have to sleep on the floor." I said grumpily, "Connolly will want to sleep in the bed he is paying for." Feeling a bit guilty over my surly manner and by way of apology, I tossed him the bedspread for warmth.

The night was cold, but the room was centrally heated and warm. I had no sooner got to sleep again, when I was conscious of someone getting into ˌthe bed.

"Come on - move over a bit." I recognised Conn's Australian accent and moved tight against the wall. I slept the rest of the night quite well, but my slumber was disturbed by a half-conscious sense that the door was opening at intervals.

Waking at about seven in the morning, the atmosphere in the room was awful. I crawled over the sleeping Connelly to reach the wall switch. In doing so I tripped over a body lying on the floor. When the light came on, I was amazed to see the number of recumbent bodies on the floor. Apart from Connelly there were five other assorted airmen lying in various postures on the floor! Conn, with an excess of generosity, must have invited all this mob to share his room. They were starting to stir after the revelries of the night before. The atmosphere in the room was unspeakable: reeking of stale beer and tobacco, to say nothing of the frequent and spontaneous explosions of wind. The window was so small, that after I had succeeded in opening it - much against its will - there was only a marginal improvement. I scarcely waited for the tap water to run hot, in my haste to wash away the grottiness.

"Alright...wakey, wakey everyone!" I called out, "Anyone got a razor?" No one had a razor. By this time everyone was more or less awake.

"Right...I'll try the night porter...but you lot had better stay pretty quiet." As Flight Lieutenant, I seemed to be senior of my mixed bag of room mates.

The night porter was still on duty, I approached him warily as I told him:

"I have left my shaving gear behind, do you think you could help with the loan of a razor?" He gave me a suspicious look and must have suspected that all those airmen who had passed him during the night, were not booked in. He was hesitant over the matter of the razor and I guessed that there had to be 'something in it for him', so said encouragingly:

"It's worth a drink you know, old chap." The thought of a tip prompted him to say:

"I think I can find one sir, I will bring it to your room...what is the number, Sir?"

"Room 27...but I'll wait for it." He knew that there was something amiss in room 27, so insisted:

"No Sir...I will bring it to your room." I had no option but to return to the room and in no time there was a knock at the door. The inmates were becoming voluble, so I hissed at them:

"Quiet you silly sods, or we are going to have trouble," silencing them immediately. As I opened the door just an inch or two, the porter tried his best to peer in as he passed me the razor. We occupied two tables in the dining room and were apprehensive as we saw the manager approaching. He came directly to me, probably as I was the eldest and said:

"Your bill, Sir," pushing it towards me. It contained a charge for seven rooms and breakfasts! After a brief conference, we decided this 'wasn't on'. Connelly and I thought it was best to see the manager jointly. He stuck to his demand for full payment - I could tell from his attitude that he did not like air force types anyway. It took a fierce argument bordering on a full scale rumpus before he agreed to a charge for one room and seven breakfasts.

*   *   *

RAF Rufforth had the appearance of an RAF Station built in a hurry. The buildings were variously sized Nissen huts, almost a mile from the airfield. The rough road to the Flight offices had a surface which had been acquired more by the marching of airmen's boots, than the work of MacAdam! Bone-shaker bicycles were issued for the use of NCO's and junior officers.

Early in the morning, there was a sea of air force blue, as the men made their way to the airfield. Against this stream of men, a solitary figure could often be seen cycling in the opposite direction. No ordinary figure this, but a delightful, curvaceous lady, with a mass of blonde hair blowing in the breeze, adding glamour and colour to the scene. It was no wonder that she received numerous 'wolf' whistles from the newly arrived 'erks' who were totally unaware that she was no less person than the Station Commander's wife! She was a charming lady and usually acknowledged the compliment with a cheery wave.

Most of the instructors were unknown to me, except Dobbie of course and Joe Ward, who had been a pupil of mine at Riccall and who had now completed an operational tour and had received his DFC. I was allocated to 'A' Flight, whose CO was Sdr Ldr Harry (Timber) Woodhatch, who had to bale out over Holland during his second tour. An interesting tale was told about him.

Having landed safely, he hid in a ditch until sunrise: peering from his hiding place, he saw a middle aged man riding a bicycle along the country road. He knew the man must be Dutch, so decided it would be safe to reveal himself. Neither could speak a word of each others language. The man indicated for Harry to sit on the bars of his cycle. 'Good ho,' thought Harry, the Dutchman was about to take him to some remote farm, where the Resistance Movement would take over and assist him to escape back to England. Harry was no light weight and the man was showing signs of strain. Harry suggested, by gesticulation, that he should take a turn at pedalling, but the man would have none of it. After cycling for at least fifteen minutes, they came to a small village. The Dutchman, determined on his mission, turned sharp left into the courtyard of a building, nearly throwing Harry off the cycle bar. It was a bitter disappointment to Harry that, instead of delivering him to the Resistance, he had taken him to the Police Station, where he was handed over to the Nazis.

The electrified fences of the Stalag prison to which he was taken were very forbidding; as the truck entered the gates of the compound, Harry's spirits had hit rock bottom. He cheered up considerably however, when a voice from one of the prison inmates yelled at him:

"This will teach you to go flying, Harry!" He knew then, that he had at least one old friend amongst the hundreds of prisoners of war.

I quickly fell into the routine of giving dual flying instruction on the Halifax and the variety of exercises, such as cross-wind landings, three-engined flying and fortunately not often, the two-engined flying demonstration I disliked so much. Not long before I arrived at Rufforth, another instructor, Geoff Thomas, died with all his crew, when his Halifax crashed whilst he was giving two engined flying instruction.

On 14 January 1944, I was told that I had been mentioned in Despatches...the parchment read:

By the King's Order, the name of Flight Lieutenant W.R. Waite
Royal Air Force Volunteer Reserve was published in the
London Gazette on 14th January 1944 as mentioned in a
Despatch for DISTINGUISHED SERVICE.
I am charged to record His Majesty's high appreciation.

Archibald Sinclair
Secretary of State for Air.

This award was in recognition of my long period of service as a Flying Instructor.

One of our aircraft had been giving trouble by swinging badly to port instead of the usual swing to starboard. Several of the pilots had only avoided a crash at the last moment. The pre-flight and engine check had disclosed nothing abnormal.

Wing Commander Dobson, who would never allow any aircraft problem to defeat him, decided he would take the rogue Halifax on test, with me as second pilot. The aeroplane swung viciously to the left, forcing Dobbie to abort the take off. Later he sorted out the problem with the Chief Engineer Officer. It was discovered that the inner port engine had great loss of power which was not revealed on the cockpit gauges. When the engine had been replaced, Dobbie flew the plane again, with Harry Woodhatch as his second pilot for a change, I took the position in the rear gun turret. The Halifax flew correctly this time.

It was a strange and fascinating experience for me, as I sat in isolation in the little perspex 'blister'. It was impossible to see the rest of the aircraft without rotating the turret. I now realised how lonely was the life of a tail gunner. When we had been flying for a while, I had enough confidence to try moving the turret by the 'handle bar' controls. Rotating the turret was easy, but I almost came to grief as I attempted to elevate the machine guns. My knees were not in the correct position and the hydraulically operated gun butts pressed down on them. I moved them just in time to avoid crushing my kneecaps.

Yorkshire in the spring-time often had the ground covered with low lying mist. Although the fog was dense, sometimes it was only a few feet deep. On one such evening, a string of airmen were cycling back to Rufforth when they suddenly hit a bank of fog, which only rose about four feet from the ground. Sitting on their bikes, they could clearly see ahead, but the ground was hidden by fog. To the bystander it was the funniest sight; their bodies could not be seen because of the mist, but their heads were clearly visible, bobbing about on a top of blanket of fog. Instead of dismounting, they pedalled on regardless, with no idea of where the wheels were going. Now and again a rider hit the verge, came off and disappeared into the fog below - to an accompaniment of expletives which could have filled a reference book!

There was another occasion, when this type of fog resulted in wide scale tragedy. Not all pupils were raw young pilots, some were very experienced and previously had been instructors on single-engined planes. At this stage of the war, Bomber Command's losses were so great that these pilots were drawn in, given a conversion course on Halifaxes and then proceeded to join an operational squadron.

On this particular night, one such Flight Lieutenant was carrying out a cross-country exercise. He returned to Rufforth in the early hours of the morning to find the airfield swathed in mist which was only a few feet deep. The pilot could see the runway lights from directly above, but when flying lower, on the approach, he lost the lights in the horizontal build-up of fog.

The Airfield Controller had the responsibility of deciding on the fitness of the airfield for landings. On this occasion, a Wing Commander Read was with him in the control tower. It appeared that some discussion about the conditions for landing took place. As it was known that the pilot had previous experience, albeit on small aircraft, it was decided to allow him to come in to land and permission was given over the radio telephone.

As the Halifax started to lose height on it's approach to the airfield, it started weaving and then veered away to the right. It seemed that the pilot had lost sight of the runway and thought it was further over to the right. At this stage, the plane was probably at a height of about 100 feet and travelling at a speed between 120 and 130 mph. Suddenly there was an almighty explosion followed by others. The dark sky became illuminated with dreadful red and yellow flames, mixed up with black smoke.

The Wing Commander and other staff drove to the airfield perimeter. The scene of carnage which they met, sickened them. A nearby farmhouse was badly damaged and blazing. Cattle and sheep, which had been sprayed with petrol, were running around on fire. Other Halifaxes which were standing on dispersal points, also Flight Offices, were smashed.

As the dawn broke, the full horror revealed that several members of the farmer's family had perished, as well as the six crew members of the Halifax. Many animals had to be slaughtered, including a pedigree bull.

Aircraft accidents were not usually reported to the public, but because of the scale of this one, it was published in the national press. My considerable experience with heavy aircraft, led me to the opinion that too much credence was given to the infallibility of very experienced pilots and too little attention to the conditions prevailing at the time. In this instance, other airfields were clear of fog and I believe a better decision would have been to divert this plane to a safer airfield.

Rufforth was the HCU chosen to train the Free French Bomber aircrews, who then joined the all-French squadron based at Elvington. Some two hundred men arrived, upon asking one of them what they would be doing that evening, with a lecherous glint in his eye and in true Gallic style he replied:

"TONIGHT...WE DESCEND ON YORK!"

An apt description - they seemed to have an even bigger lust after English girls than the Americans!

I recall that when the French Commander, Colonel Vigouroux, arrived he announced his name adding,

"I am Vigorous by name and vigorous by nature."

The French officers, when not on flying duty, looked quite glamorous in their dark blue uniforms, with corded tassels draped from gold epaulettes.

At breakfast one morning, I was the only British officer amongst a dozen sitting at a table. I wished that my French was better, so that I could have eavesdropped on their animated conversation. The nature of the Mess had changed somewhat since their arrival. Standing at the bar in the evening, whilst we were quaffing half pints of ale, our Gallic friends were tippling half pints of red vin ordinaire.

DEATH OR DECORATION

One evening in the Mess, I witnessed an incident, which would never have occurred between British officers. A French junior officer had apparently committed some small misdemeanour. He was made to stand to attention in front of us all whilst the Senior Officer dressed him down, The admonishment lasted fully two minutes, in loud, immoderate French. The French took little notice, but it made the British officers present feel very uncomfortable and sorry for the poor fellow.

I enjoyed a particularly good rapport with one of the pilots, Captain Remy Marchel, a charming man who spoke and wrote English fluently; he seemed to prefer the British sense of humour to that of his own country.

There were other foreign nationals at Rufforth with whom I made friends; two Dutchmen, exiles from the East Indies, were excellent companions. Both had held very important positions in civilian life and were very 'well heeled' financially. They regularly invited me to join them for a meal in York and obstinately refused to allow me to pay my corner. Before I left Rufforth, I insisted that they should be my guests - if only for a drink in York. Their favourite drink was Scotch whisky, almost unobtainable in those days. I telephoned around my usual haunts, but there was no Scotch to be had anywhere. The landlord of the Half Moon said:

"Did you say they were Dutchmen...your guests?"

When I replied, "Yes." he told me:

"I have got an unopened bottle of Hulskamp...do you think they would like that?" When I mentioned it to Hans, he almost exploded: "HULSKAMP...I haven't tasted that since I was in Raffles bar in Singapore."

"That will be okay then?" I asked optimistically.

"You bet," was his enthusiastic reply, so off to York we went.

The liquor was contained in a tall, orange coloured stone bottle. I had never seen it before and I was not enamoured with the flavour, which was similar to De Kuypers gin. They were delighted and took great pride in showing me how it was customarily served in Holland. In pre-war days, when work was done and before the evening meal, it was customary for the father of the family to pour the heavy liquor into tall, elegant glasses. It was important, they explained to me, that the glasses should be carefully filled to the brim, so that the surface of the liquor could be seen, slightly curved above the rim of the glass. It was then the duty of the eldest son, to propose a toast to the father and the rest of the family.

At the half moon, George the barman, found three liqueur glasses which we ceremoniously filled with Hulskamp. I appreciated the compliment, when my friends insisted the first toast must be:

"To Mickie and Diana." During the first six rounds, we adhered closely to the ritual - toasting parents, sisters, cousins and aunts. As we reached the bottom of the bottle, the ritual and our speech became more slovenly.

We then toasted every nationality we could remember - except of course the goddam Nazis.

My bill at the end of a wonderful evening was a modest forty-five bob. I never saw or heard of my Dutch friends after this night. As I did not know where they were sent, I could only hope they would survive the war.

Sometime later, when I stayed at Rufforth Hall, a strange phenomenon happened in the early hours of the morning. I was alone in the bedroom, as Joe was on duty that night. I had the strangest feeling which woke me instantly. Instinctively, I thought that an aircraft had crashed and yet there was no explosion. I had been rolled, involuntarily, slightly to one side of the bed and then the other. I was convinced that I had not dreamed it and it was quite some time before I was able to get to sleep again.

At breakfast, I mentioned it to several of my colleagues, but none of them had noticed anything unusual - it was on my mind all the morning. Listening to the one o'clock news, it was announced that a severe earth tremor had occurred, which had been violent enough to cause some structural damage and make crockery fall off side-dressers. Leeds had suffered the worst of the shock and the epicentre, the announcement said, was about fifteen miles to the east of the city. This was very close to Rufforth, so I had not been dreaming and had slept with an earthquake beneath me.

On Sunday afternoons during the summer, I had the pleasant task of taking groups of Air Training Cadets on short experience flights. None of them had flown before and some had probably never even seen an airfield. The Airspeed Oxford was used for this purpose, carrying six cadets at a time. It was a joy to see their eager young faces, flushed with anticipation; eyes sparkled with enthusiasm as each had a vision of himself - proudly wearing wings one day. I always tried to give them an adventurous flight, avoiding any violent manoeuvres, which probably would have made them airsick. One could imagine the excitement, as they recounted later, the day's adventure to their parents.

On August 10, Group Captain Young said to me:

"You are coming to Scotland in the Oxford tomorrow...we are dropping off at Lossiemouth and I want you to fly it back." The idea appealed to me as a nice change from the routine of giving dual flying and lectures on aircrew training.

On the outward flight, the Gp Capt piloted the plane, with Squadron Leader Wilson in the co-pilot's seat: I sat on a cushion behind them on the floor of the fuselage. I was not sure of the reason for the flight, but after landing they left for other destinations. I stayed at 'Lossie' overnight, which gave me the opportunity of visiting the quaint little fishing port, with its neat stone-built fishermens' cottages by the harbour side. The odour of freshly caught herrings, mingled with the salty breeze of the North Sea, assailed the nostrils with an unfamiliar piquancy!

DEATH OR DECORATION

The following day the Oxford had been serviced, refuelled and ready for the return flight to Rufforth. The seat type parachute, which served as a cushion in the pilot's bucket seat, was missing. I thought the GC must have had one when he piloted the plane. When I enquired at the Parachute Section, they were unable to provide a replacement, as they had only chest type 'chutes. Borrowing a cushion from the Mess, I bolstered up my seat in the cockpit, but I was of course still without a parachute. This did not worry me unduly, as I had always found Oxfords to be very reliable aeroplanes.

It was a fine afternoon when I left Lossiemouth for the 250 mile flight to Rufforth. The Cairngorn mountains, rugged and remote, lay ahead. One of the highest peaks, Brairmiach, almost appeared to climb to meet me. Flying at 6,000 feet, I had more than enough height to clear the peaks, but for safety's sake I gave the engines additional power. As I did so, the port engine coughed and spluttered.

"Not now," I thought, bearing in mind that I did not have many options open to me. I could not bale out and a forced landing was out of the question, in this hostile region. The immediate outlook was a bit alarming. The wing started to vibrate, making it necessary to shut down the engine. My brain thrashed round, trying to remember the nearest airfield on the route. Dyce, near Aberdeen came to my mind, as I grabbed the map to see the change of course I would have to make. It was impossible to gain height, but - thank God - I was not losing height either.

The summer-burnt heather which covered the mountains and the absence of habitation, gave the landscape below an uncharted appearance. I steered a roughly easterly course and it was not long before the mountains sloped down to a flat, green landscape. I breathed again as I saw ahead, the black hangars of Dyce aerodrome.

The Oxford was not equipped with radio-telephone, but I assumed that the airfield Control Officer would see my aircraft flying on one engine and expect me to want to make an emergency landing.

As I approached to land, a Mosquito taxied onto the runway, preparing to take off. I realised I had not been seen and I decided to land on the grass to the left of the 'Mossie'. During my final approach, the obstructing aircraft took off and I was able to make a safe landing on the runway - despite the turbulence caused by the Mosquito's engines.

The Oxford was hurriedly towed from the runway and later found to have three seized up cylinders on the 'duff' engine.

I enjoyed my stay in Dyce and was able to visit the fine granite city of Aberdeen. The Grand Hotel bar was empty when I entered and I was the only customer for some time. The barmaid, whose Scottish accent made it difficult for me to understand her at times, offered to show me a well-known beauty spot, with magnificent views of the river Dee. The following

War artist Roland Davis's impression of air battle between Nazi night fighters and Fg Off Ron Waite's Halifax during a raid on Dusseldorf 31 July 1942. Published in "Sphere" magazine.

LEAFLET DROPPED OVER BREMEN DURING RAID ON 3rd. June 1942
with purpose of destroying the morale of German U-Boat personnel.

1st. position

2nd. position after pulling insert.

Sqn Ldr Peter Dobson DFC with crew 3rd from left. Imperial War Museum photograph.

Ronnie Waite landing 'H' Harry at Rufforth. Imperial War Museum photograph.

afternoon we went there by bus and stayed for half an hour, returning in time for her evening duty.

A Reconnaissance Unit of Mosquitos was based in Dyce and I was very keen to get a flight in one. I cadged a lift with a pilot who was about to carry out an air test in one. As I sat in the navigator's position, eagerly awaiting the take-off, one of the engines developed a fault and the flight was cancelled. My luck at this time seemed bedevilled with engine troubles. I never got my flight. The Scottish episode ended when Wing Commander Neal arrived in a Halifax from Rufforth. We flew to Kinloss first, the Wingco left and I flew the Halifax back to base with a flying officer Bischoff and a fresh crew. The Oxford was left at Lossie, awaiting a new engine. I often wondered later, what had happened to the missing parachute.

June 6 1944. The news of the invasion of France came through, there was jubilation that at long last, there was action on the ground in Europe. More rejoicing followed, when on August 24, Paris was liberated.

Our French comrades, always more emotional than ourselves, were irrepressible. They went into frenzied action to decorate the Mess: tricoloured material was draped everywhere and over the roof of the bar a hastily made banner proclaimed:

"PARIS IS FREE --- SO IS THE BAR"

The celebrations began immediately the day's flying duties were finished. Many of the Non-Commissioned Officers and other ranks 'invaded' York, where no doubt there was unrestrained merrymaking - tinged perhaps, with a hint of debauchery!

As soon as the evening meal was over, the Officer's Mess became packed. Even the WAAF officers, who usually returned early to their quarters, stayed longer. Mary, a rather quiet, self effacing young WAAF officer, may have regretted staying. Two French officers took her firmly around the hips and legs and hoisted her, precariously, on to the false roof of the bar. It was as well that she was slightly built, otherwise the roof would have collapsed. She held on valiantly, entering into the spirit of the party, as a drink was passed up to her. We abandoned our usual Yorkshire beer, for the freely available French wine. As the liquor flowed, so the barriers of reserve dissolved. Within an hour we were all fairly well 'sloshed'. French voices mingled with English as with raucous voices we sang, or attempted to sing, the Marseillaise, Alouette, Sur le pont d'Avignon and lesser known ballads of dubious origin. By nine o'clock, we had drunk ourselves to a standstill - the liberation of Paris had not gone unobserved in Rufforth! We retired to our quarters, leaving the bar littered with empty glasses and smoke still drifting up from the ashtrays.

Changes in personnel were continually taking place. Sam Hartley, a very exuberant and likeable pilot, was sent as Flight Commander to 78 Squadron for a second tour: sadly, like so many others, he was killed on his second operation. Wing Commander Peter Dobson, whom I was privileged to look upon as a close friend, became Commanding Officer of 158 Squadron at Lissett. Our wives, Mickie and Nancy, became good friends too, whilst they were at Rufforth. They took a liking to each other when they first met and the fact that they were both 'expecting', cemented their friendship. Nancy had a baby girl and Mickie gave birth to Peter on 16 August.

Dobbie distinguished himself as CO of 158 Squadron and was awarded a DSO to add to his well earned DFC and AFC. A story I heard about him from several sources, pointed to his calm and courageous nature.

Whilst operating over France, his plane became the object of intense anti-aircraft fire, his plane being peppered with shrapnel. When clear of the worst of the gunfire, he called his crew over the intercom:

"Pilot to navigator...are you alright?"

"Wireless operator...are you okay?" As he called all his crew members in turn, they replied that they were unhurt. Dobbie called again:

"Then I must be the only unlucky one...I've got a piece of flak up my arse!" Despite a very painful wound in a very sensitive location, he flew his Halifax safely back to England.

A most interesting man of character at Rufforth, was Wing Commander Iles, who had invented a piece of equipment called the Silloth Trainer. It consisted of a real Halifax cockpit installed on the ground, complete with flying controls, throttles, etceteras, but with the windows blacked out. The controls, together with the appropriate gauges, were duplicated on a panel supervised by an instructor, who could simulate an engine failure, amongst other defects. These would be manifested immediately on the cockpit instruments; the trainee pilot had to be on constant alert, to take the correct action, as if he were actually flying. The Silloth was operated by a complex series of bellows and electrical contacts. Gordon - who I believe had contacts with the organ-building business - had used his special knowledge to invent the trainer: he was also an accomplished organist.

Once, on a visit to York Minster, he was given permission to play the grand organ and surprised everyone with a brilliant performance. He was an affable, comfortably built man of about forty, with an endearing quality of seeming to be aloft from the hurly-burly of the real world. His warm sense of humour was reflected by a gentle, recognisable chuckle.

It was his apparent unawareness of the practical world, which made him a frightful driver. I can vouch for this when having a forty eight hour leave pass, Gordon, who was driving to the west country, offered me a lift. It was night time, with little wartime traffic about. Once in top gear, Gordon sat sanguinely in the driver's seat, whilst the car made it's way south. When it was necessary to change direction, he made a gentle, off-handed movement of the steering wheel. The long journey had gone remarkably smoothly and hazard free, until we reached the outskirts of Cheltenham. A set of traffic lights were showing red, these he disregarded, as we sailed nonchalantly straight through them. I said nothing - we were safely through anyway. When in the centre of town another set of lights were against us, I looked at Gordon, expecting him to slow down. He was wide awake but seemed to be in another world. Before I could shout a warning, Gordon drove through the 'red', apparently totally unaware of the danger. It was not very long after this that he had a serious accident near York which could have cost him his life, luckily he was only slightly hurt.

Flying accidents at Heavy Conversion Units were on the increase and Rufforth was no exception. Within a short space of time there were several serious accidents. Some of these were unpreventable and occasionally due to the clapped-out condition of the ex-operational Halifaxes we were given to fly. In the middle of the night, whilst I was asleep in Rufforth Hall, a tremendous explosion shook the building. A Halifax with a trainee crew had flown straight into the ground from a considerable height. It took the whole of the next day to reach the front of the plane, buried deep in the ground, where most of the crew had perished instantly. The cause of this accident was never discovered. Two others, which happened about the same time had obvious causes.

The first was spectacular and miraculously, only one man was injured. Night circuits and landings were in progress; one aircraft had landed and was taxying along the runway towards the perimeter track where it would have turned off. Another Halifax was waiting for permission to take off, which the Flying Control Officer withheld until he was fairly certain the other plane cleared the runway; permission was then granted. The taking-off aircraft was at full power and well on its way down the runway, when the other pilot informed the control tower that his aircraft had burst a tyre on the runway. Too late; red Very lights were fired to try and stop the taking-off Halifax. There was the noise of an explosion, as red flames lit the sky - an unavoidable collision had occurred. It was greatly to the credit of the airborne pilot, that with a smashed under carriage, he made a belly landing in a bad cross wind. The Halifax slewed on into a manned gunpit and amazingly, no one was hurt there. The terrified crew in the aeroplane with the burst tyre, heard the roar of the other's engines and evacuated their Halifax, fleeing in all directions for some cover, thereby saving themselves.

It was not many nights later, when again, circuits and bumps were taking place, that another bad accident happened. In this instance, a pupil pilot was unable to correct a swing on take off, probably over corrected and swung right off the runway, hitting an obstruction. The starboard engine caught fire, rapidly spread along the entire wing, spraying petrol everywhere. In their haste to leave the machine, an engine was left running at full bore, causing the plane to career around in circles. In no time the whole aeroplane was ablaze. Unfortunately, the navigator was unable to escape with the rest and was burned to death.

DEATH OR DECORATION

The increasing number of crashes was seriously affecting the training programme. Group HQ decided to have a Flying Accidents Officer on every Station, chosen from the staff of instructors. At Rufforth, I was given this part-time job, which had to be integrated with my other duties. I had always taken a great deal of interest in the causes of flying accidents and was very keen to take on this duty.

I was made forcefully aware of the need for action to reduce accidents when I was walking to the Mess. Many other men were going in the same direction, either by bicycle or on foot. I was engaged in my own thoughts, when a Pilot Officer came alongside me, saying,

"Hello." I received a shock as I turned to see who was speaking. It was a young man, wearing a New Zealand flash on his shoulder. The left side of his face was covered with recent, red burn scars; from the corner of his mouth, white strands of scar tissue made it difficult for him to use his mouth fully. I quickly tried to recall him and remembered that I had given him check dual flying instruction on one or two occasions, about two months earlier. He was a youth of about twenty, but his round boyish face, with unsullied complexion, made him look even younger than that tender age. It was during a night-flying exercise that his aircraft had lost power on take off and crashed some distance from the runway.

I hoped that he had not noticed the first shocked expression on my face, but he must have seen it. I felt a sense of guilt that I had been unable to conceal it and found it difficult to talk to him, but I knew that I must - and make it appear casual.

"You seem to be getting on fine now...Which hospital did you go to?...Are you going back for further treatment?..." I tried any subject, to avoid a vacuum in our conversation. It was not as difficult as I had expected: he was anxious to talk about it and was not self-conscious about his disfigurement. Why they had allowed a burns victim of a flying accident to return to a flying-training unit, I could not understand.

In the dining room, he declined my offer to get him a meal from the servery, saying:

"I can manage...thanks."

I was ashamed of my cowardice in wishing that I did not have to act as host, particularly as I watched him painstakingly use the knife and fork with red and distorted hands. I felt momentarily sickened and thought:

"Christ!...isn't it time this bloody war came to an end?" I soon recovered my equilibrium and found moral strength from the courage of this young New Zealander.

*　*　*

All officers are liable to be called upon to perform duties at Court Martials. As a preparation they are sometimes sent as observers to study the procedure. I had twice attended for this purpose, not expecting to be called upon and it came as a surprise, when I found myself detailed to act as Defending Officer at the trial of LAC Tranter, to be held at Rufforth in August.

My preoccupation with this rather formidable task disappeared when I became the victim of a very painful disability. I could not ride the bicycle or walk without considerable pain and decided I would have to report to Sick Quarters. The thought of someone closely inspecting my 'butt end' had deterred me from going earlier. My condition was quickly diagnosed as haemorrhoids. Flight Lieutenant Corbyn was the enthusiastic young Medical Officer who treated his work very seriously. After a close examination of my affliction, he decided, almost gleefully, that an operation was necessary. I was given a bed in the small ward in the sick quarters.

The next morning the doctor arrived, clothed in a white surgical overall, accompanied by a nursing orderly carrying the tray of instruments. I had to lie on my back with my legs hoisted upwards. From this undignified position, by straining my head, I could just glimpse the doctor's head. I did not share his eagerness as he set about his task.

"Have you done this before ...Doc?" I asked.

"No...this is my first op," he replied with cheerful optimism I did not quite share. A local anaesthetic ensured that I felt no pain. I noticed a few beads of perspiration appearing on the doctor's brow, which made me worried, but it seemed that all was going well.

The next morning the doctor called to check on my condition. I was required to lie on my side, divested of my pyjamas, whilst he made the examination. Suddenly the door opened and the MO turned round sharply. I strained to see who the visitor could be and saw the startled face of a young WAAF orderly standing in the doorway.

"GET OUT...GET OUT," shouted Flight Lieutenant Corbyn at the girl, who vanished in a flash. Later the girl was telling her friend about the embarrassing situation, saying:

"You should have seen the look on Flight Lieutenant Waite's face!" To which the listener dryly replied:

"Are you sure it was his face that had the funny expression?"

Air Force regulations required that an airman under close arrest had to be visited daily by the Medical Officer. The next time Flt Lieut Corbyn called to see how I was getting along, I asked him:

"You see Tranter every day Doc...what sort of fellow is he?"

"A bit of an odd ball...he is also epileptic," was his reply.

Lying in bed with nothing to do, I started 'ferreting' into the details about epilepsy and discovered some astonishing information. Cases were quoted, although the instances were rare, where an epileptic, after an attack had carried out actions automatically, of which he had no recollection afterwards: a condition known as post-epileptic automatism. Several instances were quoted in the medical tome I was reading, one such example must have been rather amusing.

A certain French magistrate, suffering from the disease, was trying a case before him. Without warning, he left the bench, walked to the corner of the room, unbuttoned his trousers - urinated - then returned to the bench as if nothing had happened.

The information I read gave me a burst of inspiration - because of Tranter's condition this knowledge could be used in his defence. The next time I saw Dr. Corbyn, I asked if he could probe a little deeper into LAC Tranter's medical condition.

"He certainly is an unusual fellow...I will do that," he agreed.

We both ploughed deeper into the question of Tranter's responsibility for his actions. I asked the doctor if he would be prepared to give evidence for the defence and he said he would.

When I first interviewed Tranter, his answers to my questions led me to feel that this was the best defence to offer, without knowing the serious consequences of such a defence. To get the evidence I decided to visit Mrs Tranter at her home in Huddersfield.

The street where she lived was so steep that the kitchen of one house was almost on the level of the bedroom of the next. My knock on the door of the little terraced house was answered by a timid girl of about twenty with mouse coloured hair. Her hazel eyes gave the impression that she had been thrust into the turmoil of life prematurely and was afraid of what she might have to face.

As kindly as I could, smiling to try and dismiss her fears at the sudden arrival of an RAF officer on her doorstep, I asked:

"Mrs Tranter?...I am Flight Lieutenant Waite and I have come to help your husband." She looked so helpless, not knowing what to say or do, so I quickly added:

"Please don't worry...may I come in?"

"Oh, of course...come in Sir."

Over a cup of tea, she told me some interesting things about her husband.

"One Saturday..." she told me, "my husband came home from the market with his pockets stuffed with mousetraps."

"You had lots of mice in the house?" I suggested.

"No...that was the funny thing, we didn't have any mice...when I asked him about it, he didn't seem to know why he had taken them."

"Did he do any other unusual things?"

"Well..." she said almost shyly, "It was in the bedroom...I noticed a funny smell and said to Frank, 'Do you know what that funny smell is?' he said he did not...silly isn't it really," she said nervously.

"No...carry on."

"Well, later on, I found a whole box of apples he had taken from somewhere and shoved under the bed and they had gone rotten." She seemed relieved to be unburdening her problems to me. Before I left, I told her confidently not to worry and that I would do my very best for her husband. Mrs Tranter seemed in better spirits as I left, which made me feel the trip to Huddersfield was worth while all round.

On the morning of 20 September 1944, a large room was prepared for the Court Martial. At a table at one end of the room, sat the President of the Court, a Wing Commander and on either side of him sat the other members, a Squadron Leader and a Flight Lieutenant. As Defending Officer I had a table on one side of the room, facing me was the Prosecuting Officer.

On the stroke of ten, from the adjoining corridor, we heard an imperious voice commanding "...LEFT...RIGHT...LEFT...RIGHT TUR-UR-URN," then Tranter, looking paler than usual marched in, with a Corporal beside him. The Sergeant marching behind them commanded "...HALT..." and all three came smartly to attention. "STAND AT EASE..." the Wing Commander then broke in with:

"Alright...stand easy." There was a silence for about half a minute, which seemed an eternity, the charges against the prisoner were then read out. Quite an impressive list they were too - several charges of stealing; absence without leave and stealing a car. The President looked up and asked Tranter:

"How do you say...guilty or not guilty?" Owing to the unusual nature of the defence, I had received advice about the plea. Tranter, hesitantly and with some difficulty, stammered:

"Guilty with...res...reserve..." his voice faded away.

The Wing Commander appeared already to be writing 'Guilty' on his paper, when the Squadron Leader whispered in his ear. Looking at me, he asked sharply:

"What is that...what is the plea?"

I replied, "Guilty, with reservations, Sir."

"You can't plead that...what do you mean 'reservations'?"

"Well, Sir, we admit the fact of the charges, but at the time they were committed, the prisoner did not appreciate what he was doing." (The McNaughton rules on insanity states that a person 'did not know what he was doing, or if he did know, he did not know that what he was doing was wrong'.) The significance of this was that Tranter could possibly be detained 'during His Majesty's pleasure.' The Wing Commander continued:

"You realise the position the prisoner will be placed in, he could be detained indefinitely."

"Yes Sir..." I replied, "If the Court is adjourned, I will discuss it with him."

The Court was adjourned for thirty minutes. I advised Tranter to make a straight plea of 'guilty' and I would make a strong speech for mitigation because of his epilepsy.

"No Sir," he insisted "I want you to carry on with it."

I had no option; when the Court resumed, I told the President:

"The prisoner still wishes to maintain the same plea." The Wing Commander seemed very annoyed as he announced:

"The Court is dismissed and the trial will be adjourned sine die." He quickly gathered up his papers and left. Because of the nature of the defence we were pursuing - probably without precedence for relatively minor offenses - the Judge Advocate's Office instructed a senior legal officer to take charge of the defence. When we met later, I discovered he was an eminent KC.

I had suffered some guilty feelings that my enthusiastic but unskilled attempt to do my best for Tranter had misfired, so I was relieved when the Counsellor agreed that, in view of all the circumstances, he thought I had taken the best action.

There was a feeling of increased tension at the second trial. More senior officers were present, the atmosphere being similar to that of a Crown Court. The defending lawyer conducted almost the whole of the defence, but as I had interviewed Mrs Tranter, it was suggested that it might be better for me to examine her evidence. The importance of the occasion made me very nervous. I dared not hold my papers, my hands were shaking too much.

Mrs Tranter was allowed to sit down, she too, was obviously very nervous. Some of the leading questions I asked may have been improperly put to her, but because I was a non-legal officer, the President showed tolerance. The moment came for the most relevant question:

"Mrs Tranter..." I asked gently, "has your husband done anything that you think was strange?"

"What do you mean?"

"Did he sometimes bring home things which he didn't need...such as mousetraps?"

"Oh yes...he did bring home a lot of mousetraps once."

"And did you have any mice at home, Mrs Tranter?"

"Oh yes...we were overrun with them." She replied.

I was shattered! An audible titter could be heard in the Court, as it was realised my line of questioning had completely backfired. All I could do was to sit down and ask no further questions. She had obviously reversed what she had previously told me at her home, believing it would help her husband's case. The trial lasted all day. Tranter was found guilty on most of the charges against him and was sentenced to two years detention. I have no doubts that his medical condition received special treatment whilst he was in prison.

Within a few days of the Court Martial, I was sent to Upper Heyford for a short four days Flying Accident Course, which I enjoyed very much. I felt that I had done well in the final written test - the first time I had ever been confident on a course, probably because I was very interested in the subject. It had almost seemed like a holiday, so I was doubly please to find that on returning to Rufforth I had been given seven days leave.

It was close to midnight when my train pulled into New Street station, Birmingham, where the only other occupant of the compartment left. The station was unusually quiet and I hoped the guard would blow his whistle before anyone else got in. I could then travel alone and make myself comfortable. It was not to be. The door opened and glancing to see who the interloper was, I was surprised to see a diminutive figure dressed in khaki uniform get into the carriage. It was a girl of about twenty two and the single 'pip' on her shoulder indicated that she was an ATS officer. Recovering from my annoyance at having to share the compartment, I saw two large packages standing on the platform.

" Can I help you with those?" I asked. Her slightly worried expression changed quickly into a bright smile.

"Thanks," she said, as if she was not used to offers of assistance. As I placed her bags on the rack, the train started jerkily on its way. Now that I had to share the compartment, I wondered if I could still make myself comfortable in my usual way.

"How far are you going?" I asked.

"To Plymouth."

"I am going to Bristol...I have a knack of making myself comfortable and sleeping most of the journey...would you like to do the same?" Before she replied, I had already started my usual procedure of pulling the long seat up at one end and doubling it up to serve as a pillow.

"Shall I do the same for you?"

"Please," she replied, as she removed her hat. Shaking her head released some unexpected brown curls which had been neatly concealed beneath her officer's cap. Without any hint of awkwardness she unbuttoned her tunic, revealing a round little figure under her khaki shirt. After hanging up her tunic, she settled comfortably on the temporary bunk bed I had made up for her. I reflected it was only during wartime that we could take such a casual attitude to a situation, which would raise eyebrows during peacetime. After switching off the main lights - leaving the ceiling lamp glowing, we were soon asleep.

I was vaguely aware of the two stops at Cheltenham and Gloucester and only stirred when the first pale light of dawn peeped from behind the drawn blind. Peering out, I saw a mass of railway lines and points and knew we had reached the junction at Mangotsfield, near Bristol. I released the blind, which went up with a bang, waking my companion.

The last thing I wanted was to arrive home to meet Mickie, early in the morning, reeking of a stale, smoky railway carriage. Turning to the young ATS officer I suggested:

DEATH OR DECORATION

"I would like to freshen up before going home...I know of a couple of hotels near Temple Meads, where I can usually get breakfast and a bath...would you like to do the same?"

She thought for a moment before replying:

"Yes...that sounds like a good idea...I have almost two hours before my next connection." We first went to the Grosvenor Hotel, which was closed. "Shall we walk to the Grand?" I suggested, "it isn't far and I'm sure it will be open."

"Alright," she replied, as we set off for the city centre. Norma, as I discovered her name to be, was only 5' 2' tall and could not equal my stride. After an embarrassing attempt to walk in some sort of unison, we both laughed and made our own arrangements, roughly two of hers to one of mine.

At the Grand Hotel, the night porter was on duty and looked surprised as we entered.

"Can I help you Sir?" he enquired rather wearily.

"Yes please...we have had a rather long train journey and would like breakfast...first though, do you think you could fix it for us to both have a bath?" My gesture of looking for money for a tip did not go unobserved.

"Certainly Sir," he said, as he disappeared through a door. A minute later he returned with two towels, not exactly bath size, but adequate.

It was not yet 7 a.m. and there was still an atmosphere of slumber in the hotel. After surreptitiously slipping two half-crowns into his waiting palm, we were shown to the bathrooms on the first floor. Twenty minutes later we were in the large dining-room, almost deserted at this hour. It was five minutes before the waiter appeared. He was a very thin, pale faced man, who looked rather seedy in his tired-looking formal black outfit. He stood silently at the table with a small memo-pad and pencil poised for instructions. Norma ordered sausages, I had kippers, which turned out to be excellent.

Catching the waiter's attention for the bill was difficult.

"Separate bills...please." I asked. He looked suspiciously at our different uniforms, raised his eyebrows and repeated:

"Separate bills, Sir...certainly."

We left the hotel and stepped out into Broad Street, near the ancient city walls. The medieval figure on St. John's clock tower hammered the bells for eight o'clock. As we parted, Norma wished me a 'really lovely leave with my wife and little girl'. I responded, 'wishing her a safe journey'.

Now completely refreshed, I took a taxi home, eagerly looking forward to the week ahead. Some years later, I was introduced to a man who said:

"I seem to remember seeing you once with your wife at the Grand in Bristol."

"Sorry old chap, it must have been the wrong man...I have never been to the Grand with my wife." He persisted:

"I feel certain...isn't your wife fairly small, with brown hair?"

"No, she is tallish, with very blonde hair." It was then the 'penny dropped' and I was glad I had told Mickie about the journey from York.

Upon returning to Rufforth, I found my name on the Orderly Officer roster for the following Sunday. It was an unpopular duty, having to deal with every contingency on the station, from a blocked toilet in the airmen's quarters to looking after visitors. It was in the latter capacity that I was faced with a delicate situation. Under the heading 'Entertainment', the noticeboard carried the announcement of a concert to be given by a string quartette from Leeds, commencing at 7.30 p.m.

After making arrangements for the visitors to be given a meal, I went to the hall to ensure that all seating arrangements had been made. Everything was in order, rows of seats were laid out to accommodate about two hundred men. Immediately after, I received a call from the Guardroom to inform me that a small bus had arrived with the musicians. I took them to the room behind the hall so that they could prepare for their performance.

Ten minutes before the start, I looked inside the hall and was shattered to see that all the seats were empty. In panic, I dashed to the Officers' Mess, to check the date was correct. A dozen or so officers were relaxing in the armchairs, reading the Sunday newspapers. I shouted loudly:

"For God's sake come over to the hall...a group have come from Leeds to give a concert and the bloody hall is empty." Had it been a jazz concert or troupe of dancing girls, the place would have been packed. I managed to persuade - bully rather - six of my colleagues to come over.

The leader was the violinist and married to the lady cellist; a double-bass and viola player made up the quartette. They were genteel, delightful folk, which made my task of making excuses for the lack of an audience all the more difficult. I really felt dreadful, as without any truth I stammered:

"The fellows have had a tough flying programme...a lot of night flying and are resting." Actually bad weather had severely restricted flying.

"Of course...of course...we understand," said the leader, "but if only one or two would like to hear us, we will be very pleased to play for them."

"Are you sure?" I said, "We will of course, pay for your expenses in any case and a meal has been arranged for you." They all agreed wholeheartedly:

"We would LIKE to play for you."

A sergeant and corporal joined us - making the audience a total of eight. We sat awkwardly in the front row, about ten feet from the stage, any embarrassment I felt was soon dispelled. They smiled at each one of us as they announced every item, playing such favourites as Bach's Air on a 'G' string with total professionalism. At the end of the concert, there was not a hint of disappointment at the scanty audience - it might have been a Royal Command performance - they were lovely people.

After an evening spent in York, I returned to find an urgent message for me to contact the Flying Control office. The time was late - approaching midnight and I was quite mystified. The message said that I was required at Air Ministry London, for an interview at 10 a.m. the next morning. The note stated that if I could not catch a night train, an Oxford would be laid on to fly me down. I put a clean shirt and a few toilet needs into a bag and caught a train from York. I slept only fitfully, my mind too active wondering about the reason for this apparently important interview. At Kings Cross, I had time to 'wash and brush up' in the 'gentlemens'. After paying the sixpenny charge, I had a shave and freshened up. As I walked from the station into the clear morning air, my rather fearful mood changed to optimism. At the same time, I had a feeling of unreality as I made my way along High Holborn towards Kingsway and an interview which was baffling me.

Ten minutes before my appointment, I presented myself at the Air Ministry. A smart WAAF Flight Officer seemed to be expecting me and took me to the interview room. Promptly on time, a rotund, slightly balding Air Commodore entered. I stood up smartly. He smiled as he approached me, extending his hand and in a friendly manner said:

"Flight Lieutenant Waite...please sit down...did you have a good journey?"

"Very good, thank you, Sir."

He wasted no time in telling me the reason I had been called. It transpired that every week, four day courses were being held for Senior Engineer Officers, the subject being 'Flying Accidents and Causes'. I had been selected because of the good results I attained on the Accident course I had taken earlier, and was being offered the post of lecturer. The position carried the acting rank of Wing Commander and weekends would be free. I flushed with pleasure at the prospect - Wing Commander! - and weekends spent in Bristol with Mickie. The elation was short-lived however, when the Air Commodore gave details of the job - lectures to be delivered on accidents caused by metal fatigue, engine and airframe structural failure. These were specialist subjects about which I knew next to nothing. I would have been quite confident had the lecture been on the flying aspects of causing accidents. I explained this to the Air Commodore, but he still tried to persuade me to take the job.

"You could have all the previous lecturers notes and work from them," he suggested. I imagined myself facing a bunch of hard-headed, veteran Engineer Officers - particularly when it came to question time! I thought carefully before answering, as I would have loved to take the job. I decided to turn it down, I could easily end up with a nervous breakdown.

The Air Commodore sat facing me, waiting for my answer.

"Well, Sir...I appreciate the opportunity...and if the lectures had been related to flying, navigation and airfield control, I would have accepted without hesitation." With no hint of reproach, the Air Commodore said:

"I quite understand...it would be difficult for you..."

Then standing up to shake hands, he said warmly:

CHAPTER 10   1663 HEAVY CONVERSION UNIT - RUFFORTH

"I am pleased to have met you, Waite...goodbye and good luck." I remained puzzled why I had been called for the interview, perhaps it was due to the sudden demise of the former lecturer when courses had already been arranged. Within a month,I was promoted to a Flying Accidents post entirely in keeping with my ability.

Newspapers had been reporting the second evacuation of children from London. Many had returned to their homes when the blitz attacks had decreased in 1943/4. Then, the Nazis' new terror weapon, the buzz-bomb, began to strike against the capital. These winged missiles left their launching sites on the continent, with only sufficient fuel to reach London; when this ran out, the bomb, filled with high explosive, fell at random. Due to my preoccupation with my own affairs, I had paid scant attention to the plight of London, that is, until I arrived at King's Cross station, for my return journey to York.

The platform was filled like sardines with children, carrying their rather sad little parcels and accompanied by their parents. The atmosphere was tense, the strained expression on the faces of the parents told its own story, as they were about to send their children, maybe hundreds of miles away to places of safety.

The jabbering voices fell almost silent when the 'putt-putt' sound of a buzz-bomb approached. All heads turned upwards, looking for the missile with its murderous load. If it should fall on the crowded station, there would be no shelter or escape. When the sound was almost directly overhead, it stopped suddenly. There was no panic, the Londoners knew the bomb would travel some distance before it fell. About fifteen seconds later, we heard the dull scrunch as the bomb exploded on its unfortunate victims.

Soon afterwards, a long train backed into the station. The recent threat from the skies caused a change in the mood of the crowd. The calm, patient waiting, became an overwhelming urge by the parents to get their children on the train - somehow - anyhow.

Before the train came to a stop at the platform, parents - men and women, pushed and jostled one another in their attempt to open the doors and push their children into the carriages. I saw one man trying to push his child through an open window while the train was still moving. Tempers were only just kept under control in their desperation. Gradually the children were installed. The whole scene was just one more heartrending aspect of war.

My own train arrived and left before the departure of the evacuation train; I was relieved not to have to witness the harrowing separation of the children from their parents.

I had not long returned when an accident involving a trainee crew occurred near Acaster Malbis. My friend of Riccall days, Mac Agutter, had been appointed a member of the Court of Inquiry; I looked forward to meeting him again.The Transport Section provided a motorcycle combination to take me. It was a first experience for me to travel in the torpedo-shaped sidecar - damned cold on the feet. As I made my way across the field to the crash, I saw two WAAFs who looked ashen faced. Upon asking them what they were doing there, they were almost too shaken to reply. I hadn't the heart to tick them off and suggested they hurried back to the canteen for a cup of tea.

There was a trail of assorted wreckage for about 150 yards from the crashed Halifax. Amongst the bits of aeroplane, I saw a portion of a scalp, covered with light brown hair. A little further on, something snow white attracted my notice, it was a hand, wrenched off at the wrist - drained of blood - it had almost the beauty of an alabaster sculpture. As I approached the scene, smoke, accompanied by the sickly smell of carnage, drifted up from the wreck. I found Mac, exploring the starboard oleo leg of the undercarriage. As I approached him he remarked:

"Hello Ronnie, didn't expect to see you - there seems to be some unexplained damage to the oleo...not caused by the impact."

We made a few preparatory notes before returning to the Mess at Rufforth. We both gave a quick final glance at the wrecked aircraft; a small mobile crane was very gently lifting what appeared to be a crumpled bundle of RAF uniform from the mid-upper turret; it was the remains of the gunner, who, thank God, could have known nothing.

Back at the Mess, neither of us could face the usual lunch and consumed cheese on toast without much relish. I did not serve on the Court of Enquiry, which later determined the cause as 'pilot error' - a familiar finding, with which I did not always concur.

A week or two later, I was called upon again to act as the Defending Officer at a Court Martial. This came as a surprise to me after the earlier drama of the defence of Tranter. This new case was a very unusual one. The accused was a young Irishman named O'Connery, who had been absent without leave for almost a year and had been posted as a deserter. The following was his intriguing story.

O'Connery was a member of the Irish Free State army, stationed in county Cork. He deserted in order to serve in the Royal Air Force in Belfast in September 1943. In 1944, he was given leave by the RAF and as soon as he arrived home in Ireland, he was promptly arrested and charged with desertion by the Irish and was sentenced to 56 days detention, after which, he was given indefinite leave and took a job as a plasterer's assistant.

Having joined two different countries' armed forces at the same time, he was in the unfortunate position of being a deserter from one or the other! O'Connery decided to return to the RAF. He travelled to Holyhead where he surrendered to the police and was arrested and charged. I visited him at Rufforth, where he was in the guard room under close arrest. As soon as I entered, he stood up and seemed very relieved as I said to him:

"Good morning, O'Connery...I am here to try and help you."

"Sure Sor, and I'd be glad of that," was his eager reply.

Then I went on:

"I would like you to tell me all about it from the beginning." Quickly, he was about to speak when I added:

"I want the truth mind...I cannot help you if you tell me lies." I studied this fragile-looking man of twenty two, whose face bore a pale, strained look; his youth had been all too preoccupied with harsh responsibilities. He could not wait to tell me his story - told in a soft Irish brogue. Until now, his interrogators had been a company Sergeant-Major, Corporals and Sergeants of the RAF police. The story he had to tell was one of impoverishment, which, as it unfolded, made me very anxious to help him.

O'Connery was the eldest of five children and the main bread-winner. He did not mention his father, if he had ever known one, and I did not ask him. Although he had to support his family, he did not receive any allowance from the Irish Free State army - only married men were entitled to this, he told me.

"Why did you desert to join the RAF?" I asked.

"Well, Sor..." he said, quite truthfully, "I t'hought Oirland would be foiting against Hitler...I didn't t'hink they would be neutral..." and added as an afterthought, "Of course, it was better pay in the Air Force." He continued telling me about his family. His mother was too busy raising the family to do any other work - and there was little of that around. The only other provider was the eldest of three sisters who added small sums to the family coffers by doing odd domestic jobs. I found out all I needed to know about O'Connery in the one visit and warned him to expect a sentence of detention.

Later in February, a large room was made ready for the trial. Below portraits of the King and Queen, a long table was prepared for the Members of the Court; on either side, smaller tables were for the use of the Prosecuting and Defending Officers, all laid out with jugs of water and glasses. Everyone stood as the Wing Commander President of the Court and his two attending Officers entered and took their seats. I saw O'Connery briefly before the Court sat and gave him one instruction:

"If you are asked any questions, answer them in a straight-forward manner...don't add any remarks of your own."It was an 'open and shut' case; there was no way we could deny the charges made against him. The prisoner was marched in.

It was already agreed that the presence of the Company Sergeant as a witness was not necessary, his signed statement had been read to the accused and the defence did not wish to cross examine this witness. The evidence of the other three prosecution witnesses was speedily dealt with and I had no need to cross-examine them.

I had given some thought to the manner in which I would deal with my speech. I knew the history of the case by heart, but I was not a professional advocate and if I tried to be clever, I might bungle the whole thing. I decided, rather like an actor, to memorise the points I wanted to put forward and make the strongest possible plea for mitigation. The grounds for leniency were so strong, I had no difficulty in presenting them with conviction. I felt nervous as I anticipated the President's question -

"Do you wish to address the Court?" and took a drink of water. I was sure of what I had to say, but hearing my own voice saying it, made me feel tense. I was very anxious to present a good case for O'Connery and hopefully get him a short sentence.

The President, who, until now had appeared so formal as to appear almost hostile, suddenly gave me a quick and encouraging smile; which made all the difference. I felt an immediate surge of confidence. I stressed O'Connery's loyalty to the Royal Air Force in voluntarily surrendering himself - he could have stayed safely in Ireland - but wanted to continue in the fight against the Nazis. During my final remarks, I laid emphasis on the hardship and responsibility born by such young shoulders and asked the Court to exercise the utmost leniency.

Everyone, except the President and his Members left whilst they deliberated. I was on my own and able to get a very welcome cup of tea before the Court reassembled.

The President ordered the accused to be brought in. Scarcely looking up from his papers, he quickly announced:

"The sentence of the Court, is fifty six days detention." O'Connery had already been in custody for almost a month, which would be deducted from the time he would have to serve. I felt that my speech must have been quite eloquent, to have resulted in what was a lenient sentence for a charge of desertion.

The staccato voice of the Sergeant rang out:

"Prisoner, abou...t turn, qui...ck march...left, right, left, right..." That was the last I saw of O'Connery, as he marched into the corridor between the Sergeant and the Corporal, to serve the remainder of his detention.

It seemed that whenever I went flying with a leave pass in my pocket, I met some type of trouble. At Riccall it had been a bolt which jammed the carburettor - on this day it was something different. I was due to go on leave after duty on the 23rd February and was detailed to give circuits and landing instruction in the morning. I had my bag packed waiting and dressed in my uniform instead of aircrew dress, ready to leave for home.

As I walked to the Flight Office, the weather was very 'duff' with poor visibility. I went instead to the Watch Office, to get the weather forecast. The 'met' man said the fog would probably hang around most of the day.

My Flight Commander came in and we discussed the possibility of carrying out the exercise at another airfield. It was thought Holme-on-Spalding Moor might be better, so we decided to try there. With my pupil - Flt Sgt Miller - I took off into the mist. When we reached about two thousand feet, the sky had become almost clear, the ground below was still obscured by a blanket of low cloud. After flying for about ten minutes, the navigator called over the intercom:

"Navigator to pilot...we are over Holme now."

"Thank you navigator...I will call them to find out what conditions are like below."

Holme reported back that visibility was changing all the time, but never more than 500 yards. It was not possible to carry out the exercise under these conditions, so we returned to base. Back at Rufforth, the weather had improved only slightly, it was still very difficult to distinguish any ground features at all. I called Flying Control on the R/T:

"Calling Control...this is 'D' Donald...permission to land please."

"Control to 'D' Donald...OK to land...runway two eight five, we are putting on the Chance Light."

"Roger and out," I replied.

The Chance Light was a mobile, powerful light, which could be placed at the side of the runway to indicate its position in fog. On the down-wind leg I put down 30 degrees of flap and lowered the undercarriage and commenced the turn cross-wind. I could see the Chance Light but little else. I felt tense as I searched for any recognisable ground features. It was a critical time, particularly keeping an eye on the airspeed to avoid stalling - split seconds matter when travelling at 140 mph in a heavy bomber.

Suddenly, the bloody Chance Light went out! I was livid and time was not on my side. This was no time for niceties as I called Control:

"'D' Donald...WHAT THE HELL IS GOING ON...the Chance Light's gone out...over."

"Control to 'D' Donald...carry out another circuit." At this point I 'lost my cool' and let forth..:

"What the Hell's the matter with those stupid buggers down below..." I knew the terrain was flat and I could overshoot if I had to, so I continued with my descent. At about 500 feet, I saw a faint strip of light over to the left, paler than the rest. Peering forward with my nose almost on the perspex, I felt certain this was the end of the runway. Over the intercom I called to my second pilot:

"Twenty six fifty revs."

Flt Sgt Miller, who had been silent throughout - petrified no doubt - immediately raised the revs as ordered. Then - as suddenly as it had gone out - the Chance Light came back on again. It was too late to make much difference now. Through the murk I caught sight of the glidepath indicator which showed amber - I was too high. My left hand was busy adjusting the control lever, my right hand moved to the flap lever, banging down for full flap and returning immediately to the four throttle control levers to reduce power to almost zero. These actions reduced height rapidly, all that remained was to keep the Halifax straight and concentrate on the 'feel' for the touch down. I was never more grateful than when I heard the squeal of tyres on the runway.

When I returned to the Watch Office, I was told the CFI - Wg Cdr Bertie Neal - wanted to see me. I was still angry and 'up tight' and replied:

"Yes and I bloody well want to see him!" As I entered, the two WAAF radio operators, the Chief Control Officer and the CFI glared at me and I sensed an atmosphere.

"I suppose you know you were on 'Transmit' all the time...and all your bad language was broadcast?" said the CFI. My anger was subdued as I realised that with all the trauma, I had forgotten to change the lever over from the transmit position. The Wingco added,

"As you know, Group HQ in York, monitor all radio-telephone transmissions, if they heard, you will get a right bollocking." As an afterthought he added, "Mind you, Ronnie, under the circumstances I think you had provocation."

I apologised to the two WAAF girls. I heard nothing further about the incident and was glad to get away from the Air Force for a few days.

When I was at Leconfield, I kept in the Mess bar a small silver tankard, which Mickie had given me. When I left for Rufforth, it was forgotten and left behind.

A few days after I returned from leave, I decided to try and retrieve it. I was unable to cadge a lift from any of the flights, but 'A' flight told me I could take one of their pupils on an instrument flying check. I jumped at the chance, although the exercise should not have included making a landing anywhere. I knew I would never have a better opportunity to collect the tankard. The pupil flew, using instruments only, whilst I kept a watch on the accuracy of his flying until we reached Leconfield when I took over and landed.

Once in the Mess, I went straight to the bar counter and to my consternation found myself face to face with Rufforth Station Commander, Group Captain Young. He was equally surprised to see me. Removing the pipe from the corner of his mouth he enquired:

"Hello, Ronnie...what are you doing here?"

"I did not expect to see you here either, Sir...I am just collecting an important piece of equipment." I answered, as I ducked quickly away from him, before he could ask any more embarrassing questions. I knew he guessed that I was not there on any legitimate business. I collected my mug and kept out of Groupie's way for a few days.

During April, I did very little flying, then, early in May I was posted to Bottesford, 1668 HU for flying instructor duties on Lancasters. I was delighted to find that my friend Mac now held the rank of Squadron Leader and was Flight Commander. He gave me a couple of familiarisation flights in a Lancaster but, before I could begin flying duties, the news flashed across the world that Churchill had announced that hostilities in

CHAPTER 10   1663 HEAVY CONVERSION UNIT - RUF-FORTH

Europe had ceased. Group HQ gave us permission to fly over Europe and for the first time in daylight, to see the results of our bombing campaign. On 13 June, Mac and I took Lancaster 'R' and with a crew of ten, some of whom were ground personnel. We flew to the Ruhr.

The route we planned was via Amsterdam - Arnham - Wesel - Dortmund - Essen - Duisburg - Dusseldorf - Cologne - Bonn - Aachen - Rotterdam then back to base. From only two thousand feet, it was an incredible sight to see acres - almost square miles in fact, of roads lined with ruined buildings, where people had lived and worked. The sun shone through rows of glassless holes in the walls where the windows used to be. Not a single roof remained in this vast honeycomb of brick walls. Many four and five floors had collapsed into a heap of rubble on the ground. After we had returned, I could not recollect having seen a single person and assumed that all the Germans were living in the cellars.

I felt no remorse for the devastation we had wreaked, only relief that the whole damned war had ended. Any sympathy we may have felt for the Germans was quickly dispelled as the horrors of the Nazi extermination camps became revealed.

For some time, I had held the belief that it had been a mistake, after the First World War, to allow the vanquished German nation to wallow in a state of hopelessness and massive inflation. It was little wonder that they would follow a leader - any leader - who offered them hope of a better future. It was also a warning of the appalling retribution that can fall on a nation which blindly follows a policy of greed and brutality.

The following day, I was promoted to Squadron Leader and proud to be able to have the additional narrow band sewn on my sleeve.

Low Flying. Mist

CHAPTER 11

No. 7 GROUP - GRANTHAM

Within days, I was posted as the Flying Accidents Officer to No. 7 Group, which controlled all the Heavy Conversion Units - both Halifax and Lancaster.

I was introduced to my superior, Wing Commander Cattell, a tall, well built, man. His direct gaze indicated he was not a man to be fooled, at the same time, there was a friendly sparkle in his clear grey eyes. I felt assured that we would work well together, being responsible for investigating all the flying accidents in the Group.

Every morning, details of the flying accidents which had occurred, arrived on our desks. I calculated the accident rate, per hour flown, for each unit. Any Station which had an unduly high rate, was visited either by the Wing Commander or me with the purpose of finding out why, and giving guidance to the Unit's Accident Officer. For this purpose we had the use of the Communications Flight's aircraft, either a Proctor, Oxford or Dominie (which was also called the Rapide). I could usually arrange to fly the Dominie, an aircraft that I enjoyed flying very much. This de Haviland biplane, with it's distinctive pointed wings, had been extensively used before the war, as a 12 seater passenger aeroplane, with an excellent safety record. We flew from Spittalgate airfield which was situated on a high plateau east of Grantham.

One morning, a brief report of an unusual accident arrived on my desk. A Halifax had crashed on the Yorkshire Wolds, not far from Driffield. There was no one in the plane when it crashed, the crew having baled out earlier. Because of the strange circumstances, I decided to visit the scene myself. When I arrived at the rather desolate spot, I found the aircraft flat on its belly on open ground and no sign of fire. The propellers and front gun turret had been bashed around a bit otherwise there was relatively little damage. If the crew had been on board when it crashed, I doubt that anyone would have been killed. What really caught my eye was a copse of trees, a couple of hundred yards away, which had a perfect oblong sliced out of the tops of them, where the Halifax had ploughed through.

There was nothing further to be discovered from the plane, so I walked to some buildings about one hundred yards to the other side of the copse.

I found an isolated farmhouse where my knock at the door was answered by the farmer's wife. Her eyes opened wide with surprise when she saw me. Having left the car in a lane on the other side of the trees, I had obviously not been seen. I discovered their name was Joyner, and after I told her that I was from the RAF at Grantham, she said:

"Well...I don't know what you want with us, but you had better come in." After thanking her she added:

"I have just made a cup of tea for me and my husband...I expect you could do with one?" She looked every inch the farmer's wife, strong, efficient and a lady not given to idle chatter. Her husband, removing his muddy boots looked up and said:

"What did you say your name was?"

"Waite...Squadron Leader Waite...I wonder if you can tell me anything about the crash?"

"CRASH!...what crash?"

"A Halifax plane...just beyond the copse." The farm was not far from the RAF aerodrome at Driffield and they must have been very used to aircraft overhead.

"It happened in the early hours..." I told them, "did you hear anything strange?"

"Well..." said Mrs Joyner, "I heard an aeroplane fly low over the house during the night...it made such a noise, it must have been very low indeed...but it didn't sound funny."

They looked very bewildered, so with a consoling smile I told them:

"You will be pleased to know that no one was killed, and the crew have been taken to Driffield." This was not strictly true, but I dared not tell them that the Halifax had flown barely a few feet over their rooftop - like a ghost ship without a crew - while they slept below. There was nothing further I could learn from Mr and Mrs Joyner, so I left the farm after thanking them for their help, saying:

"The RAF will put a guard on the aeroplane and I expect you will hear in due course from the Ministry of Defence."

The Halifax had flown, more or less a straight course, for almost fifteen minutes after the crew had abandoned it. The fact that little fuel remained in the tanks was the reason it had not caught fire. There had been no fault with the plane, so the first question to be asked was, why had the crew abandoned the Halifax so soon?

Back at the office, I conferred with Wg Cdr Cattell and we decided that either the gauges were faulty, or what was more likely, the crew's Flight Engineer had misjudged the fuel remaining.

A Court of Inquiry was convened which included a senior Flight Engineer. The Court's findings, published later, confirmed that the Flight Engineer had miscalculated the fuel remaining. He informed the Captain who then decided that as there was insufficient fuel to reach an airfield, ordered 'abandon aircraft'. The accident was the result of human error.

Heavy bombers with four engines and six or eight fuel tanks with differing capacities, made calculations very complicated. As the result of this crash, I sent out a memorandum to all Units to tighten up the training of flight engineers, with particular regard to fuel consumption.

No.7 Group Headquarters was based in a large Victorian house called St. Vincent on the outskirts of Grantham. There was no sleeping accommodation for me in St. Vincent and I was billeted near the town centre. I bought a New Imperial 'Silver Prince' motorcycle to commute, and loved riding this lively and handsome machine every day. Lunch times in the Mess were very pleasant, although we took only the customary hour, it was more leisurely than previous Stations I had served in.

The lively conversation over coffee, was enhanced by the WAAF Officers who shared the Mess, the senior of whom was Squadron Officer Edrich. She carried her responsible rank with unobtrusive authority and was very popular. Her husband was the famous cricketer Bill Edrich. Commentaries on important matches, were frequently broadcast on radio and she accepted, good naturedly, the 'ribbing' every time Edrich's name was mentioned.

In 1945, the War in Europe was nearing its end and in a mood of optimism, No.7 Group held a Garden Party in the grounds of St. Vincent.

It was a lovely spring day and the lawns had been freshly cut and laid out with tables, chairs and refreshment tents. It had been rumoured that very important personages would be coming. Our own chiefs, Air Vice Marshal Rice and Air Commodore Kirby, were present, plus innumerable Group Captains and Wing Commanders. The afternoon got off to a good start. In our capacity as hosts, we mingled with the guests, mainly visitors from the other Services, with a few local civilian dignities.

Our own WAAF looked very smart and most of the ladies were remarkably well dressed, despite the stringent clothes rationing.

A veteran of the First World War Brigadier Sturn-March was there with his daughter. The figure he 'cut' was in contrast to the well-tailored uniforms of the rest of the Officers. His peaked military cap was immaculate. His tunic however, was crumpled as though it had been stored in a kit-bag since 1918, but still bearing the 'red tabs' and insignia of his rank on the epaulettes. His slightly bowed legs were interestingly enclosed in jodhpurs. The overall appearance was incongruous and rather sad. I learned later, that he was a well-known local character, who turned up at every official function.

I was making my way to the refreshment tent, when I felt a hand on my shoulder. Turning round I heard the deep, rich voice of Air Commodore Kirby.

"Ah...Squadron Leader Waite, I have a task for you. You see that tall lady over there, with the large white hat?"

"Yes, Sir," I replied.

"I would like you to coax her away from the group she is with, and keep her entertained." The whole idea numbed me for a moment...

" How on earth can I do that Sir?" I asked, "Surely there must be someone else." The Air Commodore beamed a charming smile - which seemed to infer it was a command rather than a request, saying:

"No, Waite, it is rather difficult I agree, but I don't see anyone else having any better chance of success." I felt that a rather pleasant afternoon was about to be ruined.

The lady in question was thin and so tall as to appear to have a permanent bend. The frock she was wearing had a very old fashioned look, and the deep-crowned hat she wore, pulled well down, was reminiscent of the twenties, making her stand out in sharp contrast to the other ladies. She was the Brigadier's daughter. I didn't have time to work out a strategy, so, sidling up to her and having the advantage of knowing her name, I ventured,

"Good afternoon, Miss Sturn-March, what a lovely day...how are you enjoying the party?"

I saw the quick glance she gave at the 'lowly' two and a half rings on my sleeve. Before she could dismiss me and doing my best to be charming, I said,

"My name's Waite...Ronnie Waite, I am a member of the staff here." Hoping that she might enquire about my work and thus open an opportunity for conversation. Instead, without looking at me - which was very disconcerting - she asked:

"Is Air Chief Marshal Harris here...I believe he is coming?" I replied that the Air Chief Marshal had not yet arrived and it was not certain he was coming. She then quizzed me about the high-ranking guests who were present. It became obvious that she was determined to meet every important person at the party. I now realised the significance of the mission Air Commodore Kirby had given me. I faced the lady, desperately trying to engage her attention, but she just looked over my shoulders trying to pick out some VIP amongst the throng.

Attempting to distract her from her obsession with meeting the 'top brass' I suggested:

"The Air Chief Marshal should be here fairly soon. In the meantime, perhaps you would like a drink and I will try and arrange for you to meet him?" I knew that there wasn't a 'cat in hell's' chance of this happening, but I thought it would buy me some time. I was relieved that she agreed and took as long as I could, accompanying her to the tent. The atmosphere inside had an odd aroma of freshly-cut grass mingling with the odour of beer and Scotch whisky. Having ascertained the drink Miss Sturn-March wanted, I asked the bar steward for:

"One pale ale and a gin and tonic," whispering "a large one please." She must have heard the order for she remarked, with unexpected humour:

"Squadron Leader Waite, I believe you are trying to get me squiffy!" A quick rejoinder did not spring easily to my mind, so I simply said:

CHAPTER 11 NO. 7 GROUP - GRANTHAM

"No, no, the measures are very small...you can hardly taste a single."

The tent was becoming quite crowded, which was fortunate because I was able to keep the lady captive a little longer. Soon, her hunting instinct came to the fore and she asked to be excused and left me. I did not attempt to follow her, to do so would have almost certainly have met with a rebuff. I watched her 'fly off' like a homing pigeon, in the direction of a group of officers wearing the broad bands of high rank on their sleeves. Feeling frustrated, I made my way back to the tent to indulge in something stiffer than a pale ale, when I bumped into Air Commodore Kirby - about the last person I wanted to meet. I was blurting out my apologies for having failed in my mission, when he interrupted...

"Not at all Waite...you did admirably well to keep the lady at bay as long as you did...go and enjoy a drink and tell the steward to place it on my account."

* * *

One sunny day in August, probably the most disastrous, single event in history happened. One small bomb, in a second's flash, incinerated the town of Nagasaki, killing 40,000 of its people. Few of us in the United Kingdom, expected the Emperor of Japan to surrender so speedily as a result. It came as a surprise when at lunchtime, the news broke. We accepted it rather dispassionately at first, but the following day, when the realisation dawned that at last it was all over, we celebrated.

A sizable party of us went into Grantham to see what was going on. The centre was thronged with people. An excited crowd had gathered outside the Town Hall and were pointing up at the building. I could not see anything unusual and asked someone next to me and was told:

"Two fellows are trying to scale the building - a soldier and an airman...to see who can reach the flag pole first."

I could not see either of the men, until the soldier appeared from the side, about two-thirds of the way up. A few seconds later, the airman appeared from the opposite side. It was a terribly risky business as neither man had any special equipment. I did not enjoy watching, but was fascinated into doing so. The soldier seemed more adept. An audible sigh from the watching crowd could be heard when the airman - having taken a more difficult route appeared over a parapet, relying upon hand grip and feeling with his feet for the channels between the stone blocks of the wall. The sense of relief amongst the crowd could be felt when the soldier reached the flag pole. Almost two minutes later, the airman could be seen picking his way gingerly across the roof to reach the pole safely. They waved from their lofty perch, to the cheers of the throng below.

When the crowd dispersed, every bar and cafe became filled with laughing people, celebrating VJ Day. I did not feel like drinking so early and joined 'Hammie' Hamilton and Paul Kenton - who felt the same way - for coffee. After I left them, I rode my motorbike to a pub in the country for lunch, arranging to meet my friends for drinks in the evening.

At around six, we met in our favourite bar in the 'Angel and Royal' soon to be joined by others from Group, including several WAAF. We drank steadily but not heavily, most of the time reminiscing about our home towns or speculating on what we would be doing once we were demobbed. By eleven I felt I had consumed enough alcohol; it had been an excellent evening, to have prolonged it might have spoilt it. The feeling must have been mutual as the party gradually broke up and we drifted our separate ways.

The next day there were fewer than usual in the Mess for lunch, possibly due to the previous night's revelling. I took my coffee - medicinally black - in the conservatory, where Paul Kenton joined me. Our paths had often crossed in recent years and we had always been very good friends, but because of his rather 'cavalier' attitude towards women, he was not always popular with his male colleagues.

From his appearance, one would have been more likely to place his peacetime occupation as being in the great outdoors, than the sedentary one of Chartered Accountant. His athletic figure and bronzed face, with eyes which were never without an amused twinkle, made him attractive to the ladies. An easy-going confidence in their presence, made him a 'hit' with them. Or, perhaps it was his pipe, which suited him and gave him an air of a charming, trustworthy brother?

During his early training, he was assessed as 'Above Average Pilot'. Instead of proceeding towards an operational squadron, he was selected to train as a flying instructor and in his first eighteen months in the RAF, was an instructor on Tiger Moths at a Unit near Oxford. He soon formed a liaison with a girl in the city and lived happily with her in a flat he rented.

I sipped my coffee, as Paul thoughtfully pressed the tobacco into his pipe; he seemed to be itching to tell me something without knowing where to start, so I prompted him:

"Come on Paul... there is something on your mind, what is it?" He replied with a question:

"What did you do after we left the 'Royal' last night?"

"I went back to the digs and listened to the wireless. Why, what happened to you?" I asked him.

"I took Bobbie back to the 'Waffery'."

'Bobbie' McBain was a rather quiet girl of about twenty-six from Edinburgh, with a delightful, lyrical, Scottish accent. The fact that she wore glasses with fairly strong lenses did not preclude her from Service.

My curiosity was roused, so I pressed him to go on:

192

"Well...I was just saying goodnight when she said,'I am on my own...Doreen is on leave...why don't you come in?'" He hesitated before saying:

"I'm not sure I should tell you."

"Oh, come on Paul...you have got to go on now."

"Well, she took me into the lounge, telling me not to put the lights on, then pointing to a chair, she said, 'I won't be long'." He paused, so I suggested:

"She went to get coffee I suppose."

"That is what I thought Ronnie, but after a time I heard water running...it didn't sound like a 'flush'...I wondered if she had forgotten about me and I ought to leave."

"I am surprised she asked you in...I thought she was timid." I remarked.

"That is what I thought." he said, as he went on to tell me:

"The door opened and in came Bobbie. Bright moonlight shone through the window and she was wearing what looked like an evening dress. She walked over, put her arm around my shoulder and sat on my lap. Actually she was wearing a silk nightie and was naked underneath! I thought I was dreaming...it was the last thing I would have expected of her! She has a lovely figure, not that you would know that to see her in uniform. She kissed quite gently and feminine, in fact, she was perfectly relaxed and natural." Although there was an obvious answer, I asked him:

"What was the running water?" He replied:

"While I was waiting, she had taken a shower...there was a subtle perfume about her. She got off my lap, took me by the hand and simply said, 'Come' as she led me to the bedroom."

Had it been anyone else but Paul I would not have believed the story. I think he knew that his story was safe with me, at least until now - 45 years later.

Due to the war ending, many changes in personnel were taking place, including my own boss - Wing Commander Cattell, who was preparing for civilian life. The need for training aircrew had diminished and a large number of those already trained were now surplus and being trained for other duties.

One morning Wing Commander Hamilton phoned me to say that the AVM had approved a flight to Germany with an overnight stop in Brussels, and would I like to share the piloting with him - I jumped at the chance. He would fly the first leg to Eindhoven in Holland and I would then take over and fly to Brussels.

On 5th September, we took off in a Dominie, with Sdr Ldr Gray, Flt Lt Jenkins and three non-commissioned officers as passengers. The weather deteriorated and we were forced to land at Cambridge. We stayed for lunch, the weather cleared later and we continued the flight. After refuelling at Eindhoven, I took off on the rather unusual runway which was made of diagonally laid bricks - millions of them. Two hours later, after our sight seeing tour, we arrived over Brussels - Evere. This had become a very important and busy airfield used by all the Allied Forces.

Having been given my turn to land, at 1500 feet, I decided to do a glide approach (without working the engines). As the aircraft crossed the aerodrome boundary, I lowered the air-brake and began the hold-off. The Dominie seemed to float a long way. I was wondering if I had held-off too high and the plane might drop heavily onto the runway. I felt a gentle rumbling from the undercarriage and realised that I had already landed.

Standing in groups around the Flying Control entrance were Service people of different nationalities, Americans, the Russians, wearing their ill-fitting basic uniforms and by contrast the French with their display of golden cords and tassels draped from their epaulettes.

My landings were not always conspicuously good, but I felt justifiable pride in the 'daisy-cutter' I had just executed. The illustrious and critical audience in Flying Control, had nothing better to do than watch every manoeuvre I had made. Our party appeared to be the only one dressed in RAF blue. As Hammie and I reported to the Watch Office, we wore an air of casual superiority - as much as to say 'that is the way to do it chaps'.

We had been booked to stay in a Transit Hotel and after cleaning up, we went to the city centre to see the sights, and what impressed us most were the lights. Whereas Britain had scarcely emerged from the drabness of the blackout, here the city streets and shops were brilliantly lit, with many flashing neon signs. Brussels seemed to have 'burst' into peace with energetic gaiety.

We found a small secluded bar - the Jean-Marie - it might have been a club. We cautiously explored inside and found the bar. The short, dark, rather rotund barman served us. After having quite a struggle trying to make our requirements understood, he served us with drinks, approximately what we had ordered. We were the only four drinking, probably being too early in the evening for the regular customers. Presently, three girls came in. They chatted familiarly with the barman but did not order drinks. Hammie returned to the bar to re-order and it was not until ten minutes later that we missed him. I went in search and found him, with the three girls grouped around him, all with drinks in their hands. It was not surprising the girls had attached themselves to the Wing Commander. He was a very good-looking, charming fellow, with black wavy hair and trim moustache. Beneath his wings he wore the DFC ribbon. As soon as he saw me he said:

"For God's sake Ronnie, don't ask these girls to have a drink...it will cost you the earth!" The girls just beamed at me, not having understood a word he had said. He told me later that when he was at the bar, the girls came over to him and chatted animatedly in a language he did not understand - probably Flemish. They might have been prostitutes, we did not stay long enough to find out.

In the morning, we all went shopping for presents to take home. At the Bon Marche, I bought a glamorous-looking nightie for Mickie. Later - after one wash - it shrunk into a long tube, instead of being gorgeous, finished up making her look like Popeye's girl friend Olive Oyle!

My second purchase turned out little better. The girl in the perfume department spoke good English. I described my wife as a 'bubbly blonde' and wanted a light perfume for her. The assistant said she understood and recommended one which she was sure would suit Mickie's type. When the stopper was removed from the bottle later, the bouquet which surged out would have knocked over a client in a Turkish brothel.

Flt Lt Jenkins was looking for a souvenir and finding a likely jewellery shop, the three of us went in. We did not stay for long. In the middle of the shop, a tough army sergeant had his left arm fully extended and he held the proprietor's starched white collar firmly in his grasp, with his right fist clenched threateningly. The skinny jeweller's face - probably never healthy looking - had a frightened pallor. We didn't know what had gone on before and assumed the sergeant felt fleeced over some deal. If it had been an RAF sergeant, we would have intervened and tried to placate him, but the different services did not like intervening in the other's problems. Two of us stayed outside, just in case, whilst the other went in search of an army NCO. The trouble in the shop subsided, so we moved on. I expect the jeweller refunded the money.

Later in the day, we returned to the airport and flew back to England with the Wingco at the controls of the plane.

We were flying over open countryside near the German-Dutch border, when I saw the black smoke from a railway engine. Looking closer, I could see that it was a long train of carriages, crowded with people. Some were hanging onto the roof, the sides - anywhere they could get a firm hold. The train was travelling slowly but the whole affair looked very dangerous. At first I wondered who they could be, then realised they were most likely to be slave labourers from Germany, who were desperate to return to their homeland, no matter what the risk.

FLYING TRAINING !! BEFORE MISSION to
HAMBURG as PILOT CAPTAIN

PILOT NIGHT FLYING — TOTAL 10 HRS 20 MIN.
which include HALIFAX — 1 HR 45 MIN

PILOT NIGHT CROSS COUNTRY FLIGHTS   NIL
HALIFAX 3 ENGINE FLYING   NIL

CHAPTER 12

AIRCREW DISPOSAL UNIT - OVER AND OUT

Early in September, the Postings Officer phoned asking me to call at his office where he told me:

"I have a posting for you Ronnie."

"Oh...where to, George?" I asked him eagerly.

"You are going to Blyton, which is an Aircrew Disposal Unit now, as Senior Administrative Officer," he informed me. It was a difficult occupation, usually acquired after years of admin. work, which entailed being responsible for the running of the whole Station, and then reporting to the Station Commander on how it was being run!

"You rotten so-and-so," I said to George, more with humour than anger, "You could have found me something better than that." He then explained:

"You should consider yourself lucky, you will retain your rank...any other posting and you would have dropped to Flight Lieutenant."

"I am grateful to you really, George...although I wonder how I will cope."!

"Oh...you'll be fine," he said with an air of finality.

Blyton lies between Gainsborough and Scunthorpe in Lincolnshire. The CO of the Station was Wing Commander 'Dixie' Dean, a distinguished and very popular airman. The work was less tedious than I had expected, with a variety of responsibilities, from dealing with WAAF who had been AWOL, to deciding with the Station Warrant Officer how to spend an accumulation of NAAFI funds. The latter was great fun. A large amount remained in the fund - far more than was necessary for a Station soon to be closed down. We enjoyed spending the money, and decided the communal Main Hall needed a new radio/record playing system for dances. We scoured the country to find the largest, loudest, most up-to-date system we could lay our hands on. This decision made us very popular with all the other ranks, as well as the NCO's.

Another duty was arranging the Pay Parades, and collecting the large sums of money required from the bank in Gainsborough. I had a 16 HP Hillman car for my exclusive use around the Camp and other official journeys - a complete change from riding old bone-shaker bicycles a few years previously.

With so many duties, I found it difficult to get any free time. However, I managed to organise the Adjutant and others, so that I could get one weekend away. It had been quite a while since I had been able to get home and I was looking forward immensely to this break. I was very disappointed when I found that I was unable to get any train from Gainsborough which would make a connection with London. The problem was - how could I reach the main line at Doncaster some thirty miles away?!

The nefarious thought flashed into my mind, "Why not take my staff car and drive there?" This would be strictly illegal, as I would not be on official RAF business, so I dismissed the idea. Then I had a second thought - if I kept to the secondary roads, it would be unlikely that I would be seen, and if I was, because of my rank of Squadron Leader, it would be thought I was on official duty. But what if I was caught? It would probably lead to a Court Martial for improper use of the vehicle, stealing petrol and other obscure charges, and perish that thought! After dithering with the problem, I decided - to blazes with it, I will take a chance. I told myself I had served the RAF well enough to justify this slight misdemeanour and in the early morning I left Blyton in the Hillman and headed for Doncaster.

Rather foolishly I drove fast, in the erroneous belief that the shorter the time taken, the less chance of being caught.

I had travelled about halfway and near the village of Misterton, I saw a group of soldiers ahead. I slowed down when a Sergeant stepped into the road and flagged me down. My heart beat faster as he approached, accompanied by a very smart, efficient young Captain, wearing a 'Sam Browne' and carrying a revolver. I lowered the window. After looking closely at the inside of the car, the Captain asked: "Where have you come from Sir?" I hoped that he had not noticed the guilty flush which came to my face.

"From RAF Blyton...why, what is the trouble Captain?"

"We are looking for two escaped prisoners, probably dressed in blue dungarees...you haven't seen anyone thumbing a lift?"

"No," I replied as casually as possible.

"Sorry to have delayed you Sir," said the Captain, as he stepped back and saluted smartly. I breathed a sigh of relief and drove on. When I arrived at Doncaster I drove into the yard of the Eagle Hotel and parked. Addressing the Manager, who was talking to the receptionist, I enquired:

"I am catching the London train, I wonder if you could let me have a lock-up garage for the car for two nights please?" It was not such a strange request as it might have seemed, in wartime few long journeys were done by car. I followed him into the yard. He raised his eyebrows when he saw the Hillman in its war camouflage paint, but asked no questions. Pointing to one of a block of four garages, he said:

"You can have number three...will you let me have the keys after, the charge for two nights will be six shillings." The journey to King's Cross and then across London to Paddington for the train to Temple Meads was comfortable but tedious. It had been eight hours since I had left Blyton. I soon forgot the hassle of the journey and enjoyed a marvellous weekend.

CHAPTER 12   AIRCREW DISPOSAL UNIT - OVER AND OUT

On my return, nothing was said about the car, although it must have been missed about the camp. If the Wingco knew I had taken it to Doncaster, he was generous enough to turn a blind eye.

On 18th September, I had to fly two VIP's to North Luffenham and Cottesmore. I did not know then that it was to be my very last flight with the Royal Air Force. I wished I had known, so that I could have savoured the pleasure of being at the controls of my favourite plane, a de Haviland Dominie, for the last time.

In order to deal fairly with the immense task of demobilisation, everyone in the Services had a Group Release number - mine was twenty six. I expected it at any time and on the 1st December, my release date had arrived. The lack of surprise did not lessen my joy.

Before leaving the Air Force, every item of equipment had to be returned to the particular Sections. This 'clearance' as it was known, took me most of a day. At the Flying Clothing Section, I made certain that the 'Airmens Portable Field Lavatory' which I had knocked down in 1942 and which Wing Commander Thompson had inserted as a charge on my clothing card, had been erased. What a load of 'crap' it would have been to have to pay for that!

As Senior Administrative Officer and nominal head of the Sections, I could have 'got away' with almost anything. In later years I regretted handing in my flying helmet and Irvin sheepskin flying jacket, which became very coveted items of memorabilia.

I had been too busy at Blyton to make close friends, so after settling my Mess bill, and saying farewell to the Adjutant and Wing Commander Dixie Dean, I left on the 4th December for Uxbridge.

After receiving my Service and Release book, I was taken to Wembley to be kitted out with civilian clothes. It was perhaps because I was so eager to get home, that I can remember little about this.

I can recall that at Wembley, there was a huge warehouse with long passages containing shelves filled with civilian suits, shoes, hats and raincoats. Dozens of men were 'milling' around, trying to choose a suit from the limited selection available. Being of more or less stock size, I was able to find a suit to fit, designated - 39L Blue Chalk Stripes SB Lapels.

I was about to leave with my cardboard box of clothes, when an immaculately dressed Flight Lieutenant stepped towards me. After five of the most dramatic years of my life, he uttered the following perfunctory announcement:

"I am directed by the Secretary of State for Air, to thank you for your efforts on behalf of the Royal Air Force. GOOD AFTERNOON."

Bumps a Bus

POSTSCRIPT

In 1984 an unexpected letter from Holland arrived. The writer was Hans Onderwater, who had been commissioned to write the story of the air war over Holland. He had access to the war records of both the Germans and the Allies. During his investigation, he discovered similarities in the German and British records of the air battle on the night of 31 July/August 1942. Hans wrote to me asking for accurate details of our air battle over Overflakkee - described in this book. His copy of the German Namenliche Verlustlitste (Personel lost in action) translated read:

JU-88C6 R4+AD Nr.360152

Pilot...Captain Herbert Bonsch CO. III/NJG2
W.O. Sergeant Otto Bottcher
A.G. F.Sgt August Wille
Poortugal. 10 kilometres south of Rotterdam.
1 August 1942. Time 0125 hours.

Patrol with 2 Messerschmitts Bf.110 attacked British bomber of type Halifax according to report Nr. 53911/15- 9/NJG2.
R4+AD shot down by tail turret gunner of enemy bomber. Bomber probably crashed in North Sea, crew of R4+AD killed in action near village mentioned in '2' (Portugal). 1 Messerschmitt damaged.

Signed Hauptmann.

DEATH OR DECORATION

Onderwater wrote "I am sure this gives final proof that your crew shot the JU88, the personal plane of Major Bosch, the CO of III/NJG2 3rd Gruupe of Nightfightersquadron 1. He was quite an ace who was active from the rape of Norway, then Holland."

It now appears certain that MacCauley inflicted the damage to the ME110 and died whilst tenaciously defending us against the enemy fighters. After the disbelief of our story by British Intelligence, I was pleased to have our version fully corroborated.

I was now very anxious to trace Sam Glasgow, if he was still alive, to tell him of the outcome of the battle that night. After considerable difficulty, Jane Reeve, the researcher for the TV film American Eagle Squadron, gave me the help I needed.

On 1st August 1989 - exactly 47 years to the day since the air battle, I received a letter from America, it commenced:-
"Dear Ronnie,
   Well - I hardly know what to say other than HERE I AM!'
         (signed) Sam.

The outcome was that Sam with his wife Margaret came from their home in North Carolina to visit us in Weymouth. We had a wonderful re-union and amongst the gifts we exchanged was a portrait in oils of Sam when he was a handsome 21-year-old Air Gunner, painted by Mickie. This made a fitting conclusion to our memorable meeting.

I have heard since that Sergeant Pool, our Canadian navigator, had become a Flight Lieutenant with a DFC and was killed on the 6th mission whilst on a second tour of operations.

Hans Onderwater's book, which has a Foreword by Prince Bernhard of the Netherlands, is entitled: 'En toen was het stil...' (Then All Was Silent).

                                        Ronnie Waite

GLOSSARY

GC	Group Captain
A/Cdr	Air Commodore
AVM	Air Vice-Marshal
ACM	Air Chief Marshal
ITW	Initial Training Wing
EFTS	Elementary Flying School
SFTS	Service Flying School
OTU	Operational Training Unit
HCU	Heavy Conversion Unit
ETA	Estimated Time of Arrival
DR	Dead Reckoning Navigation
ASI	Airspeed Indicator
Met Office	Meteorological Office
Leg	Determined steady course flown
RPM, Revs	Revolutions per minute
Prop	Propeller
Flaps	Large surface at the trailing edge of wing - air brakes
Pitot Head	Instrument below wing, registers airspeed
Drem	Ring of lights around the airfield perimeter
Gen	Considered reliable information
Gong	Decoration or Medal
Chop	Killed in action
Gone for a Burton	Killed in action
Op	Operational Mission
Sprog	New...inexperienced person
Hali	Halifax aeroplane
Lanc	Lancaster aeroplane
Flak	Anti-aircraft fire
Coned	Trapped in a cone of searchlights
Corkscrew	Flying manoeuvre to avoid fighter attack.